ACTIVIST BUSINESS ETHICS

ACTIVIST BUSINESS ETHICS

by

JACQUES CORY

KLUWER ACADEMIC PUBLISHERS
Boston / Dordrecht / London

Distributors for North, Central and South America:
Kluwer Academic Publishers
101 Philip Drive
Assinippi Park
Norwell, Massachusetts 02061 USA
Telephone (781) 871-6600
Fax (781) 681-9045
E-Mail <kluwer@wkap.com>

Distributors for all other countries:
Kluwer Academic Publishers Group
Distribution Centre
Post Office Box 322
3300 AH Dordrecht, THE NETHERLANDS
Telephone 31 78 6392 392
Fax 31 78 6546 474
E-Mail <services@wkap.nl>

 Electronic Services <http://www.wkap.nl>

Library of Congress Cataloging-in-Publication Data

A C.I.P. Catalogue record for this book is available
from the Library of Congress.

Cover design by Joseph Cory

Printed on acid-free paper.

Printed in the United States of America

CONTENTS

ACKNOWLEDGEMENTS

Following the publication of my book 'Business Ethics – The Ethical Revolution of Minority Shareholders', this new book enlarges the theoretical scope of activist business ethics. I am convinced that business ethics in its present form is not sufficient to overcome the reluctance of a large number of companies and owners to adopt ethics in their business. A more activist and militant approach is needed, and this book tries to find the origin of such an activist ethics in religion, philosophy, psychology, democracy and international contexts.

As the traditional safeguards of the interests of the stakeholders, namely the press, the law, the boards of directors, etc, are not sufficient, activist business ethics has to be enhanced by the personification of stakeholders, the predominance of the values and ethics of the CEOs and a change in the attitude of society toward ethics. In my previous book new vehicles for the safeguard of interests of minority shareholders and stakeholders were examined, namely the Internet, Transparency, Whistle-Blowers, Activist Associations and Ethical Funds.

However, we have seen in the case studies of the first book that even those new vehicles are not sufficient in many cases and my new book presents two future vehicles that do not exist yet – the Supervision Board and the Institute of Ethics. These vehicles are empowered by executive tools and can cope effectively with the existing institutions, which are controlled mainly by majority shareholders.

In view of the pertinence of the book's subject, many friends and colleagues have assisted me with their advice and support, and I would like to mention especially Henri-Claude de Bettignies, Henk Van Luijk, Meir Tamari, Jacques Levy, Francis Desforges, Genevieve Ferone, Jan Pieter Krahnen, James Weber, Samuel Holtzman, Jean-Philippe Deschamps, Andrew Pendleton, Anke Martini, Ishak Saporta, Gad Proper, Amnon Rimon, Shahar Dabach, Rachel Zeiler, Dietmar Fuchs and Nira Cory.

I also want to thank my excellent editor David Cella, who has done a very valuable job in publishing the book in record time. Special thanks also to Judith Pforr and Jill Garbi for their valuable assistance in editing the book.

Last but not least, my greatest thanks are to my wife Ruthy, and my children, Joseph, Amir and Shirly, who are the inspiration for all my academic books and novels. Ethics begins at home, and I am grateful to my family for sharing this long Odyssey with me.

ABOUT THE AUTHOR

Jacques Cory is a businessman with a background in Economics and Business Administration (MBA from Insead, France) who has encountered many cases of despoiling stakeholders and minority shareholders in his long international career in top-level positions in the high-tech industry and in mergers and acquisitions.

Cory decided to write a thesis and two books on this subject in a frank and open manner, in order to bring the subject to the forefront of the public's interest. His first book 'Business Ethics: The Ethical Revolution of Minority Shareholders' was published by Kluwer Academic Publishers in March 2001. 'Activist Business Ethics' is his second book.

He is a member of the Board of Directors of Transparency International Israel and a member of The Society for Business Ethics, and is very active in the Israeli business ethics community. Cory lectures at universities, companies and ethical organizations throughout the world on business ethics with a special emphasis on minority shareholders. Cory is also the author of the novel on ethics called 'Beware of Greeks' Presents', published in March 2001 in Israel by Bimat Kedem Publishers.

1
INTRODUCTION

"The truth can wait, for it lives a long life"
(Arthur Schopenhauer, German philosopher, 1788-1860)

The philosopher Schopenhauer believed in the eventual triumph of truth, despite the disappointments engendered by his indifferent contemporaries. Two centuries later, we live in a time of accelerated changes, and we do not have the long life to wait for the truth. Activist business ethics, business ethics with a more activist militant approach, is needed in order to remedy the wrongdoing committed to the stakeholders and minority shareholders. This will be achieved by cooperation between ethical businessmen and businesswomen, activist academics and associations of stakeholders and minority shareholders.

We should treat others as we would want them to treat us, not through interest, but by conviction. Yet this principle is not the guideline of many companies in the modern business world, although most of religions and philosophers have preconized it in the last 3,000 years. How could we convince or compel modern business to apply this principle and is it essential to the success of economy? In order to answer these questions this book examines the evolution of activist business ethics in business, democracies, Christianity, Judaism, Islam, Buddhism and other religions, as well as in philosophy, psychology and psychoanalysis. The book examines international aspects, the personification of stakeholders, the predominance of values and ethics for CEOs and the inefficient safeguards of the stakeholders' interests. The book presents new vehicles for the safeguard of those interests and future activist vehicles, such as the Supervision Board and the Institute of Ethics.

Activist ethics in business should be established in the forefront of business as a countermeasure to the crumbling of moral values. The cost of the lack of ethics and the contractual costs are much higher than the cost of ethics in business, as trust becomes more and more rare. Many businessmen perceive business as a poker game, in which cheating is condoned or even encouraged. But business is much more serious; businessmen spend most of their creative life at work; the jobs of millions of persons are at stake as well as the welfare of the world's economy. In spite of the difficulties, ethical conduct is favorable to business, as shown in numerous cases from ethical companies such as IBM, Johnson & Johnson, Levi-Strauss and others. Unlike many of their contemporaries, these companies are not amoral and their mission is not mainly to maximize their profits without infringing the law. Between unethical conduct and an unlawful act there is only one step, and this step is very easy to cross, especially if the environment is favorable. The end does not justify the means and ethics should be on an equal basis with profitability.

The democratic evolution of companies is not self-evident. After experiencing a multitude of cases where an absolute power of the companies' executives has caused astronomic losses, quasi-democratic modes of operations were adopted. It is quite far from the democracy that should be practiced in the business world, which is still mainly autocratic, but much closer than it was 100, 50 or even 10 years ago. Still, there is a contradiction between what is perceived as the basic moral principles of companies and the practice in modern business. Those principles are honesty, acting in good faith and in an equitable and just manner without betraying the trust of the stakeholders and by treating them as equals, practicing reciprocity, avoiding the exploitation of others, and acting from your own free will without forcing your will on your partners. But the practice in many cases is that the heroes of the business world are 'the smart guys', the 'street fighters', and the prevailing maxims are 'catch as you can' and 'we cannot argue with success'.

In the last 10 years there was an effervescence of Protestant Christian ethics in the U.S. business world, in order to counterbalance the immoral norms of the 80s and 90s. In parallel, there are many authors who try to prove that the ethical norms in business, according to Catholic, Jewish, Moslem, Buddhist or other religions, are the norms that should be applied in order to return to the religious ethical sources. This book will study activist business ethics developed in the main religions as well as by some of the most famous philosophers from Aristotle to modern times. A profound reading on activist business ethics throughout the centuries may prove that there are no major differences between the different ethical versions and ultimately the business world knows exactly what should be done when one advocates adhesion to ethical norms that are in many ways universal.

In Protestant morals, word of honor is sacred, a handshake is worth more than a contract, and integrity is the most precious human commodity. If a person was honest, God rewarded him, and if one was dishonest, God punished him. An immoral conduct was the cause of a profound sense of culpability. But in large bureaucratic organizations, it is no longer possible to link directly the actions with morals. In the Jewish religion the financial system is based on an absolute trust of governmental and other institutions, as without trust money has no worth, being only a piece of paper. It perhaps explains why the words 'In God We Trust' appear on the U.S. dollar bill. The culmination of Judeo-Christian business ethics is that if we invest only in ourselves we lose everything when we die, but if we invest in others - if the 'stakeholders' become an integral part of our existence - we could survive after our death.

Many theories have been proposed in order to prove that there could be a difference in the ethical norms in different countries. It is evident that there are various nuances in the practice of business ethics in all the countries of the world, but there are no major differences in the ethical concepts in the world. In the same manner that it was possible to establish universal human rights of the UN, that democratic principles are universal, and that ecological norms are known throughout the world, even if they are not applied universally, it is possible to define universal norms of ethics in business and particularly of ethics in the relations between companies and stakeholders.

Heraclitus said that everything changes 'panta rhei' and on the other hand Mme. Angot said 'plus ca change plus c'est la meme chose', the more things change the more they stay the same. Who should we believe? Is there an evolution in morals toward a more ethical world, or will the righteous be compensated only after they die, as in this world only the sharks prosper? The answer is in the proportion of the application of morals. There is a clear-cut evolution toward a better world. It is maybe a candid perception, that was common also in Europe between the two world wars, and everybody knows what happened subsequently. But it is preferable to hope that the world has arrived at the conclusion, after experiencing everything, that the best way to prosper economically is to conduct ourselves ethically and democratically.

The most important characteristic of a businessman has to be his moral integrity, especially in fiduciary positions such as CEO, vice president, or investment banker and analyst, positions that are responsible for financing tens or hundreds of millions dollars. It is imperative to broaden the humanist education in the universities, including an ethics course. The astronomical sums of remuneration to top-level businessmen are at the base of corruption. Unfortunately, there are not enough businessmen who cannot be corrupted in any case. For most of the others, it is only a relative question, as corruption and ethical deviation vary from case to case and do not have to be flagrant in each case. If executives are obliged to behave unethically, they prefer it to be toward weaker groups who cannot retaliate, and the individual stakeholders and minority shareholders are amongst the weakest groups.

The greatest danger for stakeholders and minority shareholders consists in the holy alliance between the executives of the companies and the majority shareholders who appoint and remunerate them. Those executives involve themselves in the quarry, by receiving shares and warrants of the companies in very advantageous terms that enable them to get rich with almost no risks.

This book includes also a summary of the chapters on activist business ethics from a book by the same author called 'Business Ethics - The Ethical Revolution of the Minority Shareholders'. The traditional safeguards of the rights of minority shareholders have often failed in their duty, and those shareholders have remained practically without any protection against the arbitrariness of the companies and majority shareholders. The law, the SEC, society, boards of directors, independent directors, auditors, analysts, underwriters and the press have remained in many cases worthless panaceas. Nevertheless, in the Ethics of 2000 new vehicles have been developed for the protection of minority shareholders, mainly the Internet, transparency, activist associations and ethical funds. Those vehicles give the shareholders at least the chance to understand the pattern and methods that are utilized to wrong them and give them a viable alternative for investment in ethical funds.

The new vehicles will prevent minority shareholders from using the Armageddon weapon, by ceasing to invest in the stock exchange and causing the collapse of the system that discriminates against them. The preconditions for the ethical revolution of minority shareholders do exist, but they are insufficient as other conditions are needed to be met, such as the ostracizing of unethical managers by society, appointment of ethical CEOs to head the companies, and above all giving an equal weight to financial and operational performance (the hardware), as well as to ethics and integrity (the software).

One reason for the 'clean' conscience of the managers of the companies, who despoil the rights of the individual stakeholders and minority shareholders, is the lack of personification of those groups. It is much easier to commit a wrongdoing toward somebody who you do not know and do not appreciate, especially if you are convinced that you are right.

The executives and majority shareholders who commit unethical and unlawful acts are not ostracized by society. On the contrary, very often, they are admired and envied by their colleagues who would have behaved similarly if they only had the opportunity. They are treated as 'smart guys' who take advantage of the good opportunities that they encounter. Man is before everything a social animal and it is imperative that businessmen who are unethical be treated as outcasts, banned by society and despised by their peers.

In recent years a revolution has occurred in the publication of data on the Internet. Most of the quoted companies have a site on the Internet and stock talk groups, comprised mainly of minority shareholders, where information and misinformation is shared between the shareholders who have access to the Internet. It is pure democracy, as in the agora of Athens, where all citizens had the right to participate. Information about future wrongdoing to minority shareholders can be divulged in advance and one has only to read it and sell his shares, while there is still time.

The full transparency of companies, via the Internet and ethical reports, could safeguard ethics, even if it is achieved through the assistance of whistle-blowers. Transparency compels every employee to adopt an ethical conduct, as his conduct could be published on the Internet and in the press or scrutinized by activist associations, so that his family, friends and community would learn of his conduct.

The implementation of ethics is assisted by the ethical funds. These funds were established primarily in the U.S., but are also very influential in Canada, the Netherlands and the U.K. in the last 10 years. They comprise investments of more than two trillion dollars in the U.S. and have succeeded in obtaining financial results above the average of the U.S. stock exchange, while keeping very strict ethical screening. The minority shareholders will have to collaborate with those funds and buy only shares of ethical companies.

Ethical investing is screened to reflect ethical, environmental, social, political, or moral values. It examines the social records of companies in local community affairs, labor, minority and gender relations, military and nuclear production, product quality, approach to customers, suppliers and shareholders, and avoidance of sales of tobacco, alcohol, pornography or gambling products.

In the last decade of the 20th century we witnessed in the U.S. and France, but not in Israel, effervescence in social and other activism of shareholders, and in many cases they have succeeded in changing the initiatives of very large companies, especially in the United States. But, ultimately, those organizations, the ethical funds, transparency and Internet, have not yet succeeded to change drastically the attitude of companies to stakeholders and minority shareholders. New vehicles that do not exist yet are needed.

This book proposes to establish a new organization - the Board of Supervision or Supervision Board - where the shareholders who control the Board of Directors would be able to elect a maximum of 50 percent of its members, even if they hold almost all the shares, while the other members of the Board of Supervision will be elected by the other shareholders and by the national Institute of Ethics. The Supervision Board may hire and fire the CEO of the company and decide what remuneration, bonuses, shares and warrants he will get. In this manner, the CEO will have allegiance to all the shareholders and will have only one target: to succeed in his mission without taking into consideration the divergence of interests between shareholders.

The members of the Board of Supervision will be elected by adjusted voting, as an affirmative action against the absolute rule of the shareholders who control the Board of Directors. If those shareholders hold 40 percent of the shares, they will be able to get only 20 percent of the members of the Board of Supervision. If the other shareholders present at the shareholders' meeting hold 10 percent of the shares (as the shareholders are scattered and do not attend or send their proxies), they will be able to elect 10 percent of the members of the Board of Supervision. The other 70 percent will be elected by the National Institute of Ethics.

The Institute of Ethics will be financed by a fee on each transaction in the national stock exchange. The members of the Institute, who must have an impeccable ethical reputation, will be elected by the national courts, and will not be active businessmen or hold shares in companies. This Institute will also give an ethical rating of companies, as the creditworthiness rating of companies ranking from AAA to CCC. The companies will not be obliged to obey the rules of the Institute of Ethics, but by abstaining they will not get an ethical rating and investors will refrain from investing in those companies.

Activist business ethics, assisted by the new vehicles required to impose it, is essential to the survival of modern economy in the 21st century. It is our duty to inculcate the businessmen with ethics principles, to eradicate the false maxims that business is a game and its heroes are 'street fighters', and to ensure that practice would concur with the business ethics' principles toward stakeholders and minority shareholders.

2
ACTIVIST ETHICS IN BUSINESS

"This is the land of the great big dogs, you don't love a man here, you eat
him! That's the principle; the only one we live by."
(Miller, All My Sons, Act Three)

The essence of the deontological position is the notion that actions are
morally just when they conform to a principle or a duty in question. The term
deontological is derived from the Greek *deon*, signifying a duty. The
deontology claims that the moral statute of an action should not be judged by
its consequences, as the utilitarians advocate, but by its intention, as the
consequences cannot be predicted. Therefore, we should treat others as we
would want them to treat us, not through interest, but by conviction. The
moderate deontologists, such as Etzioni, take the consequences in secondary
consideration, bringing them closer to the modern utilitarians, who take
intentions in secondary consideration.

Ethics is the science of morals, the set of moral conceptions of a person. It
includes usually the standards of practice or the categories of conduct that are
acceptable or not to a group with common interests, in order to achieve those
interests. Morals deal with customs, admitted conduct rules, which are
practiced in a society. Morals emanate values instilled by families,
communities and religious organizations. They are based on what people
understand as acts of conscience, 'con and science', or 'knowing with', as the
individual conscience is a manifestation of the influence of a group's
conscience. People think that certain acts are justified or not in comparison to
the customs of their group, family, religion, or community. "Si l'on croit les
philologues avertis, le mot ethique proviendrait de deux termes grecs, Ethos et
Itos. Le premier désignerait le 'comportement juste', le second signifierait la
'tenue de l'âme'. Vertu intérieure et attitude extérieure apparaissent ainsi
comme liées. La définition même de l'éthique attire notre attention sur une
nécessaire cohérence. Elle est un appel a une unité de vie. L'exemplarité est
au cœur de l'éthique. Elle pourrait se définir comme l'éthique incarnée,
l'éthique en mouvement." (Dherse, L'Ethique ou le Chaos, p.362) "If we
believe the renowned philologists, the word ethics comes from two Greek
terms, Ethos and Itos. The first one means 'just behavior', the second one
means 'status of mind'. The interior virtue and the exterior attitude appear
therefore as linked. The definition of ethics draws our attention on a necessary

coherence. It is an appeal to a unity of life. The exemplarity is at the core of ethics. It could be defined as ethics incarnated, ethics in movement."

The companies are under no obligation to conduct themselves ethically according to Friedman, and according to other authors they should behave ethically if they want to be profitable in the long run and increase their valorization. But the author of this book believes that companies should behave ethically and be profitable in parallel, and even if ethics diminishes the profitability of the company, they should still behave ethically. There are therefore two parameters with an equal weight, or two poles that should guide companies – ethics and profitability. Under no circumstance should we behave in a flagrant, unethical manner, even if in an extreme case the company ceases to exist. A good CEO has to ensure that his company should be profitable and ethical at the same time. From the moment that a CEO admits that the end justifies the means and in order to rescue the company he should behave in an unethical way, all the executives receive a license to conduct themselves in the same manner. All companies are threatened in one way or another: by competition, adverse economic conditions, lack of resources etc., and every excuse is valid and sufficient in order to behave unethically, as 'a la guerre comme a la guerre' – 'everything is allowed in war', 'business is like a jungle where only the strong ones survive', etc., etc.

Ethics should be established in the forefront of business because of the crumbling of moral values. The cost of the lack of ethics is much higher than the cost of ethics in business. The contractual costs get higher and higher, as trust, which is at the basis of business, becomes more and more rare. All businessmen prefer to negotiate with colleagues who behave ethically, but how many of them arrive at the conclusion that ethics cannot be unilateral? Nothing can substitute for an ethical threshold, which is at the base of modern business in the long run. But is business ethics contingent with religion, culture or the nation? What are the common lines of the ethical norms and what are the differing ones? Can we define international ethics, bearing in mind that the world is shrinking and becoming a global village, that we witness an information explosion, and that there is an evolution trend in all domains?

Are those hypotheses true or are we victims of wishful thinking? In the diamond world, where Jewish businessmen are predominant, business transactions were often concluded with a handshake and the words *'Mazal oubracha'* (in Hebrew: luck and blessing), as business in this domain, which is mostly international and discreet, cannot be concluded contractually and is based uniquely on the basis of absolute trust. Diamond merchants who transgressed the norms of trust were ostracized and could not continue to work in this field. But nowadays, we witness more and more cases where the trust is betrayed and the merchants ask themselves how to continue making business after the crumbling of the norms.

The ideal could be that like the diamond merchants, ethics and trust would become the lingua franca of the modern business world, the international language that all the 'gentlemen', 'knights' and 'Freemasons' of ethics would speak in the same manner. Many lawyers would become unemployed, but business could be conducted in a much more efficient way with substantially reduced costs.

"The goal of ethics education is not character building; but rather, like all college course work, they attempt to share knowledge, build skills, and develop minds. A course in business ethics is a useful tool to assist students when as managers they face a decision with a major ethical component attached to it... Perhaps business ethics can be best described as a not so simple method by which people can come to know what is right from what is wrong and go on and do what is right in the business arena. It simply suggests what Mark Twain once said: 'Always do right. This will gratify some people, and astonish the rest." (Madsen, Essentials of Business Ethics, p.7)

Ethics in companies has as a source the mission of the corporate, which is translated in more detailed responsibilities toward the stakeholders - the clients, employees, shareholders, suppliers, creditors, community, nation, or even the world. Those responsibilities are themselves detailed in procedures and in practice. According to Drucker, the ultimate responsibility of the directors of the companies is above all not to harm – primum non nocere. Based on this principle, an employee who learns that his employer has the intention of committing an illegal or immoral action that can harm the stakeholders of the company has the duty to disclose it to the public, the police or the SEC. But in this case, he is always treated as a whistle-blower, and he is liable to very severe retaliation, sanctions in his work, in society, and sometimes he risks also his life.

There are also theories like those of Albert Carr advocating that: "... business is indeed a game; the rules of legality and the goal of profit are its sole ethical guideline. Thus, if one is to win at the 'game of business', one must have a 'game player's attitude', which means being able to divorce one's private morality from one's sense of right and wrong on the 'playing field' of business." (Madsen, Essentials of Business Ethics, Carr, Is Business Bluffing Ethical?, p.63) According to Carr, we could find many analogies between business and poker. We cannot pretend to play poker with the ethical principles of the church. In poker it is legitimate to bluff, even to a friend, if you are not holding a good hand.

But the hypothesis that business is analogous to poker, thus justifying cheating in business and unethical conduct, is according to the author of this book completely erroneous, as in the same manner we could argue that marriage is like poker, friendship is like poker, and even the writing of this book is like poker. It is true that in poker bluffing is allowed, that is all. And even that, only if this is the prevalent norm amongst the players. But from the moment that all businessmen do not agree that it is legitimate to bluff, or rather to cheat, it should be forbidden to do so, as it means playing a game with different rules for every one of the players. It is like a husband saying that it is permitted to betray his wife, while his wife believes that it is forbidden to do so. As business, poker, marriage and the academic world operate in different dimensions it is impossible to make analogies from one dimension to the other. In one point we can agree with Carr when he attacks the businessmen who say that it pays to be ethical and in the long run we have more to lose by antagonizing our stakeholders. Ethics cannot be perceived as an item in the balance sheet of the company; we should not conduct ourselves ethically because it is worthwhile to do so, exactly as one should not be a good Christian simply in order to get to paradise. One should be moral by conviction, exactly as one should be good, generous, just, and a good Christian by conviction, and not in order to get to heaven or gain an additional profit margin of 2 percent.

Carr's worst mistake is treating business as a game. Extensive experience in business brings inevitably to the conclusion that business is much more serious and should not be treated as a game. Businessmen spend more than 50 percent of their creative time in business; the jobs of millions of persons are at stake; we could even say that it is a life and death issue for the economy and welfare of a multitude of persons, and to treat business as a game is identical to treating war as a game. We should not be willing to win in business at any cost, exactly as the Allied Forces did not win the war by committing atrocities like the Nazis. The modern world, that was reborn out of the ashes of World War II, cannot admit that everything is allowed in business as in politics. The same principles that prevailed with the Allies, and that prevail in the UN, should prevail also in business, as ethics and morality are indivisible and should be applied to all domains of life.

From the moment that we perceive business as a game, we legitimize the mentality of Las Vegas, we transform the robber barons into heroes, and the croupiers become the modern priests. Until we reach a status where 'rien ne va plus', as we have reached in the last 10 years in many investment banks in the U.S. and in many business aspects in France, Great Britain and Israel. But the robber barons of the 19th century have at least built railroads, industries and oil fields, while their modern homologues have left us with junk bonds! "No place have standards dropped more vertiginously than in the investment banking trade that is presiding over this restructuring. While other areas of business are in most respects no more ethical than ever, wrongdoing in this central arena makes a crisis of business ethics seem in full swing. And with investment banking now largely manned by the young, is the erosion of ethics here an early warning of imminent trouble elsewhere in business as this generation rises to power? Insider trading is investment banking's most widely publicized sin." (Madsen, Essential of Business Ethics, Magnet, The Decline and Fall of Business Ethics, p.136,137)

The number of companies that do not behave ethically is surprising. "Between 1970 and 1980, 11 percent of the largest American firms were convicted of lawlessness, including bribery, criminal fraud, illegal campaign contributions, tax evasion, or price-fixing. Well-known companies with four or more convictions included Braniff International, Gulf Oil, and Ashland Oil. Firms with at least two convictions included Allied, American Airlines, Bethlehem Steel, Diamond International, Firestone, Goodyear, International Paper, National Distillers, Northrop, Occidental Petroleum, Pepsico, Phillips Petroleum, R.J. Reynolds, Schlitz, Seagram, Tenneco, and United Brands. The recent Union Carbide disaster in Bhopal is well-known, as is the E.F. Hutton fiasco, the General Dynamics fraud, and of course, the Wall Street scandals involving Ivan Boesky, David Levine, and Michael Milken... Unethical behavior in business more often than not is a systematic matter. To a large degree it is the behavior of generally decent people who normally would not think of doing anything illegal or immoral. But they get backed into doing something unethical by the systems and practices of their own firms and industries. Unethical behavior in business generally arises when business firms fail to pay explicitly attention to the ethical risks that are created by their own systems and practices." (Madsen, Essentials of Business Ethics, Velasquez, Corporate Ethics: Losing it, Having it, Getting it, p. 229)

What are the reasons for unethical behavior in a company? Goals that are very difficult to achieve, a behavior that is motivated by incentive fees, a culture of a company or the industry that ignores ethical conduct, unreserved obedience to the superiors' directives, short-term goals, and others. In fact, everything can lead to unethical conduct, as it is much more difficult to conduct oneself ethically in the competitive environment that prevails in the company and elsewhere. It is therefore necessary to change the culture of companies, with an ethical commitment of the management of the company and an inflexible imposition of ethical rules at all the levels of the organization. It is said that 'crime doesn't pay', but much more often it is perceived in the business world that 'ethics doesn't pay'. "Doing what's right is not the easiest, nor the most profitable, course of action. Ethics sometimes requires self-sacrifice, foregoing personal gains or bearing significant costs and burdens. In such difficult times, people are sustained by the ethical norms that they have cultivated and that provide them with the personal incentives and inner motivations that enable them to do what is right in spite of the costs."

12

(Madsen, Essentials of Business Ethics, Velasquez, Corporate Ethics: Losing it, Having it, Getting it, p.233)

In spite of the difficulties, in many cases ethical conduct is favorable to business. The ethical conduct of IBM toward its employees results in a very high degree of motivation and loyalty. The customers of companies that are treated ethically are willing to pay a premium by buying their products at a higher price, recommending their products and remaining loyal to the firms. Hewlett-Packard has become very profitable because of its ethical conduct toward its customers. The quality of their products and their impeccable service are at the base of their high market share. Other companies that have benefited from their high ethical standards are: Borg-Warner Corporation, J.C. Penney, General Mills, Quaker Oats, Advanced Micro Devices, Chemical Bank of New York, Champion International, Levi-Strauss, Carterpillar, and others.

One of the prime examples of how a commitment to ethics pays off is Johnson & Johnson, the pharmaceutical manufacturer. When seven individuals died after consuming Tylenol capsules contaminated with poison, a massive recall of all Tylenol capsules was launched, a move that cost the company an estimated $50 million after taxes. This conduct was according to the company's credo, which states 'our first responsibility is to the doctors, nurses, hospitals, mothers, and all others who use our products'. Following its brave and costly ethical conduct, the company has recovered its losses, sales have reached record levels, and the firm is prospering, benefiting from the trust and confidence that its response has created. This crisis might have destroyed the company, but its ethical conduct boosted its image in the eyes of Johnson & Johnson's millions of customers.

In the 60s and 70s the student revolution prevailed. The author of this book, then a student at INSEAD business school, had difficulty understanding in May 1968, during his frequent visits to the Sorbonne and the Odeon, what the subtle differences between the Maoists and the Trotskyites were, as all of them had absolute social and ethical convictions. But in the 80s and 90s, when the sons of the 'revolutionary' students grew up, the norm has become that it is right to get rich at all cost and the sooner the better. There is no longer time to participate in the Peace Corps or to spend a few years in a Hindu Ashram. If you're not a millionaire at 26, you've missed your career. In Israel, many of the 'nouveaux riches' are young people of 25 to 35 who have founded start-ups and earned millions or even tens of millions of dollars, when their companies were acquired by American companies, or when they sold part of their shares at public offerings. For many young businessmen, Las Vegas personifies the United States instead of the Grand Canyon or Lincoln Center, thus forgetting that after the roaring 20s the world has suffered the worst depression of modern times. We return to social Darwinism, where the law of the fittest prevails, and we forget that this ideal was at the basis of the Fascism and Nazism. 'We cannot argue with success' has become the leitmotiv a la mode, even if the success was obtained to the detriment of the weak - the customers, suppliers and minority shareholders.

Theories, such as those of Milton Friedman, prevail, stating that a company is amoral, and that it should only maximize its profits without infringing the law. Another distinguished professor, Theodor Levitt, has written in the Harvard Business Review that business has to fight as if it was at war; and as in a good war, it should be fought gallantly, valiantly, and especially immorally. But amoral or even immoral beliefs could lead to a conduct illustrated in the famous business case of the Ford Pinto. In 1978, three young women were burned to death when the Pinto that they drove was hit in the rear and the gas tank exploded. Ford Motor was sued for criminal homicide for the first time in its history. In 1980 the jury decided that the company was not guilty. However, the company has lost in the public opinion and paid millions of dollars as damages. It was disclosed that Ford knew that the tank was vulnerable, but when it analyzed the cost of the change it appeared that it would amount to $11 per car. They made an economic analysis, which showed that it would be less costly to pay damages for the few deaths and injuries that statistically would occur rather than to introduce the change in all the cars. As Ford behaved legally, it was impossible to convict the company, although ethically they were responsible for the deaths. This case illustrates blatantly the difference between ethics and law, as ethics maintains never to cause unjustifiable harm and do only what we would want others to do to us.

Twenty years later, an American jury decided that General Motors has to pay damages to six persons, who were severely burned in a car accident, the astronomical amount of $4.9 billion. The plaintiffs accused the company of installing the gas tank of the Chevrolet Malibu only 20 cm. from the car's rear, causing an explosion of the tank as a result of an accident. General Motors calculated that the cost of the repair would be $8.5 per car, while costs of damages would amount to $2 per car only. From there, they came to the economic conclusion that they should not repair the cars. One of the jurors said: 'We are only numbers for them, statistics'. The verdict is a breakthrough in the attitude of the American law toward ethical considerations, which should be adopted and put at the same level as the economical considerations. It proves how business ethics has evolved in the last 20 years, at least in the United States.

But even if we confine ourselves to examine the damages committed by infringements to the law and not to ethics, we can find that "Details of white-collar crime which costs the US at least $40 billion annually (while street crime costs are estimated at only $4 billion) are documented." (Madsen, Essentials of Business Ethics, p.147-148) The only ones who are to be blamed for this situation are the authorities that spend billions of dollars against street crimes and only minimal sums against white-collar crimes. If we could change the priorities of governments and invest considerable amounts against economical crimes we would be able to generate many more funds for social causes. But individual stakeholders have never financed electoral campaigns of presidents or congressmen and why should someone be interested in their fate? On the contrary, those who finance the politicians are in many cases those who commit the economic crimes against the law or ethics.

Between an unethical conduct and an unlawful act there is only one step, and this step is very easy to cross, especially if the environment is favorable and if we feel excited by the flirtation with danger. Many businessmen are convinced that while they are winning nothing could happen to them. One could imagine himself at the court of Napoleon at the eve of the Russian campaign! They start to wrong individual stakeholders; they finish by wronging all the other stakeholders. They start with millions of dollars, they continue with tens or hundreds of millions of dollars. They start with unethical acts; they finish with unlawful acts. As ethics is at the fringe of the law, from the moment that we sacrifice the outposts, the capital becomes an open city. This is the reason why it is so important to inculcate ethics in business, and those who want to safeguard legality in business have to favor the adherence to ethical norms, especially when we observe, as it will be explained at length further on, that legality ultimately does not succeed to prevent in many cases the wrongdoing to the rights of the stakeholders.

Those facts are at the foundation of this book, as the wrongdoing to the rights of shareholders has its origin in certain investment banks, its legitimization in the erroneous notion that business is like a game, where everything is permitted because 'catch as you can', and where the virtues of the CEOs get lost in their interests as the rivers disappear into the sea.

According to Etzioni, "The neoclassical paradigm is a utilitarian, rationalist, and individualist paradigm. It sees individuals as seeking to maximize their utility, rationally choosing the best means to serve their goals... The coming together of these individuals in the competitive marketplace, far from resulting in all-out conflict, is said to generate maximum efficiency and well-being." (Etzioni, The Moral Dimension, p.1) But he continues: "... the approach followed here is one of codetermination: It encompasses factors that form society and personality, as well as neoclassical factors that form markets and rational decision-making... Where the neoclassical assumption is that people seek to maximize one utility (whether it is pleasure, happiness, consumption, or merely a formal notion of a unitary goal), we assume that people pursue at least two irreducible 'utilities', and have two sources of valuation: pleasure and morality... The neoclassical assumption that people render decisions rationally... is replaced by the assumption that people typically select means, not just goals, first and foremost on the basis of their values and emotions." (Etzioni, The Moral Dimension, p.3-4)

Therefore, the end does not justify the means, and morality is on an equal basis with pleasure and utility. This paradigm is quite far from the maxim of La Rochefoucauld, and concurs completely with the ideas of the author of this book. The dynamics of economy cannot be understood without integrating social, political and cultural factors. Those different assumptions are at the basis of what Etzioni calls the paradigm of I&We. This paradigm is in contradiction to the theories of laissez-faire and the invisible hand of Adam Smith and the utilitarian theory of Bentham. It rallies with the theory of Durkheim that maintains that: "morality is a system of rules and values provided by society, imbedded in its culture, and that individual children acquire these as part of the general transmission of culture." (Etzioni, The Moral Dimension, p.7) And from this point, Etzioni elaborates his thesis on a community that is responsible and gives the same status to the individual and to his union with the community. But one has to be careful not to subjugate individuals to society, which could result in Fascism. "A responsive community is much more integrated than an aggregate of self-maximizing individuals; however, it is much less hierarchical and much less structured and 'socializing', than an authoritarian community... Individuals and community are both completely essential, and hence have the same fundamental standing... The individual and the community make each other and require each other... The I's need a We to be." (Etzioni, The Moral Dimension, p.8-9)

If we conduct ourselves in a strictly utilitarian mode, we can enjoy $1,000 that was stolen in the same manner that we enjoy $1,000 earned honestly. The utility is the same, the consequences are identical, but the intention is different. In the same way it is worthwhile to sacrifice Iphigeneia in order to enable the Greek ships to sail to Troy, what is the value of one soul in comparison to the welfare of the whole army? We can also sacrifice the freedom of the black slaves to increase the richness of the American colonies and the lives of millions of Jews for the glory of the Third Reich. Many actions based on morals do not result in pleasure and utility. We go to the army out of duty (at least in some countries), we pay our taxes out of conviction (at least some of us), and we do not betray our wives out of fidelity (unfortunately less and less). In the same manner we treat our customers honestly, not only in order to increase our market share; we do not pollute rivers, not only in order to avoid being fined; and we treat fairly our minority shareholders, not only in order to increase our company's valuation.

The businessmen who conduct themselves ethically do not do so for interest or utility, but mostly because of deep conviction. Interests may change, but convictions are normally part of the personality. If you can bribe an official and get away with the pollution of a river for a minimal sum, knowing for sure that your act will never be discovered, is it to the interest of the company to do so? Furthermore, if you can increase your profits by wronging the stakeholders, is it not legitimate to do so? The answer should be categorically negative, because when you adventure in the moving sands of interest, it can bring you to riches, bury you or send you to prison. Only if you act according to your conscience you become directed by a compass, which always points to the north. It is very difficult to understand how so many businessmen adhere to the theories of the utilitarians when it is impossible to measure 'the maximum of utility for the maximum of persons' and that it is immoral to disregard the interests of the minority shareholders who have to sacrifice themselves for the sake of the welfare of the majority shareholders. Probably it is convenient for them to quote great philosophers such as Bentham in order to conceal their selfish motives, which are to maximize their benefits as majority shareholders or executives who are remunerated by them.

David Warsh analyzes in his article "How Selfish Are People – Really?" (Ethics at Work, Harvard Business Review, p. 23-27) the theories expressed by Robert Axelrod in his book "The Evolution of Cooperation" and by Robert H. Frank in his book "Passions Within Reason: The Strategic Role of the Emotions". There are therefore two main historical ways, which contribute to notions of just and unjust. One is the ancient tradition based on religion, philosophy and morals, the Golden Rule, the Ten Commandments and the precepts of Jesus Christ, the humanistic tradition. The other is the recently modern tradition of social and biological sciences. The economists claim that people try to maximize the satisfaction of their interests and Darwin further justified selfish conduct in his theory of natural selection and the survival of the fittest. The economy according to Axelrod is based on mutual interests and on cooperation based on reciprocity. There is no reason to have scruples or to feel embarrassed. One has to make a calculation without sentiments and decide on a course of action with maximum benefits, cooperate if we need the partner, or leave him if we do not need him anymore. Frank thinks that emotions shortcut conduct, which is based on mere interests, because honest people are those who are preferred as partners. Virtue is not only its own reward, it can also result in material rewards. The Quakers got rich because they earned a reputation of honesty in the business world. People do not live on desert islands and their conduct is not based, after all, uniquely on egoism and interests. If one follows the theories of Axelrod, a stakeholder who was wronged will try to seek revenge and we enter into a Machiavellian perpetuum mobile requiring an exorbitant price for the lack of trust, while an ethical 'Quaker' conduct allows us to concentrate on the vital issues of business, production, sales, research, and not on protection against abuse of trust.

The theory of Etzioni is in fact a symbiosis between the utilitarian theory of Jeremy Bentham and the Categorical and Absolute Imperative of Immanuel Kant. Kant was convinced that ethics has nothing to do with consequences or human welfare, but comes uniquely from a sense of duty and obedience to a moral law that every rational person has to accept. For a law to be moral it has to be universal. When we lie we do not want everybody to lie, and when we steal we do not want everybody to steal. Therefore it is immoral to steal and lie, as it would be impossible to live in a world where everybody steals and lies. And especially, it is not reasonable to wish that all moral laws would be applied toward everybody except you. There are many businessmen who are convinced that this should be the rule and what is permitted to them should not be permitted to anybody else, but probably they have not read Kant, and they are convinced that as God is with them they are untouchables and above everybody else in society. They transgress the universal and impartial maxims of Kant, scorn the dignity of human beings that Kant preconizes to safeguard above all, and succeed in not being apprehended by the law, public opinion, or the stakeholders of the company.

This is the reason that the theory of Etzioni is more practical than the theory of Kant, as it takes into consideration utility, but subjugates it to morality. This compromise allows us to deny the utilitarian theories, which are in complete contradiction to this thesis, as those theories cannot advocate the welfare of the minority shareholders, which is to the detriment of the excessive gains of the majority shareholders, therefore opposed to the utilitarian theory. Utilitarian theories legitimize in many cases the conduct of large companies that transgress the rights of minority shareholders, as the majority should always be preferred to the minority.

The majority shareholders rely on the minimal odds that if they act to the detriment of the individual stakeholders, it will be discovered, and even if it will be disclosed – they benefit from a large number of employees, consultants and lawyers, who will practically prevent the individual stakeholders from stopping the wrongdoing. If, however, the individual stakeholders sue them, the court will first of all try to reach a compromise, which is always less than the sum gained by the companies, and if the latter arrive to the conclusion that they are going to lose their case, they try to settle outside the court. In any way – the odds to repay the complete sum wronged from the stakeholders, or even more, are so slim, that every CEO who is a utilitarian has to decide to transgress the rights of the stakeholders on behalf of the owners of the companies, who also appoint him and remunerate him. He even has a fiduciary duty to do so, according to Milton Friedman, if it is legal, as the CEO has only one duty to maximize the profits of a company, which is amoral. One could arrive therefore at the conclusion that there could be no compromise between Friedman and Etzioni: either we advocate that a company, and its executives, employees and shareholders, have to conduct themselves ethically, even if it is to the detriment of profitability, or we declare that a company, a country or a person have only one duty – to maximize their welfare and utility even if it is to the detriment of others and of ethics.

To sum up, against the 'classical' economical theories suggesting that we should conduct ourselves ethically only if it is worthwhile to do so, we have to develop another theory based on a moral education, communitarian values and public opinion. Nevertheless, we should not overlook completely the utilitarian rationalizations of honesty, cost effectiveness, penalties and bonuses on honesty. We should not behave like Don Quixotes, completely detached from society searching for virtue at all cost, but we should blame especially the 'rational' businessmen who examine all their actions through the prism of profit and losses deriving from them. Ultimately, we should take into consideration pleasure and utility on the one hand and ethics and moral on the other hand, while trying to find the possible symbiosis between the two, if we do not insist on maximizing the two basic principles. The company could be analyzed at the same time as: "(1) a profit-maximizing organization operating in a more or less competitive environment, (2) a social contract defining the rights and duties of different stakeholders, and (3) a community sharing a common mission and value system. This tripartite definition of the firm means that an enterprise combines the three models of social co-ordination. It is an economic, political and moral institution." (Harvey, Business Ethics, A European Approach, Bouckaert, Business and Community, p.159)

Hasnas develops further this analysis as well as the lack of communication between ethical theorists and businessmen. "Critics of the discipline often point out that business ethicists are usually academics, and worse, philosophers, who speak in the language of abstract ethical theory... Business people, it is pointed out, express themselves in ordinary language and tend to resist dealing in abstractions. What they want to know is how to resolve the specific problems that confront them." (Business Ethics Quarterly, January 1998, Hasnas, The Normative Theories of Business Ethics, p. 19) "Far from asserting that there are no ethical constraints on a manager's obligation to increase profits, the stockholder theory contends that the ethical constraints society has embodied in its laws plus the general ethical tenet in favor of honest dealing constitute the ethical boundaries within which managers must pursue increased profitability... Few contemporary business ethicists have the kind of faith in the invisible hand of the market that neoclassical economists do. Most take for granted that a free market produces coercive monopolies, results in damaging externalities, and is beset by other instances of market failure such as the free rider and public good problems, and thus cannot be relied upon to secure the common good." (same, p. 22-23) Thus, "as an empirical theory, the stakeholder theory asserts that a business's financial success can best be achieved by giving the interests of the business's stockholders, customers, employees, suppliers, management, and local community proper consideration and adopting policies which produce the optimal balance among them… This, of course, implies that there will be times when management is obligated to sacrifice, at least partially, the interests of the stockholders to those of other stakeholders. Hence, in its normative form, the stakeholder theory implies that businesses have true social responsibilities. The stakeholder theory holds that management's fundamental obligation is not to maximize the firm's financial success, but to ensure its survival by balancing the conflicting claims of multiple stakeholders." (same, p. 25-26) "The social contract theory asserts that all businesses are ethically obligated to enhance the welfare of society by satisfying consumer and employee interests without violating any of the general canons of justice." (same, p. 29)

Almost all the large companies in the United States and a large number of the other companies have Codes of Ethics that have been written in the last ten years. Nevertheless, "codes of ethics are not a major factor in important decisions involving ethical questions. Codes may communicate the specific rules…, but they have little impact on what might be considered the important problems of business." (Madsen, Essential of Business Ethics, Robin Donald et al, A Different Look at Codes of Ethics, p.223) Those Codes of Ethics can be grouped in a few clusters:

"Cluster 1
'Be a dependable organization citizen.'

#1- Demonstrate courtesy, respect, honesty, and fairness in relationships with customers, suppliers, competitors, and other employees.
#2- Comply with safety, health, and security regulations.
#3- Do not use abusive language or actions.
#4- Dress in business-like attire.
#5- Possession of firearms on company premises is prohibited.
#6- Use of illegal drugs or alcohol on company premises is prohibited.
#7- Follow directives from supervisors.
#8- Be reliable in attendance and punctuality.
#9- Manage personal finances in a manner consistent with employment by a fiduciary institution.

Cluster 2
'Don't do anything unlawful or improper that will harm the organization.'

#1- Maintain confidentiality of customer, employee, and corporate records and information.

#2- Avoid outside activities which conflict with or impair the performance of duties.

#3- Make decisions objectively without regard to friendship or personal gain.

#4- The acceptance of any form of bribe is prohibited.

#5- Payment to any person, business, political organization, or public official for unlawful or unauthorized purposes is prohibited.

#6- Conduct personal and business dealings in compliance with all relevant laws, regulations, and policies.

#7- Comply fully with antitrust laws and trade regulations.

#8- Comply fully with accepted accounting rules and controls.

#9- Do not provide false or misleading information to the corporation, its auditors, or a government agency.

#10- Do not use company property or resources for personal benefit or any other improper purpose.

#11- Each employee is personally accountable for company funds over which he or she has control.

#12- Staff members should not have any interest in any competitor or supplier of the company unless such interest has been fully disclosed to the company.

Cluster 3
'Be good to our customers.'

#1- Strive to provide products and services of the highest quality.

#2- Perform assigned duties to the best of your ability and in the best interest of the corporation, its shareholders, and its customers.

#3- Convey true claims for products.

Unclustered Items

#1- Exhibit standards of personal integrity and professional conduct.

#2- Racial, ethnic, religious, or sexual harassment is prohibited.

#3- Report questionable, unethical, or illegal activities to your manager.

#4- Seek opportunities to participate in community services and political activities.

#5- Conserve resources and protect the quality of the environment in areas where the company operates.

#6- Members of the corporation are not to recommend attorneys, accountants, insurance agents, stockbrokers, real estate agents, or similar individuals to customers."

(Madsen, Essential of Business Ethics, Robin Donald et al, A Different Look at Codes of Ethics, p.219-220)

Unfortunately, many codes remain vague. "Many thoughtful executives have tried to address the vagueness issue – 60 percent of American companies now have detailed codes of conduct, designed to translate basic company values into specific terms. One-third of American firms have ethics training program or ethics officers. Many are now working with law firms and public accounting firms to make these programs as effective a possible. But even these comprehensive ethics programs are of little help with right-versus-right issues." (Badaracco, Defining Moments, p.30) Do we need Codes of Ethics, if they remain vague and if they are not applied in many cases, or even worse if they are the source of double standards – the theoretic standard and the practical standard, which is often in contradiction to the theoretic standard? The answer is straightforward – we need Codes of Ethics, because even if their efficiency is only partial, they might change the attitude of persons who do not behave ethically and enhance the implementation of activist business ethics in companies.

3
ETHICAL AND DEMOCRATIC EVOLUTION

"It is often easier to fight for principles than to live up to them."
(Adlai E. Stevenson in a lecture in New York City in 1952)

The evolution of business ethics in the last ten years has been accomplished in parallel to the political, social and economical world developments. It is not a coincidence that in the decade where the Iron Curtain has collapsed, most of the world conflicts have been resolved, and the western world has accomplished unprecedented economic achievements, business ethics has started to become an inevitable norm in most of the developed world, especially in the United States. The notions of quality, ecology and service have become predominant, employee harassment has become illegal, companies contribute more and more to the community, and ethics in business has ceased to be an oxymoron.

Heraclitus said that everything changes 'panta rhei' and on the other hand Mme. Angot said 'plus ca change plus c'est la meme chose', the more things change the more they stay the same. Who should we believe? Is there an evolution in morals toward a more ethical world, or will the righteous be compensated only after they die, as in this world only the sharks prosper? The answer is in the proportion of the application of morals. If in the ancient world only the Athenians were democratic and Aristotle was more or less a priest in the desert; if Moses gave his Ten Commandments in a world that was 99 percent pagan and immoral, the majority of the western world is today democratic and applies more and more ethical norms in business. There is therefore a clear-cut evolution toward a better world. It is maybe a candid perception, that was common also in Europe between the two world wars, and everybody knows what happened subsequently. But it is preferable to hope that the world has arrived at the conclusion, after experiencing everything, that the best way to prosper economically is to conduct ourselves ethically and democratically.

Fukuyama describes this development as the end of history. The 'happy end', the utopist end, or the beginning of another history, is a subject that is treated extensively by ethicists. "Today virtually all advanced countries have adopted, or are trying to adopt, liberal democratic political institutions, and a great number have simultaneously moved in the direction of market-oriented economies and integration into the global capitalist division of labor. As I have argued elsewhere, this movement constitutes an 'end of history' in the Marxist-Hegelian' sense of History as a broad evolution of human societies advancing toward a final goal. As modern technology unfolds, it shapes national economies in a coherent fashion, interlocking them in a vast global economy. The increasing complexity and information intensity of modern life at the same time renders centralized economic planning extremely difficult. The enormous prosperity created by technology-driven capitalism, in turn, serves as an incubator for a liberal regime of universal and equal rights, in which the struggle for recognition of human dignity culminates." (Fukuyama, Trust, p. 3-4)

The democratic evolution of companies is not self-evident. After experiencing a multitude of cases, where an absolute power of the companies' executives has caused astronomical losses, quasi-democratic modes of operations were adopted. It is quite far from the democracy that should be practiced in the business world, which is still mainly autocratic, but much closer than it was 100, 50 or even 10 years ago. "I have already mentioned the worst leader of the kind of Hitler-Napoleon-Henry Ford. The one whose nerves lose their sensibility. A leader who surrounds himself by yesmen is like a pilot in a 'blind' flight, who is assisted by instruments indicating him only what according to them he would have wanted to see, in lieu of showing him the real data. Furthermore, a dictator of this kind fires from the organization all the strong, independent and original men and forbids any critical discussion on his policy, in a way that when the collapse occurs there is normally no alternative policy that someone has defined and imagined, and there is no competent leader that could receive the command." (Jay, Management and Machiavelli, p.126 in the Hebrew translation) From Henry Ford to the 21st century the business world has evolved and the majority of the modern business world theories promote a democratic and ethical environment in business.

The ethical evolution has accelerated in the last few years and it tends to become democratic. The interests of all parties involved can coincide without being in evident contradiction. We talk more and more of 'win-win situations'; that we should not necessarily win to the detriment of the others. The basic moral principles are honesty, acting in good faith, in an equitable and just manner, without betraying the trust of the stakeholders, practicing reciprocity and equality, avoiding exploiting others, treating the stakeholders as equals, acting from your own free will without forcing your will on your partners. The experience of the author of this book is that we tend to use maxims such as 'win-win', while in practice we behave in the opposite. We talk about trust, mid-west ethics, Christian or Jewish morals, while the heroes of the business world are always the 'smart guys', the 'street fighters', and the prevailing maxims are 'catch as you can', and 'we cannot argue with success'. "The concept of win/lose as opposed to win/win is too often prevalent in business. We assume winning is the only way to function. Wars are probably society's extreme example of this concept. We fight for what we believe in. We translate this into business and use war terminology such as 'guerilla tactics', 'killer instincts', 'the corporate battlefield', and so on. If we continue to promote war-related words, we will continue to see business as a 'fight'. In such a mentality, there is little room, even in a minor disagreement of the day, for others to win. If someone else wins, then we perceive the situation as if we have lost; losing is viewed as unacceptable." (Chatfield, The Trust Factor, p. 80-1)

Surely, there is a large gap between the ethical theories and practice in business. In wanting to achieve too much we could discourage the businessmen who want in good faith to conduct themselves ethically but find that it is practically impossible to implement all the indicatives of the Codes of Ethics. We have also to take into consideration that businessmen do not operate in a vacuum, and it is impossible to behave impeccably while your colleagues behave without scruples. Therefore, this book suggests introducing ethics gradually into business in order not to discourage those who want to behave ethically and to enable them to function in an efficient and profitable manner. We could abstain from performing actions that are flagrantly unethical. In the second stage, progressively we could advance in the path of ethics, and even if we evolve gradually the improvement will be monumental in comparison to the prevailing situation. For example, if instead of having a ratio of 1 to 100 between the salaries of the CEO and the lowest paid employee, you would reduce the difference to 1 to 50, it would be an important achievement.

An encouraging step in the moral support and cultural validation of the American business world was taken in 1989 by the "Business Enterprise Trust, an independent nonprofit organization led by prominent leaders of American business, labor, academia, and the media... like Warren E. Buffet, chairman and chief executive officer of Berkshire Hathaway Inc.; Katharine Graham, chairman of the executive committee of The Washington Post Company; Ambassador Sol Linowitz; and Henry B. Schacht, ... chairman and chief executive officer of Lucent Technologies... Each year the Trust honors five awardees who have shown bold, creative leadership in combining sound management and social conscience." (Bollier, Aiming Higher, p.VIII - IX)

Three of the awardees are:
- Jack Stack and the company Springfield ReManufacturing, which have installed an 'open books' system, where all the financial results of the company are accessible to all its employees. As a result of this system, the financial results of the company have improved radically, and the community of employees has become cohesive, laborious and enthusiastic. The philosophy of Stack is to treat the employees as human

beings who want to contribute their intelligence, creativity and energy to the company.

- The ice-cream company Ben & Jerry's, which was founded by Ben Cohen and Jerry Greenfield, contributes 7.5 percent of its pretax profits to the communities of Vermont, compared to an average of 1 percent in the United States. In order to evaluate rigorously the social performance of the company, external auditors prepare social audits each year, which are published with the financial reports of the company. The audit includes the morale of the employees, the environmental performance, the customers' satisfaction, and the contribution to the community.

- The pharmaceutical company Merck, which has developed and distributed for free Mectizan, a remedy for river blindness sickness, which is widely spread in Africa amongst populations who do not have the means to buy this medicine. Merck was cited by Fortune as the most admired company in seven consecutive years. With a sales turnover of $16.7 billion in 1995 and a net profit of $3.3 billion, Merck is very sensitive to its social responsibility mission. The value of the free donation of Mectizan in 12 years is estimated at $250 million.

We should elaborate in more details the example of Ben & Jerry's, as it is significant for a company behaving ethically by conviction. According to the founders of the company, Ben Cohen and Jerry Greenfield: "By incorporating concern for the community – local, national, and global – into its strategic and operating plans, the values-led business can make everyday business decisions that actualize the company's social and financial goals at the same time. Instead of choosing areas of activity based solely on its own short-term self-profitability, the value-led business recognized that by self-addressing social problems along with financial concerns, a company can earn a respected place in the community, a special place in customers' hearts, and healthy profits, too... Unlike most commercial transactions, buying a product from a company you believe in transcends the purchase. It touches your soul. Our customers don't like just our ice creams – they like what our company stands for... Our experience has shown that you don't have to sacrifice social involvement on the altar of maximized profits. One builds on the other. The more we actualize our commitment to social change through our business activities, the more loyal customers we attract and the more profitable we become." (Cohen and Greenfield, Ben & Jerry's Double-Dip, p. 30-1)

The ethical evolution follows the ecological evolution, which has followed the democratic evolution and the evolution of human rights. Those movements are in direct correlation and will become in the near future the norm of conduct of all civilized countries. "The socially responsible business movement is in its early stages. It's at a critical point in its development. There's a lot of questioning going on – some of it cynical, some well intentioned – about where it's headed and whether it can actually work. The same thing happened in the early days of the environmental movement. The mainstream pooh-poohed it. People called environmentalists 'tree huggers' and 'crazy hippies'. Now there's curbside recycling in most major American cities. There's a steady stream of environmental legislation moving through Congress. Environmental considerations are a part of the normal planning process today. Many corporations have environmental coordinators on staff. Most Americans know there's no 'away' to throw things. Concern for the environment doesn't seem so crazy anymore. That's the way social movements change what the norms are. Our guess is, it'll be that way with values-led business. It won't be long before the idea that business should be a positive force in society won't seem crazy either. We know the world won't change overnight. What we're talking about here is taking small steps. The important thing is to take them in the right direction – and in the company of a lot of good people." (Cohen and Greenfield, Ben & Jerry's Double-Dip, p. 53-4)

In spite of the optimism of Ben & Jerry, and of many other ethical businessmen, it is still difficult to discern which tendencies will govern the business world of the 2000s. Will it be a democratic and ethical world, or a cynical and hypocritical world, which will render lip service to ethics while continuing to be brutal and selfish, or rather a world in slow transition, that will last a century as did the transition from the autocratic world at the beginning of the 20th century to the democratic world of today? One cannot also ignore the regressions, and many businessmen who have started their career as ethical men have come to the conclusion that in order to progress and manage a company selling hundreds of millions or billions of dollars they have to behave in an unethical manner. To alleviate their conscience they can become philanthropists like the robber barons, and finance a cathedra at the university, buy a few Renoirs for a museum, or found a billion dollars fund for charitable causes. Is there a threshold beyond which it is impossible to behave ethically? Is it possible to found a financial empire while remaining ethical? This theme could be the subject of another book.

One of the preconditions for ethical evolution, democracy, the welfare society and human rights, is an affluent economy that enables us to conduct ourselves ethically, while the basic needs of existence are already provided for. We can behave in an unethical manner even in rich countries like the Roman Empire in its decadent period, and we can behave humanely even in extreme situations as in some Nazi concentration camps, but in general the rich countries can afford to behave ethically and democratically. One extreme example of inhuman conduct is the one of the Iks, an extremely poor tribe of Uganda, which was studied by Colin Turnbull, an anthropologist who lived among them from 1964 to 1967.

"Turnbull came to describe the Ik as 'the loveless people'. Each Ik valued only his or her own survival, and regarded everyone else as a competitor for food. Ik life had become a grim process of trying to find enough food to stay alive each day. The hunt consumed all of their resources, leaving virtually no reserve for feelings of any kind, nor for any moral scruples that might interfere with filling their stomachs. As Margaret Mead wrote, the Ik had become 'a people who have become monstrous beyond belief.' Scientist Ashley Montagu wrote that the Ik are 'a people who are dying because they have abandoned their own humanity... Both morality and personality among the Ik were dedicated to the single all-consuming passion for self-preservation. There was simply 'not room in the life of these people,' Turnbull observes dryly, 'for such luxuries as family and sentiment and love.' Nor for any morality beyond 'Marangik', the new Ik concept of goodness, which means filling one's own stomach... America now faces a wilding epidemic that is eating at the country's social foundation and could rot it. The American case is much less advanced than the Ik's, but the disease is deeply rooted and is spreading through the political leadership, the business community, and the general population. Strong medicine can turn the situation around, but if we fail to act now, the epidemic could prove irreversible." (Derber, The Wilding of America, p. 5-6)

Savage, inhuman and immoral conduct is never justifiable, but in the case of the Iks it could be comprehensible. In today's France, Israel, Great Britain and the United States it is unjustifiable and incomprehensible. In 1990, 70 percent of Americans have contributed to charitable works and 50 percent have acted as volunteers in social works. What is dismaying is that probably some of those people behave in their business life in a manner that is often immoral and they do not see the contradiction in their double standards. An ancient proverb in Ladino, a Spanish-Jewish dialect, describes those people who 'rovan pitas y bezan mezuzot', who rob while being religious, and this hypocritical conduct is probably the most dangerous and difficult to fight.

We know where we stand after spending two hours with the Iks, but it is much harder to beware of a respectable businessman with an impeccable reputation, who is Doctor Honoris Causa or Officer of the Legion of Honor, yet who behaves like a highway robber in his business dealings. This comes largely from greediness, although it is difficult for us to understand what is the difference in the quality of life between a fortune of $5M and one of $15M. Nevertheless, many crimes and unethical acts are conducted by majority shareholders who wrong individual stakeholders in order to gain a few million dollars more, money they probably will not be able to spend in their lifetime. Do we have to wait for an extreme crisis in order to recover ethics and values, as has happened in the past? To avoid such extreme cases, we have to act today, at the risk of being ridiculed like Don Quixotes, booed like Zola, or perhaps even gain respect afterwards like Gandhi did.

"Over the last hundred years, American history can be read as a succession of wilding periods alternating with eras of civility. The Robber Baron era of the 1880s and the 1890s, an age of spectacular economic and political wilding, was followed by the Progressive Era of the early 20th century, in which moral forces reasserted themselves. The individualistic license of the 1920s, another era of economic and political wilding epitomized by the Teapot Dome scandal, yielded to the New Deal era of the 1930s and the 1940s, when America responded to the Great Depression with remarkable moral and community spirit. The moral idealism of a new generation of youth in the 1960s was followed by the explosion of political, economic, and social wilding in the current era... The prospect of the death of society gave birth to the question symbolized by the Ik: What makes society possible and prevents it from disintegrating into a mass of sociopathic and self-interested isolates? This core question of sociology has become the vital issue of our times." (Derber, The Wilding of America, p. 14-5)

"Criminologists Fox and Levin define sociopaths as 'self-centered, manipulative, possessive, envious, reckless, and unreliable. They demand special treatment and inordinate attention, often exaggerating their own importance... On their way to the top, sociopaths ruthlessly step over their competitors without shame and guilt.'... A sociopathic society is one, like the Ik, marked by a collapse of moral order resulting from the breakdown of community and the failure of institutions responsible for inspiring moral vision and creating and enforcing robust moral codes. In such a society, the national character-type tends toward sociopathy, and idealized behavior, although veiled in a rhetoric of morality, becomes blurred with antisocial egoism." (same, p. 24)

The business world is more and more conscientious of the necessity of ethics. In the annual polls of the Gallup Organization, the number of persons who insist that a 'strict moral code' is 'very important' has increased steadily from 47 percent in 1981 to 60 percent in 1989. But on the other hand, "Asked in a Harris Poll in 1992 to name the groups with good moral and ethical standards, American adults said: small business owners (64 percent), journalists (39 percent), business executives (31 percent), lawyers (25 percent), members of Congress (19 percent)." (Kidder, How Good People Make Tough Choices, p.48).

Do people in general and businessmen in particular have a tendency to cheat and conduct themselves in an unethical manner? "The baseline research on cheating was done in the 1920s by Hartshorne and May, and published by Macmillan under the title, Studies of the Nature of Character. Their research question was, 'Do people who have received character education (later called moral education and now often known as ethics training) cheat less frequently than those who have not received character education?' One activity they used to investigate the question was to administer tests to different groups of students (religious, private, and public schools) and monitor the cheating rates. Their conclusion? They found that character education had 'no influence on producing a general moral character trait which consistently resists opportunities to cheat.' One of their assumptions was that cheating in school indicated future cheating as an adult.

Since their controversial reports were published, the research methodology has been repeated over 700 times in the United States, Canada, United Kingdom, France, Germany, Israel, and in many Eastern and Spanish-speaking countries. What does over 60 years of research in over 30 countries have to say about whether teaching right from wrong influences behavior? Hartshorne and May were right! Cheating is situation-based for 90 percent of the population. At one time or another, depending on the situation, 90 percent will cheat. The other 10 percent? They will cheat all of the time, unless it is too easy! When the stakes are high and the supervision is low, somewhere between 20-25 percent will cheat. It is not always the same 20-25 percent; and over a period of time, 90 percent will cheat in that situation. Where the stakes are high and the supervision is high, the cheating runs from 8-12 percent. This includes the hard-core cheaters and those driven by desperation.

Does this 60 years of research hold true for adults? The Roper Organization conducted a nationwide survey on cheating in the workplace. They found that 25 percent of the people surveyed admitted to the pollsters on the telephone that they cheated on their income taxes, 20 percent admitted to lying to their boss, 22 percent thought there were circumstances in which stealing from an employer was justified, and 18 percent admitted padding expense accounts. Corporate, independent and government auditors might place some of the percentages higher… The same cheating rates hold consistent at community and junior colleges. Consistency seems to be the theme from age to age, geographic location to location, and time to time… Thus, simply having a code, teaching it to people, and increasing supervision will not eliminate all the cheating. Enforcement is required." (Ward, A Code of Business Ethics, p.6-7)

In a poll conducted by Professor Donald McCabe of Rutgers University among 6,000 students in 31 universities, the highest percentage of students who admitted cheating at least once in an examination or a major paper was among the business administration students – 76 percent, compared to 63 percent among Law students or 68 percent among medical students. In order to change those alarming findings we have to change the attitude of the business students and the managers of companies. "Ethics is not a blind impartiality, doling out right and wrong according to some stone-cold canon of ancient and immutable law. It's a warm and supremely human activity that cares enough for others to want right to prevail." (Kidder, How Good People Make Tough Choices, p.59).

Wuthnow cites in his book 'Poor Richard's Principle' that a study conducted by the National Accounting Association in the U.S. has revealed that 87 percent of American managers were ready to commit a fraud in one or many cases that were presented to them. Another study conducted among 400 salesmen revealed that it is the fear of being discovered, and not moral principles that prevent people from transgressing the laws. Wuthnow, himself, has discovered in a study that 48 percent have maintained that it is justifiable to bend the rules from time to time at work, and 32 percent have disclosed that they have seen colleagues commit unethical acts in the last month.

Derber in his book 'The Wilding of America' writes about a poll made by Professors Kanter and Mirvis of the Boston University, showing that the wilding state of mind has spread all over the country. "Self-interest, Kanter and Mirvis believe, has become such an overwhelming urge that it is pushing empathy and moral sensibility into the far background. They describe an American landscape in which close to half of the population takes as its basic assumption 'that most people are only out for themselves and that you are better off zapping them before they do it to you. Many Americans, Kanter and Mirvis report, believe that their fellow Americans will cheat and lie to get what they want, especially when money is concerned. Sixty percent say that they expect 'people will tell a lie if they can get by it,' and 62 percent say that 'people claim to have ethical standards, but few stick to them when money is at stake.' About half say that 'an unselfish person is taken advantage of in today's world', and slightly under half believe that people 'inwardly dislike putting themselves out to help other people.'

As among the Ik, who take positive pleasure in hurting others, none of this strikes Americans as particularly noteworthy or surprising. Forty-three percent – and more than half of young people under 24 years of age – see selfishness and fakery at the core of human nature. Millions of Americans, Kanter and Mirvis conclude, are hard-boiled cynics who, 'to put it simply, believe that lying, putting on a false face, and doing whatever it takes to make a buck' are all part of the nature of things… Making reference to the culture of the Reagan-Bush era, Kanter argues, 'The tendency to behave cynically is being reinforced to an unprecedented degree by a social environment that seems to have abandoned idealism and increasingly celebrates the virtue of being 'realistic' in an impersonal, acquisitive tough-guy world.' He could be talking to the Ik when he concludes that 'in citizen and country alike, there seems to be a loss of faith in people and in the very concept of community." (Derber, The Wilding of America, p. 90-1)

One of the reasons of this state of mind could stem from the alarming findings of the National Center for Health Statistics, showing that stress afflicts 59 percent of the workforce at least once a week, that 44 percent seldom get enough time for themselves and 46 percent feel sometimes that they are burned out in their jobs. In recent surveys it was revealed that "Most Americans still work hard and feel it is meaningful and important to do so, but a majority (77 percent in one study) also worry that they have become workaholics – addicted to something that may be preventing them from realizing the full measure of life. Despite their interest in material possessions, a large majority (72 percent) readily admit that they 'want more from life than just a good job and a comfortable lifestyle.' Most (78 percent) say they do think a lot about their values and priorities in life, but a sizable minority (35 percent) also claim they 'need more time to think about the really basic issues in life.' Economic progress, it appears, has produced material abundance but not enough time to think about how to translate this abundance into qualitative improvements of life itself. How to rein in our economic commitments – or at least steer them in more desirable directions – is the question we seem increasingly to be asking." (Wuthnow, Poor Richard's Principle, p.36)

Trust has a predominant role in the business world, although the erosion of trust costs exorbitant amounts to the modern economy. "It is ironic, then, that at a time when there is increased trust between the superpowers, there seems to be less trust by many within and between businesses. Downsizing, mergers, outsourcing, and reengineering have led to mistrust by many employees of the business for which they work (or worked). Dangerous products, invasive marketing, and efforts to pressure people to agree to unneeded repairs have fostered mistrust between customers and businesses. Takeovers, leveraged buyouts and corporate espionage have fostered mistrust among businesses. And yet the importance of trust within and between business organizations, both nationally and internationally, is increasingly recognized. Trust is said not only to reduce transaction costs, make possible the sharing of sensitive information, permit joint projects of various kinds, but also to provide a basis for expanded moral relations in business. Indeed, many (such as Gewirth and Hosmer) have claimed that ethics and trust are bound up together." (Business Ethics Quarterly, April 1998, Brenkert, Trust, Business and Business Ethics: An Introduction, p. 195).

But trust also has its limits and risks, and having an absolute trust in a leader or a fuhrer has caused in the past severe repercussions. One has to find the middle way between trust and suspicion, as unfortunately it is still impossible to have unreserved trust in the business world, even if we possess the best intentions. "A trust relation implies very little with respect to organizational ends. Parties to a trust relationship can engage just as easily in unethical and even illegal behavior as they can in ethical behavior (Koehn, 1996; Baier,

1986). Witness such groups as the Mafia where members of such ethnically homogenous groups prefer to do business in 'old boys' networks (Landa, 1994). Fanaticism may take place on the basis of trust relationships due to shared values. Howell and Avolio (1992: 47) describe the trust that employees of Michael Milken had in the junk bond king. They report that, according to one former subordinate, 'if he walked off the cliff, everyone in that group would have followed him.'" (Business Ethics Quarterly, April 1998, Husted, The Ethical Limits of Trust in Business Relations, p. 239)

Trust has its national nuances. Japan, Germany, and even the United States until not so long ago, are societies with a very high level of trust and social orientation; while France, Italy and China are societies which are more individualistic and mistrusting, especially toward the authorities. Fukuyama maintains that the United States is a country in transition from trust to mistrust, with a very high budget of police protection, more than 1 percent of the population in prison, a very high percentage of lawyers and an exorbitant cost of mistrust deriving from those tendencies and amounting to many percents of the national product. This mistrust tax, including the transaction costs, is imposed also on the French and Italian economies, while the trust of the German and Japanese societies are at the basis of their accelerated growth in the past.

"Law, contract, and economic rationality provide a necessary but not sufficient basis for both the stability and prosperity of postindustrial societies; they must as well be leavened with reciprocity moral obligation, duty toward community, and trust, which are based in habit rather than rational calculation. The latter are not anachronisms in a modern society but rather the sine qua non of the latter's success." (Fukuyama, Trust, p. 11) Nevertheless, the United States could succeed to make a spectacular turnaround as we saw at the turn of the century, in associating individualism and communitarism, which are inherent in its society, causing an interaction that joins together the advantages of the individualistic and communitarian societies.

The economic repercussions of trust exist in the Japanese keiretsu, like Sumitomo and Mitsubishi, which are groups allying many companies, often around a bank, each one possessing shares in the other companies as in a gigantic spider web, treating each other in a preferential mode. With the Koreans we find the chaebol, like Samsung and Hyundai. On the other hand, the Americans and the British have arms-length regulations obliging the different groups of companies to treat each other equitably, as with an unaffiliated company. In the Chinese society, the private companies are almost always family companies. The CEOs of the Japanese companies are professional executives while the Chinese executives are almost always members of the families that control the companies.

"The true essence of Chinese Confucianism was never political Confucianism at all but rather what Tu Wei-ming calls the 'Confucian personal ethic'. The central core of this ethical teaching was the apotheosis of the family – in Chinese – the jia – as the social relationship to which all others were subordinate. Duty to the family trumped all other duties, including obligations to emperor, Heaven, or any other source of temporal or divine authority. Of the five cardinal Confucian relationships, that between father and son was key, for it established the moral obligation of xiao, or filial piety, which is Confucianism's central moral imperative." (Fukuyama, Trust, p. 85) Here also, we see the predominant place that religion and national morals have over the ethical conduct in the business world. Trust and ethics are perceived as the outcome of modern economy, democracy and evolution. But they are also inherently linked to thousand years old religions and philosophy, as we shall see in the following chapters.

4
ACTIVIST BUSINESS ETHICS IN CHRISTIANITY

"No servant can serve two masters. Either he will hate the one and love the other, or he will be devoted to the one and despise the other. You cannot serve both God and Money." (The Bible, The New Testament, Luke, 16:13)

In the last ten years we witnessed an effervescence of Protestant Christian ethics in the U.S. business world, in order to counterbalance the immoral norms of the 80s and 90s. In parallel, there are more and more books and articles that try to prove that the ethical norms in business, according to Catholic, Jewish, Moslem, Buddhist or other religions, are the norms that should be implemented in order to return to the religious ethical sources. On the other hand, secular authors are in favor of the ethical norms of Aristotle, Adam Smith or other philosophers. A profound reading on the business ethics of the principal religions and of the humanist philosophers can prove that there are very slight differences between the different ethical versions and ultimately the business world knows exactly what should be done when one advocates adhesion to ethical norms that are practically universal.

In order to understand the importance of business ethics in the 20th century, one should analyze the Protestant ethical precepts, elaborated principally by Max Weber, a German economist, sociologist and philosopher who lived from 1864 to 1920 and published in 1901 a well-known article: 'The Protestant ethics and the spirit of capitalism'. In his article he proves that the behavior of individuals is understood only if we take into account their beliefs on the world, which include their religious beliefs. If there is a homology between Protestant ethics and capitalism, it is the puritan that realizes it, existing only in the western civilization. The Protestant middle class advocated frugality based on work. Nevertheless, the tendency to tie up the basis of ethics and modern business on the Protestant foundations should also bear in mind that the same foundations prevailed also in the Catholic, Jewish or secular middle class.

In Protestant morals, word of honor is sacred, a handshake is worth more than a contract, and integrity is the most precious human commodity. If a person was honest, God rewarded him, and if one was dishonest, God punished him. An immoral conduct was the cause of a profound sense of culpability. But in large bureaucratic organizations, it is no longer possible to link directly the actions with morals. An individual is no longer directly responsible, as responsibility is divided throughout the hierarchy. A person does not go anymore to the priest to seek moral guidance, as the manager replaces the priest. However, one should not be too carried away by the idealism of these morals, as in many cases it describes an utopist theory, which was not followed by all businessmen, and a large number of them behaved hypocritically and rendered only lip service to those Protestant ideals. At best, we could accept the ideals of the Judeo-Christian morals as a guide, without establishing that practice followed the guide, as the Tartuffes exist in all peoples and in all religions, and probably in the same proportion, as human nature is identical.

Laura Nash in her book 'Believers in Business' describes evangelist businessmen as having a sense of sin and salvation emanating from a personal and continuous relation with Jesus Christ, an obligation to testify the love of Christ and the divine nature of Trinity, a conviction that all aspects of existence obey Biblical authority. Their conduct is based on the writings of Weber, who describes the conservative Protestant as living a diligent, frugal, punctual, and equitable life in all its aspects. We have to compare two ethics: the ethics of self-interest, of Adam Smith, Friedman, Bentham and others, which maintain that everything is interest in life and especially in the business world, as it is not out of benevolence of the butcher and the baker that we eat our dinner but out of interest; and on the other hand the ethics of alliance, engagement and love, stating that the aim of business is to create values, establish human relations, and render services. The author of this book suggests to all those who read it to make a list of all their actions performed in a typical day or in several days and to classify them as actions motivated by interests and actions motivated by duty, love, sociability, sympathy or sentiment. They would probably find that the majority of actions are not motivated by interests, and that the simplistic theories of the Smiths and Benthams are much less sophisticated than the Judeo-Christian theories that will be elaborated in this book.

"The role of faith is to reestablish the proper perspective, but that perspective is itself full of paradoxical viewpoints that combine a deep sense of the immediate with a calm sense of distance... The believer CEO has the decisiveness and courage to act, and yet chooses to lead according to more relational, participatory input... Keeping these paradoxes in tension is what keeps the ego in check, and yet it creates the self-confidence to take risks, handle failures, accept short-term sacrifice for long-term value." (Nash, Believers in Business, p.193-4) There is for example in the United States - Christian Yellow Pages in the most important cities for those who want to favor Christian suppliers that allegedly share their same convictions. The evangelist managers often prefer to receive professional services from lawyers, members of Board of Directors, or colleagues from the same congregation, although it is very difficult to abstain in the modern business world from an association with members of other religious faith.

If we go back to the origins, we find that Jesus Christ blesses the poor and offers them the Kingdom of Heaven, preaches against the greed of wealth, as it is easier for a camel to go through a needle hole than for the rich to reach the Kingdom of Heaven. One cannot serve at the same time God and Mammon, or money. The poor have no duties toward the rich, but the rich have a duty to be charitable. Saint Augustin preconizes that it is forbidden to get rich by making others poor. Trade was perceived by the first Christians with a certain disdain, as it was associated with fraud and greed. It was forbidden to charge interests, but it was allowed to make a profit on an investment.

The religious importance in the United States is evident even today. 85% of Americans have received a religious education in their childhood, 84% believe in God as a Celestial Father, to whom they can pray, 75% believe that Jesus was the Son of the Lord, 71% believe that there is life after death, 67% are members of a church or synagogue, 40% go to church every week and 38% define themselves as new evangelical Christians. But the number of Americans stating that religion is very important for them has declined from 75% in 1952 to 56% today, and the belief that the Bible is literally the word of God has diminished from 65% in 1963 to 32% in 1992.

Church is perceived in the business administration faculties as the enterprise that is managed in the best manner in the last 2000 years. "The all-time greatest management entrepreneur is Jesus Christ. Just look at what he accomplished. By any measurement standard, the empirical evidence bears witness that the organization founded by Jesus is the most successful of all time. Longevity? Two thousand years are counting. Wealth? Beyond calculation. Numbers? Beyond counting. Loyalty of adherents? Many give their lives for it. Distribution? Worldwide, in every country. Diversification? Successfully integrated into all kinds of enterprises. Ergo, Jesus Christ reigns supreme as the greatest manager the world has ever known." (Briner, The Management Methods of Jesus, p. xi)

Jesus has always insisted on the differentiation between true and false, just and unjust, good and bad. "A lack of absolutes can lead to all kinds of corporate problems, from petty thievery to major crimes. It leads to shoddy products and shoddy practices in the marketplace." (Briner, The Management Methods of Jesus, p. 17) "When there is clear, irrefutable evidence of corruption within the corporation, move immediately to handle it. Never, never try to cover it up... Jesus' decision to drive the goons out of the temple wasn't based on rumors or unsubstantial reports. He knew what was going on. He saw it. Gather your facts, then act. Don't put it off. Get it over with and move on." (Briner, The Management Methods of Jesus, p. 22-23) Those precepts are identical to the precepts that should be implemented by ethical managers who have to differentiate between just and unjust and intervene without delay against every act that is not ethical in their companies.

One of the cardinal problems of companies is the information that independent directors receive from their companies, the flattery exercised on them, and the necessity they have to discern between true and false statements. Here also we can take example from what Jesus said to the Pharisees: "You hypocrites! Isaiah was right when he prophesied about you: 'These people honor me with their lips, but their hearts are far from me.' " (The Bible, Matthew, 15:7-8) Briner describes the analogy: "Board members are too often brought in, wined, dined, and entertained and given only the brightest of pictures as to the state of the enterprise…. The easiest thing to do as an outside director is to take all the reports of the corporate executives at face value and never ask questions. A rule of thumb is that if you are only getting good news, you are not getting the whole picture…. Jesus provides the greatest of all examples. He continually dismissed insincere flatterers, but accepted honest praise graciously…. In business as in life, we need to be sure that we discern the difference between honest praise and insincere, self-serving, sycophantic flattery. We need to do as Jesus did: Seek the truth in all things and in all people." (Briner, The Management Methods of Jesus, p. 54-55)

Honesty is at the base of the Judeo-Christian ethics. "For the Lord detests a perverse man but takes the upright into his confidence. The Lord's curse is on the house of the wicked, but he blesses the home of the righteous." (The Bible, The Old Testament, Proverbs, 3:32-33) "Above all else, guard your heart, for it is the wellspring of life. Put away perversity from your mouth; keep corrupt talk far from your lips. Let your eyes look straight ahead, fix your gaze directly before you. Make level paths for your feet and take only ways that are firm. Do not swerve to the right or the left; keep your foot from evil." (The Bible, Proverbs, 4:23-27) Honesty is therefore rewarded and dishonesty is punished.

"A radical Christian (by my definition) is one who will put God first in all decisions, even when putting God first is costly. In the business world, this means putting God first even when doing so costs money. That is true freedom – spiritual freedom – as opposed to business bondage." (Burkett, Business by the Book, p. 29) "Clearly God's Word says that a deception will always be found out: 'He who walks in integrity walks securely, But he who perverts his way will be found out' (Prov. 10:9) Total honesty is the minimum acceptable standard for a Christian. If a business cannot survive in total honesty, then it's time to do something else." (Burkett, Business by the Book, p. 63)

We find in the Bible answers to ethical problems that preoccupied business philosophers from Adam Smith to Friedman. "Every Christian in business – employer and employee alike – should work to maximize profits, but not to the exclusion of the other elements of a biblically based business. For an employer to maximize profits by underpaying employees, for instance, is a violation of the second function of a Christian business: meeting needs." (Burkett, Business by the Book, p. 52) This is therefore the Biblical solution to the double allegiance toward the shareholders and the other stakeholders. The Bible refers especially to suppliers: "Without a doubt those who provide materials on credit have the first right to any available income from a business. I realize this runs contrary to current business logic, which says, "When money is tight, string out your accounts payable." But consider Proverbs 12:22: 'Lying lips are an abomination to the Lord/ But those who deal faithfully are His delight.' When someone orders materials with an implied promise to pay, but does not do so, that person is simply lying." (Burkett, Business by the Book, p. 55)

It is estimated that the annual loss of the American economy due to employees' theft amounts to $160 billion, but there are no statistics on the losses incurred by the wrongdoing of executives and majority shareholders. Those losses could be estimated by the Institute of Ethics, and should include the losses incurred to companies, stakeholders, minority shareholders and the state. The losses per capita could be enormous, and some executives could incur to their companies huge losses as was proven in some cases in the last few years. A Judeo-Christian or secular ethics of the executives of the companies could reduce substantially the losses to world economy. In the business environment, where keeping a promise is just a question of economic worthwhileness, and where ethical conduct is favored only in cases where it assists in maximizing profits, it is necessary to recall what were the norms in a recent past. "Yet only a generation ago, keeping a vow was the norm in our society. Those who would not keep their word were shunned by those around them and few people would do business with them. I doubt that most of our grandparents knew anyone who had gone bankrupt or even defaulted on a loan to a local merchant. Debtors' prisons were still in operation as late as the 1920s in America, and divorce lawyers would have had a hard time earning a living in our grandparents' day… What our society needs is a good dose of biblical ethic from God's people – the kind of ethic that requires us to keep our word no matter what the costs. Situational ethics have so shaped our society that even God's people have lost the concept of absolutes when it comes to keeping our word." (Burkett, Business by the Book, p. 68)

This book will deal extensively on the cost of mistrust in business. It is inconceivable that astronomical sums are squandered every year in order to prepare in many cases ambiguous contracts with the sole intention of breaking them and getting away with it. Imagine what we could accomplish allocating all those billions toward ecology, growth, struggle against poverty, unemployment and disease. If the businessmen would have an almost complete trust in their dealings with stakeholders, if they would participate in an ethical league, similar to the Free Masons, we could resolve all the problems of mistrust, which are completely superfluous and counter-productive. "In my father's generation when a man gave his word to do a job he did it! If he didn't, no one would do business with him again. Today, if you reach an agreement on almost anything, you need several attorneys to review the contract to make sure it contains no loopholes that could allow the other parties to escape fulfilling their part of the bargain. In fact, the highest-paid, most successful attorneys are often those who can weave the most ambiguous language into a contract so that the actual intent is assumed but not mandated." (Burkett, Business by the Book, p. 70-71) Truly, Burkett idealizes a lot, as the previous generations were those of the robber barons, the Tartuffes, who while going assiduously to church, exploited in the worst manner their workers in sweat shops, but at least the norms were different. As this book is not a historical book, we will not deal further on what was the situation in the past but rather on what should be the behavior in the future.

The Bible is full of precepts, which guide us on the conduct toward business partners, employees, the community, etc. The New Testament favors Activist Business Ethics and attacks mainly the rich who wrong the rights of the poor, "Now listen, you rich people, weep and wail because of the misery that is coming upon you. Your wealth has rotted, and moths have eaten your clothes. Your gold and silver are corroded. Their corrosion will testify against you and eat your flesh like fire. You have hoarded wealth in the last days. Look! The wages you failed to pay the workmen who mowed your fields are crying out against you. The cries of the harvesters have reached the ears of the Lord Almighty. You have lived on earth in luxury and self-indulgence. You have condemned and murdered innocent men, who were not opposing you. Be patient, then, brothers, until the Lord's coming." (The Bible, James, 5:1-7) It is with a great sympathy and conviction that we read those citations, which are much more extreme than those of Mao Tse Tung, with the sole difference that Saint James exhorts us to wait the Lord's coming, while Mao and other revolutionaries lost their patience after their people have been waiting for 2000 years and have decided to take the fate of their people in their hands. This is therefore the great dilemma of Christian businessmen, should they wait for the Lord's coming in order to remedy the ethical norms and practice or should they do it by themselves in the present.

The Old Testament suggests also waiting until the Last Judgment in order to see the dishonest succumb, as it does not give an exact date for solving the day-to-day problems that annoyed the Hebrews thousands of years ago as they do nowadays. "The Lord abhors dishonest scales, but accurate weights are his delight. When pride comes, then comes disgrace, but with humility comes wisdom. The integrity of the upright guides them, but the unfaithful are destroyed by their duplicity. Wealth is worthless in the day of wrath, but righteousness delivers from death." (The Bible, Proverbs, 11:1-4) The author of this book will try to illustrate how difficult it is to find fundamental differences in the domain of business ethics between the different religions, the modern secular theories or the precepts of Aristotle. Nevertheless, as we have mentioned before, there is a large number of Christian businessmen who are tempted to do business exclusively with their coreligionists, as apparently they share the same ethical convictions. "Few knowledgeable Christians would marry a nonbeliever (although some foolishly do). Yet many Christians will enter partnerships with nonbelievers, thinking they can make them work. If they succeed, it is generally because they aren't committed to applying God's principles to their business. Usually these partnerships are rationalized on the basis of economic necessity – not biblical principle." (Burkett, Business by the Book, p. 195) Therefore, according to Burkett, if partnerships between Christians, Jews or Japanese succeed it is generally because they did not commit to apply God's precepts in business, and the only way to apply the biblical precepts is to do business exclusively with Christians.

The Bible assures a reward on honest behavior in this world or in the next. "It is also within God's power to grant material blessings to those who truly follow His directions. 'Riches and honor are with me, enduring wealth and righteousness.' (Proverbs, 8:18) But many times God elects to store those riches for distribution in eternity, in which case the rewards are multiplied a thousandfold (see Matthew 6:20)" (Burkett, Sound Business Principles, p. 39) Luke has said: "No servant can serve two masters. Either he will hate the one and love the other, or he will be devoted to the one and despise the other. You cannot serve both God and Money." (The Bible, The New Testament, Luke, 16:13) The seculars probably believe that it is worthier not to serve any master at all, not to be a servant, to be a free man or woman, free in conducting yourself ethically not for God's glory, not for receiving in the future a better return on investment, not for paradise, but only for humanistic reasons, for the love of your neighbor and friend.

According to Burkett, the secular could succumb to drugs, immorality and divorce: "In our society most people are looking for guidance and unwavering commitment to principles. Unfortunately, when these can't be found, many people are duped by the humanist's argument that 'values are established by society.' The end result of this lie can be seen in the abuses of our day – drugs used to escape reality, sexual immorality, a high rate of divorce – and ultimately in the collapse of society itself… A Christian must decide either to follow Christ or to follow Satan. There is no middle road. A business will be dedicated to the furtherance of either God's kingdom or Satan's." (Burkett, Sound Business Principles, p. 44-45) And to reinforce his arguments, Burkett continues: "Secular business philosophy teaches that 'to the victor belong the spoils.' That translates into a trait the Bible calls selfishness. 'He who shuts his ear to the cry of the poor will also cry himself and not be answered.' (Proverbs 21:13)" (same, p. 55).

Burkett generalizes therefore that the secular philosophy advocates selfishness and ignoring the cries of the poor, and to reinforce his arguments he cites once more the Old Testament. However, this book advocates the secular theory of Etzioni, which stands in complete opposition to the perception of Burkett on the secular theories of business ethics. Furthermore, the ethical theories of many other Jewish, Buddhist or pagan philosophers like Aristotle, who are no more Satanic than the witches of Salem, are no less humanistic than the Christian precepts preconized by Burkett, and fully concur with the Christian business ethics.

Activist Business Ethics is therefore strongly linked with Christianity, but Christianity in its fundamental approach, preached by Jesus and the Apostles, which was open to all mankind, and not only to sectarian Christianity.

5
ACTIVIST BUSINESS ETHICS IN JUDAISM

"Do not exploit the poor because they are poor
And do not crush the needy in court,
For the Lord will take up their case
And will plunder those who plunder them."
(The Bible, Proverbs, 22:22-23)

"על דאטפת – אטפוך, וסוף מטיפיך – יטופון"
Al deateft atafouh - vesof metifaih yetoufoun (Aramaic).

"Because you have drowned others - you were drowned, and those who have drowned you - will be drowned."

When Hillel the wise, as told in the Jewish Mishna, saw the head of a robber whom he knew, floating in the river, Hillel said: "Because you have robbed and murdered your victims and thrown their bodies into the river, your murderers who are also criminals have murdered you, and their crime will be punished by other criminals who will also kill them and throw their bodies into the river."

The Mishna says in Sanhedrin (kof, ain aleph):
"במידה שאדם מודד – מודדין לו"
Bemida sheadam moded – modedin lo.

"A criminal is punished by the same measure of his crime."

Haman wanted to hang Mordachai and he himself was hanged. The Egyptians drowned the Hebrew babies and were themselves drowned while chasing the Hebrews who fled from Egypt.

The Talmudic rabbis considered fraud, particularly if it is committed against the weak, as an odious crime, equivalent to murder, although it was not punished so harshly as violent crimes. The rabbinical courts treated fraud with a particular harshness, prohibiting the swindlers to conduct business, and in exceptional cases by confiscating their property.

In Judaism, poverty is not a virtue, but poor people are not blamed for their poverty. Land could be bought, but propriety expired in the next Jubilee. A luxurious life is not treated favorably and moderation is recommended for the just. The Bible forbids charging interests on other Jews, but Yitschak Abarbanel, the erudite Jewish financier of the era of Ferdinand and Isabelle, did not see any difference between a financial benefit and a commercial gain. Jewish law compels treating the gentiles honestly. One should obey the laws of the country in which he resides, as according to the Halakha – *Dina de malkhuta dina*, or - the law of the kingdom is the law.

A subject that preoccupies the religions is the charging of interests for money lent. The Jews maintain that when you lend money you do not possess it anymore and you become like the salaried who do not receive their salary on time. Time is an essential dimension and you have to be compensated for the time in which you are no more in the possession of the money, as well as for the risk that the borrower will go bankrupt.

The Jewish tradition says: "The longest way is the one who goes from the heart to the pocket." You cannot in fact go from the heart to the pocket without examining the philosophy of life and its significance. The Jews were stigmatized by the Christians as people who have an excessive love of money.

"Jews, as creators and promoters of what was to become the ethical heritage of the West, fell prey to a reaction against the restrictions it imposed on human behavior. They originated the fundamental law 'Thou shalt not kill', and yet they are charged with the great historical 'murder'... Despite being bound by severe dietary prescriptions, they are accused of cannibalistic rituals involving Christian children. And finally, Jews are saddled with a reputation for being obsessive about money. Their God, of whom they are not permitted to make images, is assigned the shape of a dollar sign. And yet it is true that the Jews respect money; for in it they see a content which speaks of the true distance between the heart and the pocket. The deeper meaning of money – and, in the broader sense, of earning a living (parnasah, livelihood) – is dealt with in Jewish tradition both ethically and with courageous humanity. The Kabbalah of Money is an offering of rabbinical and mystical insights into an ecology of money, involving the health of all forms of exchange, transaction, and interdependence." (Bonder, The Kabbalah of Money, p. 3-4)

The origin of the word Kabbalah comes from the Hebrew word *kabel*, to receive, which represents the tradition that was transmitted from generation to generation. The Kabbalah teaches that from the simple you can reach the complex, from the concrete the abstract, from the detailed the general. This concept is applied in the Kabbalah to money as to all other corporal aspects of life. The Jews respect money earned honestly as it permits them to satisfy the basic needs of life and it enables the spiritual study that is the essence of life. There is a story of a Rabbi who was permitted to visit purgatory, where he heard horrible cries coming from people sitting at a banquet. On the tables was the best food imaginable, but unfortunately the elbows of the guests were inverted, preventing them from bringing the food to their mouths. Then, he was brought to paradise, where he heard happy laughs. The same sight greeted him, but unlike in purgatory the guests were not trying to nourish themselves, rather each other... "Purgatory is a world with no Market, where a certain difficulty is enough to destroy our ability to enjoy the banquet. In paradise, besides the pleasure of the delicacies we enjoy, we soothe our frustration each time we bring food to our neighbor's mouth... In the popular collection of rabbinical sayings known as The Ethics of the Fathers (Pirkei Avot), we read: 'Where there is no flour, there is no Torah. Where there is no Torah there is no flour.' " (Bonder, The Kabbalah of Money, p. 9)

The financial system in the Jewish religion is based on an absolute trust of the governmental and other institutions, as without trust money has no worth, being only a piece of paper. Contrary to Christianity, the Jewish religion perceives poverty as a terrible tragedy. In the Midrash (Exodus Rabbah 31:14) we read: 'Nothing in the world is worse than poverty; it is the most terrible sufferance.' In order to fight poverty, the Rabbis have developed the concept of yishuv olam, the effort to regulate the world. We have to try always, while safeguarding honesty, to augment the quality of life, to augment the wealth of the community and of the individual, or in the language of the rabbinical Market, the ideal condition is – 'where a party does not lose and the other one wins'. In other words, a few millenniums before the most sophisticated management theories have invented the ideal of the 'win-win situation', the Jewish Rabbis preconized basically the same thing. For example, in the law of neighbors 'dina de bar-metzra', if a person has a plot of land that is near another, his neighbor automatically has an option to acquire the plot at the market price. One does not lose, as he receives the market price, and the other gains as he enlarges his property and increases its value.

If we prevent somebody from receiving a possession, it is equivalent to stealing it from him, as we act against the values of the Market. This principle, which is fundamental in the Jewish religion, should be reminded continuously to companies that make takeover bids or shares offerings addressed only to some of the shareholders. According to the Jewish tradition this is equivalent to fraud. "The sinful cities of Sodom and Gomorrah described in the book of Genesis represent a society that is sick because it is unable to help itself towards the 'settling of the world'. In refusing to help one another in such a way that one doesn't lose and another gains,' the citizens of Sodom and Gomorrah created a miserable market, similar to the purgatory described in (this) chapter, in which inverted elbows don't cooperate." (Bonder, The Kabbalah of Money, p. 18)

Time is one of the limits that are imposed on wealth. Time is money, but one does not need to occupy all his time in making money, as the essential purpose is not to make money but to study, and money is only a means to enable studying without worry. The Talmud asks – Who is really rich? Rabbi Meir answered: "The person who derives the internal peace out of his fortune." (Shabbat 25b) "Rabbi Meir draws from common knowledge when he says that the truly rich are those who acquire maximum quality of life without creating scarcity for themselves or others, who live up to their responsibilities, avoid 'wasting time', and do not draw livelihood from Nature beyond what is truly necessary." (Bonder, The Kabbalah of Money, p. 25-26)

In order to respond to the eternal question of *'Tsadik ve ralo, rasha ve tovlo'*, 'The just suffers while the unjust prospers'; the Rabbis of the Kabbalah describe a world that comprises four levels. The elementary level is that of Action – Assiya, of logic – Pshat, of the material, the material goods – Nekhes. The second level is the one of the formation – Yetsira, of the allusive – Remez, of the emotional, the quality – Segulah, which is the internal force coming from the soul that determines who we are. In the business world, good Segulahs can bring you much further than good decisions. The third level is the one of the creation – Beriah, of the symbolic – Drash, of the spiritual, the merit – Zekhut. The supreme level is the one of the emanation – Atsilut, of the secret – Sod, of the connection with the infinite, Lishma – for itself, with no aim of benefit, just for studying and doing good per se. The merits of our ancestors are coded in our conduct and determine largely the justice and injustice of this world. It is a long chain, which goes from generation to generation. Our actions have repercussions not only on our lives and the lives of the people surrounding us, but also on future lives of our descendants, and this is why we have to try to be just, as injustice can have cosmic repercussions.

As a great "admirer" (…) of the Kabbalah and Judaism, Voltaire concludes: "Pangloss disait quelquefois a Candide: 'Tous les événements sont enchaînes dans le meilleur des mondes possibles; car enfin, si vous n'aviez pas ete chasse d'un beau chateau a grands coups de pied dans le derriere pour l'amour de Mlle Cunegonde, si vous n'aviez pas ete mis à l'Inquisition, si vous n'aviez pas couru l'Amerique a pied, si vous n'aviez pas perdu tous vos moutons du bon pays d'Eldorado, vous ne mangeriez pas ici des cedrats confits et des pistaches. – Cela est bien dit, répondit Candide, mais il faut cultiver notre jardin." (Voltaire, Candide, p. 164-6) Pangloss would say to Candide, 'All events are connected in the best of all possible worlds; for, after all, if you hadn't been driven off from a beautiful country residence with great kicks in the backside for the love of Miss Cunegonde, if you hadn't been brought before the Inquisition, if you hadn't lost all your sheep from the good land of Eldorado, you wouldn't be here eating candied citrons and pistachios.' 'That's well said,' replied Candide, 'but we must cultivate our garden.'

"The Bible (Leviticus 19:13 – Do not withhold that which is due your neighbor. Do not let a worker's wage remain with you overnight until morning) classifies interactions related to theft into two groups: 'withholding' (oshek) and 'misappropriation' (gezel). Our social awareness singles out and punishes situations of misappropriation, but we rarely impose limits upon transactions that involve withholding. The difference between these two kinds of theft is defined by Maimonides. He states that gezel is the forceful appropriation of something that doesn't belong to us or that isn't available to us. By contrast oshek can be (a) the act of not returning something that has been taken, even with the owner's consent, or (b) the withholding of something that belongs to another, even if we don't mean to keep it. In committing these thefts, we interfere, act as obstacles, and keep things from being returned to their legitimate owners." (Bonder, The Kabbalah of Money, p. 53)

There are a multitude of cases in modern economy with situations of withholding or oshek, such as the withholding of information which is disclosed only to some of the shareholders, a takeover bid which is offered only to part of the shareholders, the differentiation between majority and minority shareholders who hold nevertheless the same shares, etc. According to Jewish law the dimensions of space and time belong to God, and if we cause a shareholder to lose time in trying to obtain information, which is accessible only to insiders, we commit a crime against God. In the same manner the management, which does not pay on schedule its employees or its suppliers, cause them severe losses, which is condemned by the Bible. 'Love your neighbor as yourself' (The Bible, Leviticus, 19:18) is undoubtedly the most important precept of the Judeo-Christian heritage, and the good that we want to occur to us is at the basis of the good that we must do to others, without committing oshek or withholding time, information, and so on, as we would not want it to occur to us also.

"From the well-known biblical saying (Leviticus 19:14) 'Do not put a stumbling block before the blind' (lifnei iver) the rabbis draw an important concept: it is our duty to pay attention not only to the interactions we engage in, but also to the people we deal with in these interactions… To begin with, who is 'blind'? All those whose 'vision' is less than ours." (Bonder, The Kabbalah of Money, p. 59) A large number of managers of companies cause their employees to make misappropriation, by withholding from them information, by intimidation, oral order, or any other means equivalent to putting a stumbling block before the blind. One could find analogies in many cases, where independent directors approve decisions without having all the data available. In those cases, the majority shareholders benefit from the blindness of the shareholders, or of the directors in the Board of Directors, who are often treated as blind, deaf and mute.

The way that the wrongdoers fight the disclosure of the truth to the blind by the whistle-blowers is often by spreading slander (lashon hara), which is false information widely spread in order to affect the credibility of the whistle-blowers. Maimonides says that slander is the worst of crimes equivalent to the forsaking of God. Unfortunately, slander and defamation are very widespread in modern economy, especially on the Internet. At the other side of human conduct is charity, or tsedakah, from the Hebrew word tsedek – justice, as doing charity is doing justice. Wealth without charity impoverishes the Market and reduces liberty. Tsedaka is another example of 'how to become rich while having less'. Midrash Tanhuma states that *'Tsedaka tatsil mimavet'*, charity avoids death, literally or figuratively as it saves us from the anguish of death. Can we imagine any companies, which instead of slandering their opponents would try to be charitable? If so, could they survive?

If businessmen would believe in the different cycles of life, we could obtain a radical change of attitude. "The Mishnah is even more precise and gives us step-by-step instructions on how to deal with our evil impulses in interactions: know (1) where you are coming from, (2) where are you going, and (3) whom you must answer to. In other words: understand the Market deeply. Remember that in each of these infinite cycles of return there is an Eternal Eye that sees everything, an Ear that hears all, and a Book where everything is recorded." (Bonder, The Kabbalah of Money, p. 92) Those maxims, which are relevant to pious people who really believe in God and who are not Tartuffes, could apply to the secular in the same manner, by replacing God with their conscience and humanism. We rediscover here the notions of transparency, sense of proportion, long term, ultimate goal of our existence, and all the other notions that will be developed in this book. If we feel transparent, humble, being part of a long chain of humanity, we would be bound to conduct ourselves ethically toward the stakeholders, the community and the shareholders of the companies.

The majority shareholders and the CEOs of the companies should always remember that the last would be the first. "In long-term livelihood, in less immediate cycles of return, our 'failures' (falls) are part of our success (rise)... This 'whole', this interconnection, resembles a wheel: the side that rises does so while the opposite side falls. The highest point signals the beginning of the fall, and the lowest point means we're beginning to climb again. Thus, falling is an essential part of the rising mechanism.... What is on the top must descend and what is on the bottom must rise." (Bonder, The Kabbalah of Money, p. 102) In reality, the mighty are almost always intoxicated by their strength; they despise the weak and are convinced that they will never fall. In most of the cases it is this intoxication that causes their fall, as we cannot act in a void; illegitimate actions almost always bring about direct or indirect reactions.

If we invest only in ourselves we lose everything when we die. But if we invest in others, if the stakeholders become an integral part of our existence, and the others become an integral part of our being and everything is amalgamated in an entity, we could survive after our death. Money and selfishness distort our point of view. "The rabbis saw this. Not because they had magic, but because they understood the lens through which we look at things. They used to say that when you look at a glass, you can see right through it. Put a little silver on the glass and it turns into a mirror, so that the only thing we see is ourselves. With a little money, what was once transparent becomes immediately obscure and we can no longer tap into any external reality." (Bonder, The Kabbalah of Money, p. 170)

We could not analyze the ethical aspects of Judaism without mentioning the anti-Semitism that has festered during thousands of years of prejudices against the Jews and their alleged lack of ethics: "In the popular imagination, there seem to be three major factors militating against the acceptance of these Jewish perspective on the moral and ethical issues in modern business and economic behavior. 1. A general acceptance of the anti-Semitic slurs regarding Jewish avarice and business immorality, which are often reflected in the literature and culture of almost all of the Christian societies. The myth of Jewish capitalism and exploitation fostered both by Nazi Germany and by the writing of Karl Marx was built on age-old biases. These either saw in Jewish frugality, hard work, and entrepreneurship the implementation of a national materialistic obsession, or were based on jealousy, the desire to avoid contractual obligations, and the need for scapegoats to explain social or economic distress. 2. The association of biblical and talmudic regulation with a simple agrarian economy, far distant from the modern world of international finance, sophisticated patterns of merchandising, and constant technological changes... 3. An understandable yet unfortunate current overemphasis on spiritual behavior that, following primarily Christian religious patterns, has meant a disassociation of Judaism from so-called secular aspects of life as economics, political organization, and social change." (Tamari, The Challenge of Wealth, p. xiv-xv)

The same qualities, that the Jews shared with American Protestants, frugality and savings, were interpreted on the Jews' behalf as avarice and exploitation and on the Protestants' behalf as honesty and compassion. The Jewish religion has founded the basis of business ethics and all those who adhere to its principles have to conduct ethically: "The Divine origin of wealth mandates that it not be earned through immoral or unjust ways. Even where they are legal, therefore, exploitation, abuse of power, undisclosed conflicts of interest, and oppression through withheld information cannot coexist with a God-given morality. So, Judaism rejects the concept of 'let the buyer beware' and places the primary onus for full disclosure on the seller, who is usually more knowledgeable. The biblical injunction against placing a 'stumbling block in the path of the blind' is understood as forbidding advice or selling goods and services that are to the physical or spiritual detriment of the other party." (same, p. xxii) The talmid khakham, the religious Jew, has to comply fully to all those obligations and keep all his promises, even if he can avoid them legally, he should act with clemency toward the debtors, abstain from acting cruelly toward his associates in business, and strive to act ethically toward every one. All religions, including Judaism, have therefore about the same ethical principles, but the practice of some of the believers is often in total contradiction to the religious precepts.

Rabbi Israel Salanter, the founder of the mussar (morals) movement of the 18th century, has stated that the transfer of funds from one person to the other without his consent is a theft according to the Torah, no different from the theft of a burglar. He put therefore the ethical theft, even if it is legal, at the same level as the brutal theft. The Jewish community of Lublin has stated in 1624 that if a debtor does not pay his debts and goes bankrupt he should be excommunicated: "If a bankrupt debtor should offer to make a settlement for his debts (instead of paying them in full) then the cherem, ban of excommunication, is to be published against him... He is to be considered to be unfit to give testimony or to take an oath. He is to be imprisoned for a whole year and shall not be appointed to any religious position... and he shall not be called up to the Torah for a whole year (or) until he repays his creditors. The creditors may take away all the clothes that the bankrupt has made (even) for his wife within the year that he became bankrupt. He shall lose the rights of citizenship in the community (which limited his right to remain and do business in that town). When the cherem is pronounced in the synagogue the bankrupt person's wife and children must be present (so as to a priori educate against fraud through the fear of such shame)." (same, p. 30) One could only imagine the fantastic repercussions of such a conduct on the modern business world. If we could ostracize the members of the community who do not act ethically and who prefer going bankrupt than repaying their debts from their personal funds, we could raise substantially the ethical level of the business community. We could put to the pillory all the members of society who do not behave ethically, publish it through the Institute of Ethics and the Internet, exactly as we do for the solvency of the companies.

One of the most common sentences in the business world, said when a party of a contract decides not to fulfill his contractual obligations, is - 'sue me', knowing that a trial is very costly and it is almost impossible to win it if the parties are not of the same strength. Therefore, it is necessary that the party who breaks the contract, does not fulfill his promises, or does not pay his debts, should not be able to act in such a banal way and would have to run the risk of suffering from a much heavier 'fine' than a monetary payment after many years of trial. Rabbi Eliezer states in the Talmud (Shem Mi Shmuel, Parshat Shelach) that a person who does not fulfill his business promises commits an odious crime similar to idolatry. "Each Jew is a standard bearer of the dignity of the Jewish people and their God, so that morality in the marketplace leads to the sanctification of His Name, and dishonesty, to chillul HaShem, the desecration of His Name." (same, p. 36)

The relative success of the adhesion to ethical precepts by the Jews in the Diaspora and by the Americans in the Protestant communities in the previous centuries was based principally on the religion and on the cohesive structure of the community. A member who was ostracized received the worst punishment, and the social aspect was much more important than the legal aspect. This social supremacy could also end in abusive cases such as the excommunication of Spinoza and the executions of the witches of Salem, and therefore it is recommended to follow a moderate path, as proposed by Aristotle.

Thousands of years after the Bible and the Talmud, the ethical precepts of conduct in business are as pertinent as the most recent books on the subject. "The Bible closes the verse in Leviticus 19:14 forbidding placing a stumbling block in the path of the blind by adding 'and you shall fear the Lord.' Wherever this phrase appears in the Bible, it is understood by the Rabbis to refer to actions hidden from the human eye and operating in the recesses of the human heart. Since white-collar crime, economic oppression, and misplaced trust operate primarily in secret, this affirmation of the fear of God is Judaism's major defense against them. All the spiritual underpinnings of Judaism's moral business and economic framework, as distinct from its halakhic legislation, are strengthened by the concept of pattur aval assur – not liable to punishment but forbidden. As often as not, many immoral acts in business are carried out within the letter of the law; fear of judicial punishment being the primary restraint. Jewish sources, however, based on all the aspects discussed in this chapter, ruled that in order to be clean before God and man, there are acts that although perfectly legal are nevertheless not permitted." (same, p.44) And it is exactly those precepts that are very often violated by the insiders who place a stumbling block in the path of the 'blind' minority shareholders, who do not know of the information that is shared uniquely by the insiders. Those insiders are convinced that they act legally, although not ethically, but they have no fear of the wrath of God, who - according to the Bible - does not allow mankind to conduct those wrongdoing in secret.

In contrast to the Roman concept of caveat emptor, the law of the Halakha states that it is the seller who should advise the buyer and divulge everything that he should know. Moshe Chaim Luzzatto writes in Mesillat Yesharim in Italy in the 18th century that it is honest to cite all the advantages of an article to a buyer but it is forbidden to hide the defects, which is equivalent to fraud. This law does not apply probably to Jewish matchmakers (...), but it should be applied to all shares issues, all financial reports, and all consultants' opinions. Nevertheless, reality is in many cases completely opposed to those precepts in order to benefit the companies, often to the detriment of the stakeholders.

"It is well known, both in the accounting and consulting professions, that financial reports can be represented so as to give a desired picture that may or may not always be absolutely true. The window dressing of financial data would therefore seem to be a clear case of geneivat daat. The current Hebrew accounting phrase, leyapot – to make beautiful – makes this clearer than the polite English window dressing. The techniques are many and varied but all of them have the same purpose in mind, which is to present a picture favorable to the seller, underwriter, or entrepreneur and to hide any flaws, defects, or liabilities from the potential investor.

For example, changes in the way inventory is calculated, the shifting of income or expense from one period to another, and alternative methods of calculating the depreciation of fixed assets all change the profits of the firm without any relationship to the results of its operations. So, too, hiding the true personality of the major investors through straw corporations or offshore corporations, together with a lack of disclosure concerning future earnings and past performance or other weaknesses and strengths, creates a different price for the shares of the corporation, thus leading to a different behavior." (same, p. 65-6)

The Halakhah condemns the argumentation of a *shaliach ledvar aveirah*, an agent who commits forbidden acts, which could be applied nowadays to the directors who act unethically in the name of the shareholders. Orders to commit such immoral acts are not allowed according to Jewish law. Tamari finds analogies between gneivat daat, defacement of knowledge, as stated in the Halakhah and modern business, such as misrepresentation of financial results to the minority shareholders as compared to those presented to insiders, such as actions of investment bankers, auditors and consultants in favor of the majority shareholders, insider trading, award of shares and warrants to executives in order to induce them to carry on resolutions to the benefit of the majority shareholders, takeover bids where the minority shareholders are forced to sell their shares at prices fixed by the management and majority shareholders, and so on.

"The entry of current management into the LBOs is a major area of halakhic concern, raising issues ranging from gneivat daat, through lifnei iver, down to the negation of the rules regarding bailees' din shomrim, literally, the laws of watchmen. The moral issues arise even before the MLBO occurs. The price that will be paid to the existing stockholders, will, inter alia, be affected by the economic performance of the corporation prior to the sale. It is obviously to the interest of the management during this period to operate the corporation as badly as possible; low profits, low sales, and inefficient performance all contribute to a lower price that they will ultimately have to pay. This is simple geneivah, theft, defined by Maimonides as 'removing another's wealth without him (the existing stockholders) being aware of it. Since the executive officers are the agents of the stockholders, they are halakhically bound to operate so as to maximize their benefits.... During the negotiations regarding the MLBO, the management is in the potentially immoral situation of being simultaneously both the buyer and agent of the sellers. In order to be clear of transgressing lifnei iver, they have to make sure that this conflict of interest is clearly defined and publicized, even if the stockholders understand it by themselves." (same, p. 105-6)

Millenniums have elapsed since those ethical precepts were written, Jews were deported from their homeland and were dispersed throughout more than 100 countries in the Diaspora, they have returned to Israel and founded an exemplary state, and still the same cases occur.

The fear of the generation of the Flood to have to share their assets was so great that theft became a norm, and therefore God sent them the Flood. It is beyond the scope of this book to find analogies between the generation of the Flood and our generation, as every generation is convinced that the Flood is near, but it is edifying to cite once again Tamari: "Now crimes against property spread, bloodshed and murder became commonplace, as corruption and immorality became the hallmark of society; therefore God decreed destruction through the waters of the Flood. Recognition of the impossibility of maintaining a moral and ethical society within the parameters of 'more is better than less' and without acknowledging man's egotistical uses of wealth determine much of Judaism. It has made the moral parameters of the limited use of wealth the pillar of its religious, spiritual, and communal tradition.

The Aggadah tells of the gentile who came to study Judaism with Hillel the Elder, whose school of Torah represents the definitive basis of the Halakhah. The gentile's condition for such study was that it be given while he stood on one foot. Unhesitatingly, Hillel answered, 'That which is repugnant to you, do not do to your fellow; That is the basis of the Torah, now go and learn its implementation...' Most of the basic injunctions and teachings of the Torah are found in Kedoshim, where the verse 'Thou shall love thy neighbor as thyself' appears. Rabbi Akiva taught that this verse is the essence of the whole Torah. This is the pillar, as it were, on which the Jewish treatment of the use of wealth rests. The essence of such treatment lies in the ability of the individual and society to understand and accept that there is a stage of 'enough' regarding economic activity and wealth." (same, p. 129-130)

This book develops extensively the necessity to disclose or reveal actions, which are not ethical or legal, and tries to legitimize this disclosure of information that is often perceived as an unforgivable denunciation. The main focus of the book is on activist business ethics, and it proves how Jewish law is indeed activist in its ethical approach. Jewish law favors those denunciations, as is written in Leviticus 19:16 'Do not go about spreading slander among your people. Do not do anything that endangers your neighbor's life. I am the Lord.' We have therefore to disclose the actions that endanger people but we are not allowed to slander people. One has to be sure that the disclosure is not a slander and that it could really save a person. This commandment is relevant today, as it was a few thousand years ago, and if businessmen had followed it, many frauds would have been prevented, the criminals would have been punished, and the innocents would not have lost their investments.

"The Midrash states, 'One may not withhold knowledge or evidence that may cause a loss of his fellowman's money, as it is written, 'Do not stand idly by your brother's blood.' We are also obligated to inform others of shoddy workmanship or loss suffered through a business deal in order that others not suffer the same loss. This is not considered to be lashon hara (talebearing), which is strictly forbidden. So, too, if one hears somebody plotting to cause another harm, one is obligated to tell them, so they can prevent it, or alternatively, one should persuade the plotters not to carry out their plans.

The prevention of damage is not only directed to individuals, but applies also to public welfare as may be seen from the comment of the Shulchan Aruch, 'Even more so, is one obligated to prevent damage to the public. Therefore, if one knows that people intend to do such damage, one has to protest to the best of one's ability.' These injunctions would seem to have special significance for those possessing knowledge of planned corporate takeovers that are to the detriment of the shareholders, as well as for workers who have knowledge of fraud within their corporation, to make their knowledge public. Modern whistle-blowing would seem to be in keeping with these rabbinical injunctions and was even institutionalized in many communities." (same, p.144)

Jewish law, which has given to all mankind the Ten Commandments, is pertinent in its precepts on business ethics as it was millenniums ago. The largest number of moral dilemmas, which are treated in this book, were already treated by activist Rabbis, who have given solutions to those problems, which could have been written by the most modern ethicists. Nobody condones recurring to those laws in the business world, as the application of them even among the religious Jews is unfortunately as ineffective as among the seculars. Human nature is the same, and the religious Jews, Christians or others are not more moral and ethical than the secular people. But, the norms of the Jews, Christians, Buddhists, Moslems, and others can assist us to guide ourselves by the lighthouse, which lights up the route of the businessmen wanting to return safely to their convictions.

6
ACTIVIST BUSINESS ETHICS IN OTHER RELIGIONS

"And We showed them the two highways. But they have not embarked upon the steep road. And what will convey to you what the steep road is? Emancipating a slave, or feeding on a day of hunger an orphaned relative or a pauper in misery. The one will be of those who believe, and enjoin patience on one another, and exhort each other to kindness: they are the company on the Right Hand. But those who repudiate our signs, they are the company on the Left Hand: over them will be a vault of fire."
(Koran, The City, 10-20)

In order to analyze activist business ethics, which is common to most religions, we should try to compare it to the teleological and deontological precepts already discussed in another context previously. Kidder describes in his book - 'How Good People Make Tough Choices' the different aspects of ethical dilemmas compared to the precepts of the philosophers of ethics. We have already mentioned utilitarianism, which is a teleological philosophy, from the Greek word teleos meaning ends or issue, which gives predominance to the results, results oriented. What matters is the result of an action and not its motives, and whether a certain law or ethics give more utility or welfare to the largest number of persons. According to this theory, 'Ends-Based Thinking', it is probably justifiable to sacrifice the lives of a few passengers of a hijacked plane in order to save the lives of the rest of the passengers, or to abuse the rights of minority shareholders if the majority of shareholders benefit from it. This theory was conceived by the British philosophers Jeremy Bentham (1748-1832) and John Stuart Mill (1806-1873). It is superfluous to analyze in this book the absurdities to which such a theory can lead. How is it possible to measure utility? Are all persons equal, all nations equal, etc?

The opposed theory is the deontological theory, from the Greek deon, which means duty or obligation, 'Rule-Based Thinking', requesting us to act according to our conscience and duty without taking into consideration the results. This theory was conceived by the German philosopher Immanuel Kant (1724-1804), and adheres to the categorical imperative, requesting that our actions have to conform to universal principles. All our actions have to be conducted according to what we would want others to do in similar circumstances. According to this theory, we have to always keep our promises without taking into consideration the sacrifices; we can never agree to exceptions to the rules; everything has to be uniform for everybody, etc. Do we have to remain loyal to a company, even if it commits immoral actions? Who decides that an action is unethical? What do we do when two actions are just but incompatible? As it is practically impossible to foresee all the circumstances of an action, which is never similar to another, and as absolute theories are always dangerous, it is very hard to follow this theory a la lettre.

The third theory, which is preferred by the author of this book, is a theory which is at the basis of almost all religions, and which proclaims 'do to others what you would like them to do to you'. This precept known as The Golden Rule, or Care-Based Thinking, is based on reversibility, which asks you to test your actions by imagining how it would feel if you were the recipient, rather than the perpetrator of your actions. This precept is at the basis of business ethics toward the stakeholders, employees, minority shareholders, customers, suppliers or members of the community. It appears in Matthew 7:12: 'All things whatsoever ye would that men should do to you, do ye even so to them.' Jews find it in the Talmud: 'That which you hold as detestable, do not do to your neighbor. That is the whole law: the rest is but commentary.' Or as it appears in the Islam precepts, 'None of you is a believer if he does not desire for his brother that which he desires for himself'. Why is this rule 'golden'? The word suggests that it ranks as the first and most valuable rule – 'the law and the prophets', as Jesus said, or 'the whole law' according to the Talmud.

"But the label 'golden' was applied by Confucius (551-479 B.C.), who wrote: 'Here certainly is the golden maxim: Do not do to others that which we do not want them to do to us.' Similar formulations appear at the center of Hinduism, Buddhism, Taoism, Zoroastrianism, and the rest of the world's major religions. As philosopher Marcus G. Singer writes, the Golden Rule is 'a principle of great antiquity' that has 'played a key role in the moral teachings of nearly all cultures and religions and continues to play a key role in moral education.'… More important is the point, made by Augustine and others, that the Golden Rule not only sets limits on our actions but encourages us to promote the interests of others." (Kidder, How Good People Make Tough Choices, p.159).

It is regrettable to notice that the best way to adhere to this precept is by finding ourselves in situations where people treat us in an unethical way causing us serious harm. As long as we see our colleagues acting in an immoral way toward others we do not feel the acute pain as when the acts are committed against us. It goes without saying that when we act toward others unethically, only those who are scrupulous and who can imagine what will be the consequences of their acts can feel the pain caused to the others, and even then it is mitigated, as naturally we suffer less from committing unethical acts than from feeling them ourselves. In many cases some businessmen don't even have scruples and prefer to remain indifferent to the pain inflicted by them onto others. But when they feel for themselves the pain it is at maximum amplitude, because they are not accustomed to being victims. As it is often mentioned in this book, the abundance of cases against ethics is ultimately beneficial to ethics, 'the worse it gets the better it is', because sooner or later everybody will be abused in one way or another and the companies that do not conduct themselves ethically will arrive at the conclusion that it is impossible to abuse everybody all the time, and they will conduct themselves ethically maybe not out of conviction, but surely out of necessity.

The precept not to do to others what you would not want others to do to you is so fundamental in all religions as in business, that even if it is not self-apparent, everybody will have to reach the same conclusion sooner or later. Today, only the pioneers go in front of the masses and preach that companies should behave ethically. Their unethical colleagues are convinced that they are immune to unethical conduct, as they know how to beware. But afterwards it will happen inexorably to them also, as there is no ethical code among companies that are not ethical. Even the codes of the Mafia are ephemeral, as we saw in the famous Godfather. From day to day, the cases of abuses augment, and more and more people conclude that the pioneers were right, regretting that they did not follow their advice. The conclusion should be never to compromise with unethical companies, which ultimately abuse all the stakeholders, and even the accomplices of their unethical acts.

The Japanese culture is profoundly rooted in Confucianism. This philosophy is wholly lacking in individualism and claims that adhesion to the group rather than the success of the individual is the most important virtue. Only when natural human affection, which exists in the family, is extended outside the family to include complete strangers, can human nature reach perfection and social order be maintained. The Japanese companies are at the same time capitalists and Confucianists, and are based on the loyalty of the employees who perceive the company as their second family. The Confucian Market is not the Market of Adam Smith, as the members of society operate in favor of others, of the company, of the community, and are not motivated uniquely by their own interest as preconized by Smith. This philosophy under many variables was adopted by the Germans, Swedes, Danes and Austrians. The Germans, especially after having suffered from the consequences of a society that became completely wild during the Nazi era, have developed like the Japanese a Social Market, which rallies the government, companies and employees in common interests, in order to achieve social justice together with prosperity. The Germans have developed a model of co-determination obliging companies of more than 500 employees to elect the representatives of the employees to up to 50 percent of the members of the Board of Directors. Co-determination is a version of economical democracy, which functions very well for more than 40 years.

In Islam, the prophet Mohammed was very attentive to economical justice and obedience to the business laws. He had 'insider information' on the subject, being himself a merchant in his youth. "There is much more space in the Koran devoted to economic matters than in the Bible. Over 1400 of the 6226 verses refer to economic issues, as the Koran provides a complete recipe for all aspects of life, material as well as spiritual. It is quite specific about the duties and obligations of believers, as well as their economic rights and entitlements." (Wilson, Economics, Ethics and Religion, p.117) In Saudi Arabia as in Iran, the Shariah law is the prevailing law, and even in other Moslem countries the Koran influences very much the constitution. Trade is perceived as a noble occupation, and fraudulent and dishonest practices are strictly forbidden. As in the Bible, the Koran condemns covetousness of others' wealth. Wealth is justified as a source of generosity toward the poor. The Koran does not condemn wealth, but only the way to obtain it if it is fraudulent, as God does not distribute wealth equitably between his believers. The fruits of obedience to Allah are received in the hereafter.

Interests, riba, are forbidden in the Koran as they are in the Bible. On the other hand, distribution of profits, mudarabah, is encouraged, and the benefit of the financier has to come from the profits of the investment that he has financed. Speculations are forbidden, as they are perceived as a game, qimar. The Koran favors profits, if they are not obtained by harming others, as we should pay reasonable salaries and make reasonable profits, while remaining moderate and abstaining from alcohol. Loyalty is very appreciated in Moslem countries, in relations between company and its owners. Competition is limited; the companies are more family-owned and smaller than in the western countries.

Buddhism has always advocated the 'moderate way' in its attitude toward economy, based on rejection of extremes – satisfying of desires and asceticism. It favors trade and profitability, while giving to economy a moral and ethical goal. There is an interdependence between humans and nature, production and consumption, management and work. "For the Buddhist, the ideal state involves release from this ego-mind through Enlightenment which is nirvana. One Zen proverb runs: 'The way to Enlightenment is easy – just avoid picking and choosing.' Picking and choosing reveals the human tendency to prefer one thing over another for oneself alone, often at the expense of other people and other living things. This tendency is a manifestation of the ego-mind. In Buddhism, release and freedom from this process is called Enlightenment." (Inoue, Putting Buddhism to Work, p. 20) One has to be detached from all human desires in order to obtain nirvana, as after satisfying the needs, other desires appear which are impossible to be satisfied and ultimately we live a life of suffering in all levels of the economy classes. If on the other hand we live a moderate life with moderate desires and we are satisfied from our own lot we can reach the moderate way. The Buddhist economy is based on three principles: an economy which benefits oneself as well as the others (opposed to the capitalism of Adam Smith advocating the pursuit of your own interest), an economy of tolerance and peace (opposed to the cut-throat competition in the western world), an economy which safeguards ecology (opposed to the attitude of 'Apres moi le Deluge, after me - the Flood').

"The Buddha became a spiritual seeker because he was concerned with how to be free from suffering. In that he tried to deliver people from suffering and give them happiness, his path might well be called 'the path of happiness'. Although he emphasized the need for a minimum level of material wealth to sustain oneself, the goal itself is a form of happiness that is entirely unconnected to how much wealth one has. All too often, capitalism has overlooked the goal of happiness in favor of competition for competition's sake. If we use the following formula to understand happiness, we can see the difference in the Western and Eastern approaches. Happiness = Wealth/Desire. In the West, the general orientation has been to attain happiness by increasing wealth so that one can get more of what one desires. In contrast, Buddhism emphasizes the happiness that comes from being detached from desires, i.e., happiness is increased by reducing our desires. Western civilization has been dominated by the Descartian 'I think, therefore I am' philosophy of self-autonomy. From this perspective it is quite natural that the ego automatically fulfills its desires by an increase in wealth. But the Buddhist philosophy of 'non-self' points to the undeniable reality that a given 'self' cannot live independently but only in relation to other people. Both physically, and psychologically, humans are dependent on other human beings as well as on the natural environment (sunshine and water, for example). When we recognize that our lives are dependent on other beings and that our lives are interconnected with those of all beings, thought of gratitude toward other people and the earth will naturally arise." (Inoue, Putting Buddhism to Work, p. 89-90)

At Ryoan-ji, the Buddhist temple of Kyoto, a poem is engraved in the stone, saying: 'Know what you really need'. Buddhism advocates that you have to possess strength to reject superfluous desires and products and to be delivered from the chains of consumption. Happiness is achieved by enjoying the simple pleasures of life and not by accumulating wealth and products. We do not need to go on a diet in order to rid ourselves of excessive gastronomical, sexual, or consumption desires. We do not titillate appetites and desires, consumption and wealth; we seek the moderate way, moderation, simplicity. We do not waste nature or money, and we contribute part of our gains to social causes, religion and society. This act is called a 'shared heart'. We have to work to live but also to contribute to society and to work with others. "To put Buddhism to work is to see that economics and a moral and spiritual life are neither separate nor mutually exclusive. Buddhist economics is based on the premise that when we move beyond the compartmentalization of our lives to a more holistic vision of life, economics can operate in a way that is spiritually rich, socially beneficial, and environmental friendly. While the twentieth century has been marked by materialistic, self-centered consumerism, the next century needs to be focused on the quality and spirituality of life itself." (Inoue, Putting Buddhism to Work, p. 126)

Before resuming this analysis of business ethics and religions, we should return to the origins, to the primitive and savage tribes, which existed long before Moses. Even in those tribes we could discern ethical foundations that have not changed fundamentally after many thousands of years. "According to Sahlins, traditional 'primitive' tribes divided their human environment into three concentric circles. The inner circle was their own greater family group. Here the non-calculated gift is the natural way of dealing with one another. In family relations altruism and sacrifice of private efforts were highly valued. The intermediate circle covers the relations with the clan, the neighbors and eventually a part of the tribe. Here the basis of relationships is the exchange of gifts, which has to be balanced in a precisely equal way. Sahlins calls this balanced reciprocity: 'The gift is the primitive way of achieving the peace that in civil society is secured by the State' (Sahlins, 1974, p.169). The exterior circle contains the people that do not really matter, one can cheat and twist them as much as possible. Toward these outsiders one applies negative reciprocity." (Buckley, The Essence of Business Ethics, p. 126)

In the year 2001 we still have on the one hand relative ethics of the primitives and on the other hand Judeo-Christian ethics, which preach 'love thy neighbor as yourself' or according to Kant 'an action is morally just if its maxim can become a universal law for all those who act in a similar situation'. It is between those two poles that the activist ethics of business vary even today, although many recent events prove that there is a rather acute tendency of many modern businessmen to recur to the precepts of the Sahlins, of the Iks, and of the primitive tribes, and to forget the Judeo-Christian precepts which founded the morals of their countries.

7
ACTIVIST BUSINESS ETHICS IN PHILOSOPHY

"Dr. Stockman: Well, but is it not the duty of a citizen to let the public share in any new ideas he may have?
Peter Stockman: Oh, the public doesn't require any new ideas. The public is best served by the good, old-established ideas it already has."
(Ibsen, An Enemy of the People, Act II)

After the Bible, Aristotle is the founder of the philosophy of ethics in his book 'Ethics' or 'The Nicomachean Ethics'. According to Aristotle man aspires to be happy, in the sense of eudaimonia, happiness, as the summum bonum of his existence. Happiness is not identical to pleasure, and the ethical man will aspire to live a happy life but not necessarily a pleasurable life. Happiness is not the end of each action, but it is nevertheless the supreme goal of life. "For even if the good of the community coincides with that of the individual, it is clearly a greater and more perfect thing to achieve and preserve that of a community; for while it is desirable to secure what is good in the case of an individual, to do so in the case of a people or a state is something finer and more sublime." (Aristotle, Ethics, p.64) Aristotle maintains that wealth is certainly not the happiness that we are looking for, as it is only a means to obtain other goods. Money does not bring happiness, but it helps to obtain it. Man is by nature a social creature and his good should include his parents, his wife, his children, his friends, and his compatriots. "The conclusion is that the good for man is an activity of soul in accordance with virtue, or if there are more kinds of virtue than one, in accordance with the best and most perfect kind." (Aristotle, Ethics, p.76) "And if, as we said, the quality of a life is determined by its activities, no man who is truly happy can become miserable; because he will never do things that are hateful and mean. For we believe that the truly good and wise man bears all his fortunes with dignity, and always takes the most honourable course that circumstances permit." (Aristotle, Ethics, p.84)

Virtue has two faces – intellectual and moral. The intellectual virtue is acquired by education and experience. But the moral virtue is acquired by habit and ethos. "The moral virtues, then, are engendered in us either by nor contrary to nature; we are constituted by nature to receive them, but their full development in us is due to habit. Again, of all those faculties with which nature endows us we first acquire the potentialities, and only later effect their actualization." (Aristotle, Ethics, p.91) A man is not ethical or unethical by nature, he can become so by habit, and the social role of humanity is to develop the ethical aptitudes of all humankind. One cannot be wholly happy without being wholly ethical and moral, and if we could inculcate these notions to the business world, and prove that it is not only a philosophical theory, but also a reality, which is proved in many cases, we could change the aptitudes of a large number of businessmen. As the businessmen at the start of their career are not good or bad, it is circumstances, milieu, ambiance of their companies, example of their superiors, influence of their families, which make them more or less ethical. The businessmen who remain ethical in spite of an unethical environment are very rare. A very strong character is needed, serious convictions and a vast intellectuality.

The good conduct is incompatible with excess, one has to be moderate in order to preserve his moral qualities. An excessive or insufficient sportive activity is harmful, and it is the same with food, drink, courage, pleasure, and all other human activities. Moderation is not equal to everybody and everybody has to aspire to find his equilibrium in the moderation that suits him. Aristotle treats ethical ignorance with indulgence "When a man repents of an act done through ignorance, he is considered to have acted involuntarily." (Aristotle, Ethics, p.113)

This book will refer to the feigned or true ignorance of businessmen who do not behave ethically. If we oversee it, if we do not publish it, if we do not dissect it, if we do not blame it in the press and on the Internet, in a nutshell - if we are not activist ethicists, these businessmen will continue to abuse the rights of the stakeholders or the minority shareholders without feeling an iota of guilt. If they are treated like spoiled irresponsible children, they will never regret their acts, and they would say that they did not know. If there is a certainty that resulted from the atrocities of the Nazis, it is that we cannot let the world remain in ignorance, feigned or real. The Allied Forces could always say that they did not bomb Auschwitz because the atrocities were not published, the Poles in Krakow, at 70 kilometers from the camps, could always say that they did not know what happened beneath their noses. But in the modern world, it is impossible to ignore atrocities, and what happens in Rwanda, Kossovo or Bosnia, or in the recent past in Argentina, Chile, Kuwait or Greece, is known throughout the world, which cannot feign ignorance and is obliged to intervene. This book affirms that in the same manner we should not let the ethical wrongdoing committed by companies remain hidden from the public eye and we have to publicize them through the Internet, press, books, articles, theses, the Institute of Ethics, university lectures, shareholders' assemblies, courts, parliament, literature, theatre and cinema.

According to Aristotle, the unjust men have chosen deliberately to be so, and now that they are so, they cannot change. This theory is in contradiction to Christian theory, which enables followers to repent even at their dying breath.

It would be interesting to analyze how the modern unethical businessmen tend to repent or not. We only know that the robber barons have founded philanthropic institutions, the bankers who were condemned recently for insider trading have engaged in community activities, etc. But what is the conduct of those who were not apprehended, or those who do not think that they are rich enough to contribute money to society? Here again, if we would disclose their ethical wrongdoing, it would increase the probability of their penance, and activist business ethics would prevail!

We can reach truth according to Aristotle in five ways: through science – episteme, art – techne, prudence – phronesis, intelligence – nous, and wisdom – sophia. How many business administration faculties give courses or try to develop those qualities? They teach mathematical models, which are almost never applied in practice and are completely irrelevant, but who gives courses or case studies, which could develop those qualities that are so necessary to businessmen? One of the most striking features of modern businessmen is the intellectual superficiality of many of them. How many businessmen read classic literature, philosophical dissertations and poetry? How many go to the theater, to concerts, to museums? A business dinner consists almost always of talking about business matters, or often about the best restaurants in New York, Dallas, London or Singapore. With such a limited scope of interests, how can we wonder that some businessmen are not ethical, do not seek truth, moderation or wisdom? Are those qualities incompetent to businessmen? But the fact that this situation prevails in some cases does not mean that it should be so. Furthermore, we cannot allow ourselves to leave any domain of business without ethics even if it is difficult today to converge ethics and business. We are dealing with the salvation of the modern world, and all the world economy depends on it. This is the reason why it is necessary to inculcate ethics actively by all means at all levels.

In the same way that many people state that ethics in business is an oxymoron, we could state another one - that friendship in business is an oxymoron. Aristotle describes three kinds of friendship – friendship based on interests, friendship based on pleasure, and friendship based on goodness. The first two friendships are quite common in the business world, but the third is very rare, in spite of the maxims 'love thy neighbor as yourself'. Friendship based on goodness is like love, as it accepts the others as they are, they want their good in all cases, even if they do not derive utility or pleasure from the friendship. It is 'for better and for worse', even if the businessman loses his job, his high level and his influence, or he gets sick or becomes poor. This friendship is permanent; they like to remain with each other, and they have complete trust in the friend. How is it possible that the Germans can be friends with the French, after centuries of animosity, and that unethical businessmen cannot establish true friendships and behave ethically towards their stakeholders and colleagues?

Why does everything have to be based on interests and pleasure? We could save hundreds of billions of dollars which are the worldwide costs of the lack of ethics and trust; extremely high bills of lawyers would be eliminated, as will security measures, endless negotiations and due diligences which decorticates the bowels of companies. Why can't we say in purchasing a company 'trust me that all what I have stated is correct'? Then we shake hands, and we save millions in lawyers', auditors' and consultants' expenses, months of negotiations causing an immense loss of management attention, as well as public and private funds.

The author of this book witnessed cases where investments were made and companies bought after one day of negotiations based on complete trust, and others that were concluded after more than a year, not to speak of those which were not concluded at all because of mistrust. And the results obtained were often contrary to what was foreseen. From the moment that we start to act in friendship and trust in modern business life, as proposed by Aristotle 2,500 years ago, we could establish an unshakable economy, which will conform to the modern world of cooperation and the 'end of history and wars'.

According to Aristotle, fortune is desirable but not if it is obtained at the price of treason. If we analyze the conditions of happiness in Aristotle's Ethics, we have to conclude that most businessmen cannot be happy, as "it is evident that self-sufficiency and leisuredness and such freedom from fatigue as is humanly possible, together with all the other attributes assigned to the supremely happy man, are those that accord with this activity; then this activity will be the perfect happiness for man." (Aristotle, Ethics, p.330) It is very difficult in the modern and competitive business world to possess the virtues required by Aristotle in order to achieve happiness, live a moderate life, without excessive fatigue and 15-hour work days, be content with what you possess, and have enough time to enjoy life and develop your intellect and culture.

Aristotle like Marcus Aurelius understood the value of detachment from day to day life and proposed examining periodically the chosen path and the price that we have to pay in order to pursue it. We need to obtain a psychological, emotional and spiritual equilibrium in order to be happy. There are very few businessmen who can find such equilibrium and find the time to examine the cost of doing it 'my way'. In the excessive way of life that most of us live it is impossible to think and examine the ethical values. At the high speed that we travel in the modern business world we cannot stop and try to obtain the peace of mind necessary to be happy. And if businessmen will not be happy they could never conduct themselves equitably toward others, as it is very difficult to be good to others if your own life is miserable. According to Solon only those who possess moderate goods could be happy, and they will accomplish the best actions in living a moderate life, as it is possible for those who have an average wealth to be just.

How do we follow the precepts of Solon and Aristotle nowadays? According to American statistics stated in the "The Hungry Spirit" of Handy, 69% of Americans would like to conduct a more relaxed life, the per capita consumption has increased by 45% in the last 20 years, but the quality of life, as measured by the Index of Social Health, has deteriorated by 51%. Only 21% of the youth think that they have a good life, compared to 41% 20 years ago. In Great Britain, in a poll conducted in 1993 – 77% have considered their working hours as stressful, 77% were preoccupied with the effect that their working conditions had on their families. The stress costs in 1996 - 40 million working days and $10 billion in social security costs. The costs of nervous breakdowns in the U.S. are according to a study of MIT $47 billion, identical to the costs of cardiac diseases. We have therefore completely departed from the model of a happy life developed by Aristotle!

Furthermore, the richest one percent in the U.S. earned in 1989 - $600,000 per person, and as a group they earn more than the income of the poorest 40 percent of the population. The 1,000 best paid CEOs in 1992 earn on the average 157 times more than the average salary. The 400 richest men in the world have according to Forbes in 1993 a capital that is equal to the combined GNP of India, Bangladesh, Nepal and Sri Lanka. Seventy percent of international trade is conducted by 500 companies. Can we imagine that such an inequality and such a stressed population could subsist in the long term? Le Monde Diplomatique comments on the pessimism that prevails in France, where 80 percent of the French do not think that the economy can improve. Unemployment augments, especially among the youth, the nation does not have any more trust in the elites, who are often guilty of corruption, and there is much hostility toward the technostructure. Ironically, the French economy has improved, but nobody feels better about it; they do not even believe the statistics. There is therefore a large gap between the theories of Aristotle on ethics, happiness and welfare, and the actual condition of the world, which is much richer and more developed than Aristotle's world. But let us check if the current situation conforms better to theories of more 'practical' philosophers.

Two thousand years after Aristotle, Machiavelli advises the princes to recognize reality as it is, at least as it was at the epoch of Machiavelli. 'The way that we live is so different than the way we should live, that those who neglect what is done for what should be done, are ruined rather than preserved, as a man who wants to act completely according to his virtues finds soon his destruction in the midst of what is wrong'. Ethics is therefore unpractical and even dangerous. Machiavelli does not maintain that we have to conduct ourselves immorally by ideology, but rather by necessity, as otherwise we cannot survive in the immoral world in which we live. In the same manner, the managers, politicians, and practically all members of organizations have to do what is necessary in order to protect themselves. In a world acting unscrupulously the only way to survive is to ignore scruples when it is necessary.

Some people even say, that in order to conduct ourselves ultimately in an ethical manner, we have to do unethical actions and gather enough power and wealth that would enable us to conduct ourselves as we really want - ethically. This oxymoron, which consists of legitimizing immoral conduct in order to be able to conduct oneself in the future ethically, advocates that the end justifies the means. We have seen and will see in this book where those ideas can lead. Of all the enemies of ethics in business, the most dangerous ones are the Machiavellists, who blame the others of hypocrisy, because they see the world as it really is and not as it should be. They forget that from the moment that you start to behave unethically you fall with vertiginous speed and you can never climb back and be ethical. You become dependent on fraudulent actions, addicted to wrongdoing, like drugs and liquor addicted, and it is almost impossible to redeem yourself.

"In all important aspects, states and large companies are identical – especially in the framework that they create, and which include an interaction between the economical and political needs and between the wish and knowledge of men... The wisdom of princes is open for the managers. And that is how we return to Machiavelli. It is a pity that his name has dark and unscrupulous connotations, which are called 'murderous Machiavellian acts'. It is not even true; our initial intention was simply to examine which rules and habits have brought about a political success in the past, and to conclude which principles it is needed to apply in order to succeed in the present political world. This was a true experience of the scientific investigation and request; nevertheless, it is not surprising, that many paths, which according to those precepts have obtained a political success, are not part of the category that benefits from moral gratitude. As says Francis Bacon: 'He has proved openly and honestly what people do, and not what they should do'... The only effective way to examine organizations and their mode of conduct is to see them simply as a fait accompli; and not as a moral or immoral act." (Jay, Management and Machiavelli, in Hebrew, p. 19, 30, 32)

We have therefore businessmen who claim that we have to conduct ourselves immorally like the Prince of Machiavelli out of necessity, or as their colleagues in the Cosa Nostra say: 'nothing is personal', before murdering someone. If it is not me who will do it, it will be somebody else and I could do it in a much more humane manner, or if I do not do it to another he will do it to me, and it is better that I will be ahead of him. But there are also other philosophers, such as Kant or Schopenhauer, who teach that malice is innate in human nature and cannot be fully eradicated, although men have other qualities such as altruism. Malice is done for its sake and not in order to benefit the one who does it, and it is done in full conscience that those acts are immoral. Therefore, this kind of immoral person cannot even hide in his ignorance as in the cases cited by Aristotle, and not even in necessity as in the Prince of Machiavelli. He does malice for malice, rejoices from seeing his victim suffer and has no scruples, although he knows that his act is immoral.

We tend to think that conducting malice for malice exists only in the criminal environments, in fascist or communist totalitarian regimes, in certain couples, or with certain psychopaths. "Kant and Schopenhauer preconized that man has an innate sense of radical malice which is part of his nature, and in other terms, he is innate of viciousness, which it is impossible to eradicate (and this in the vicinity of other factors which act in the opposite direction). According to Kant there is in the human race a tendency to deviate consciously from goodness, in other terms: act consciously against the moral law, or revolt against it. The material context is underlined with Schopenhauer: in every man (although in different measures) there is a tendency to harm others without deriving any benefit from it, and even at the price of some harm caused to himself." (Strauss, Volition and Valuation, p.233)

Experience proves that Kant and Schopenhauer have described quite a large number of businessmen, that, in spite of the Machiavellian image that they have, do harm for harm, rejoice from it and do not even get from it any benefit. Under the rational and decent appearances of the modern business world, we can notice excessive emotions and vices that can be expressed only in the business world, which is the last bastion of the totalitarian regimes, and where the 'subjects' – the employees – are completely subjugated to their employers, who have over them absolute power. Those cases are elaborated in books such as "Brutal Bosses", and in the psychological analysis that follows. They may not be the rule, but they are nevertheless very frequent.

The only way to eradicate and reduce the absolute power of the managers is by rendering the company more democratic. "Bosses' cruelty adversely affects employees' initiative, commitment, motivation, anxiety, depression, self-esteem, and productivity, and may also be implicated in the occurrence of headaches, heart disease, gastrointestinal disorders, sleep disturbances, dermatological problems, sexual dysfunction, and even murder. And it is on the rise... The statistics are staggering. An estimated 90 percent of the workforce suffers boss abuse at some time in their careers. On any given workday, as many as one out of five subordinates report to bosses from whom they expect harmful mistreatment." (Hornstein, Brutal Bosses, p.xii-xiii)

The employees who were interviewed in 'Brutal Bosses' have mentioned that their organizations perversely protect the bosses who cruelly abuse their employees, although the law protects employees against sexual, racist, religious and other abuses. The bosses think that they are almighty, 'l'etat c'est moi' is a maxim very common in the business world, and the Darwinist evolution analogy is adopted there too, justifying the abuse of the weak who have to disappear (or be terminated) or to submit fully to the absolute will of their superiors. From the moment that certain bosses do not respect their own employees, how can we expect to ask them to respect the rights of the stakeholders of the company, such as the customers, minority shareholders or suppliers, who are not so close to them and personified as their own employees, whom they see every day? And if this becomes the norm, it does not stop at the executives, but it goes down to all levels of the hierarchy.

Respect is a fundamental right of the employee at the office, of the wife at home, of the minority shareholders in the company, of developing countries, and so on. It is impossible to trace a demarcation line, which stops at the threshold of the companies, and the same democratic evolution that has occurred in the last 50 years in all other domains has to be implemented also within the companies. The Talmud considers public humiliation of a person as equivalent to death. The bosses who maltreat their employees kill them gradually and are responsible for an unforgivable offense. It is therefore necessary to foster especially the ethical conduct toward the employees, who have to be respected, as part of the democratization process of the companies.

But is it really necessary to render the company more democratic? There are many elitist philosophers who despise the masses, which they perceive as mean and stupid. Yeshayahu Leibowitz, one of the greatest Israeli philosophers, who is known also as having called the Israelis Judeonazis in their relations to Palestinians, despises openly the masses: "The masses have all the rights. The human rights in society are not derived from their level, and this is democracy. It does not say that men are equal, but that everybody has equal rights. Does democracy preconize that a man with a low intellectual level has less rights than a man with a high intellectual level? But that does not mean that I respect the two men equally. I give both of them the right to vote and therefore the result will be catastrophic, as has said Socrates, and because of that the Athenian democracy has executed him. Because the majority of men is mean and stupid, the power of majority is a power of mean and stupid men, and we can see it all over the world." (Leibowitz, On Just About Everything, p.156)

We arrive here to the height of absurdity, a Jewish philosopher, who names his compatriots Nazis, proclaims that democracy is the power of the mean and stupid, while the same Nazis have exterminated six millions Jews in the Holocaust, in a fascist regime which preconized that the masses were mean and stupid and that only a dictatorship of the chosen people could lead the masses with the whip. He says it in Israel, where the conduct toward the

Palestinians has provoked fundamental and democratic changes, which have brought about the Oslo agreements. We started with Aristotle, continued with Machiavelli, Kant and Schopenhauer, and end up with Leibowitz. It is the human evolution but in the opposite direction. Fortunately, mankind evolves toward humanism, human rights, democracy, social-capitalism, and ethics in business. The democracy of the so-called ignorant masses is always better than a liberal autocracy and monarchy, in spite of what Leibowitz and others may say, and the masses are today much more educated than were the aristocrats in the totalitarian regimes. And the same evolution that has occurred in the political world will happen also in the business world, as nothing can stop it, not even retrograde theories.

"The grand theories of the philosophy of economics, however intriguing they may be in their own right, are not adequate for business ethics, and for many of the same reasons that the classic theories of Kant, Locke, and Mill are inadequate. The theories themselves are incomplete, oblivious to the concrete business context and indifferent to the very particular roles that people play in business. Their inaccessibility or inapplicability to the ordinary manager in the office or on the shop floor is not just a pragmatic problem but a failure of theory as well. What we need in business ethics is a theory of practice, an account of business as a fully human activity in which ethics provides not just an abstract set of principles or side-constraints or an occasional Sunday school reminder but the very framework of business activity. The heart of such a theory will not be a mathematical modes but a down-to-earth, matter-of-fact account of the values that do and should govern business and business enterprises by way of motivating the people who actually live and work in business." (Solomon, Ethics and Excellence, p. 99-100)

To conclude, certain philosophical theories are often incomplete and irrelevant to the practice of business. We need therefore practical and activist theories, as those devised by some of the authors of ethics in business in the last ten years, who are cited in this book. The author of this book tries as well to contribute his humble participation to the application of new activist practical theories to business ethics, based on vast experience and extensive empirical research. The empirical theories are not based on mathematical models, which are completely irrelevant to the practice of business, but on down-to-earth values, which have to govern and motivate the businessmen. And those can be found in their purest form in the texts of Aristotle written a few thousand years ago but ringing as true today, making him perhaps the best modern empirical, activist and practical philosopher.

8

PSYCHOLOGICAL AND PSYCHOANALYTICAL ASPECTS

"I tell you the truth, unless you change and become like little children, you will never enter the kingdom of heaven. Therefore, whoever humbles himself like this child is the greatest in the kingdom of heaven."
(The Bible, Matthew, 18:3-4)

In order to prepare an omelet you have to break the eggs; in order to build a house you have to break the stones; and in order to succeed in the business world you have to break your principles. Those ideas prevail in parts of the business world of today, which is very competitive, and where you can win it all or lose it all. The rates of unemployment, especially of executives, are very high, and on the other hand the remuneration of brilliant executives is very high. Therefore, the temptation to conduct oneself in an immoral way is very strong. You have much to lose if you have too many scruples; if you come from a rich family you have to prove to yourself that you can surpass the achievements of your father, and if you come from a poor family you have to do your utmost to succeed in life and not be like your father. Business is a profession where you start out as an idealist and end up as a cynic. The managers and the consultants ask themselves frequently what is the market price for their conscience. They perceive themselves as mercenaries who are paid by the highest bidder. Society is ruled by wealth and power. Truth and ethics have nothing to do with it. We have to accept the world as it is.

But things are not as simple as they appear; we cannot remain cynical without feeling guilty about it and without perturbing our emotional and even sentimental life. This can result in excessive drinking, acute anxiety, nervous breakdowns, excessive rage, disgust, and tension with wife and children. Do we have to decide to leave the business world in order to cultivate our garden, or can we try to change the norms by evolution or revolution?

One of the most striking psychological aspects is the fact that most of the executives and owners of companies do not feel that they are to be blamed for transgressing the rights of stakeholders and minority shareholders. We have learned recently that one of the richest men in the world, whose company was sued for monopolistic behavior, is a fervent admirer of one of the most important books of the 20th century 'The Great Gatsby'. His admiration is so acute that his wedding was designed in the roaring 20s-style described in the novel and his very expensive home is decorated with citations of the novel. It would be interesting to learn if the following citation, which is practically the conclusion of the novel and its main moral, appears also on his walls.

Tom Buchanan, the capitalist tycoon who comes from a very rich American family, perceives Gatsby as a nouveau riche, a newcomer, who on top of this was the lover of his wife Daisy. He causes the death of Gatsby and after that washes his hands and his conscience, without any scruples, as those inferior creatures who do not belong to our clan do not matter. The author concludes: "I couldn't forgive him or like him, but I saw that what he had done was, to him, entirely justified. It was all very careless and confused. They were careless people, Tom and Daisy – they smashed up things and creatures and then retreated into their money or their vast carelessness, or whatever it was that kept them together, and let other people clean up the mess they had made... I shook hands with him; it seemed silly not to for I felt suddenly as though I were talking to a child. Then he went into the jewelry store to buy a pearl necklace – or perhaps only a pair of cuff buttons – rid of my provincial squeamishness forever... Gatsby believed in the green light, the orgiastic future that year by year recedes before us. It eluded us then, but that's no matter – to-morrow we will run faster, stretch out our arms farther... And one fine morning - So we beat on, boats against the current, borne back ceaselessly into the past." (Scott Fitzgerald, The Great Gatsby, p.107)

As long as the world will continue to treat the Buchanans as spoiled children who are not responsible for their actions, it will be impossible to change fundamentally the situation. But we should blame those who forgive them - usually because of cowardice. We hesitate to condemn the mighty. And we continue to shout at the donkey, as we are too afraid to confront the lion, the wolf or the fox. We cannot hope that the Buchanans of this world will all of a sudden be overcome by remorse. They will always continue to retreat in their wealth and appease their conscience by buying a pearl necklace. Therefore, it is necessary to fight and not condescend their immoral conduct, exactly as we condemn crimes performed by highway robbers. There is no difference between a bank robbery and a stakeholder or minority shareholder wrongdoing. And we have to define as theft every unethical act, even if the law cannot punish it. We could always sanction ethical crimes publicly, as this book advocates.

Charles Derber describes in his book 'The Wilding of America' the modern heroes, whom he calls sociopaths and savages, and compares them to the Iks of Uganda, known for their inhuman conduct. Boesky was proud of his greed, declaring in the 80s before a students' assembly at Berkeley that 'Greed is healthy. You can be greedy and still feel good about yourself.' Milken, the God of Wall Street in the 80s, is described by some authors as the ultimate savage, in fact the greatest financial criminal of history. "One of Milken's favorite sayings was, 'If we can't make money off our friends who can we make money off of?' Milken did not favor either buyers or sellers of junk; he took both under his wing and found, as described in the SEC indictment, exquisite ways to extort money from them, whether it was taking exorbitant commissions, demanding 'warrants', a type of financial sweetener for the deal-maker, or distorting the price of offerings often by ingenious schemes involving unethical if not illegal buy-backs and trading on the extraordinary inside information available to him. Milken, virtually omnipotent, saw himself as outside both moral and legal constraints, regarding them as 'mere conventions... for the foot soldiers of the world – the less creative, less aggressive, less visionary.' Bruck writes that the King would make his own laws: 'For whether it meant procuring women, or threatening would-be clients, the resounding credo at Drexel was to do whatever it took to win.'" (Derber, The Wilding of America, p. 46-7)

The precepts of Buchanan, Boesky, Milken, and others are followed assiduously by some executives in the business world of today, who do not perceive themselves as guilty of anything and when they are accused, they feel outraged by the arrogance of the accusers. If you cannot get rich at the detriment of your friends and colleagues, from whom can we get rich, and what chutzpah have the wronged to sue them, the untouchables? They are beyond conventions, constraints, morality. They are the aristocrats of finance, half-Gods, or at least the lackeys of the omnipotents. They make their own rules, as the conventional rules and ethics are good only for the ignorant masses that always have to lose. The individual stakeholders and minority shareholders have to understand that they have only one goal in life – to fill in the treasury coffers of the insiders, without having any right to complaint. Everything is permitted in order to win, and the rights of the weak are none of their concern.

The cynical individualists of the business world today think that they are the true capitalists defined by Adam Smith, and if every one pursues his own interest there would be an invisible hand that will translate the individual interests into the common good. "Adam Smith, the first great economist of the modern age, articulated the idea of the 'invisible hand', the mysterious market mechanism that automatically translates the selfish ambition of each person into the good of all. Always a problematic doctrine, the idea of an invisible hand has now been spun into a dream with almost surreal dimensions. In the good society, a market society, Americans now learn, the supreme virtue is to concentrate feverishly on one's own interests, for by doing so one not only maximizes one's chances of getting ahead, but also performs what George Gilder, whose book Wealth and Poverty is discussed in Chapter Three, calls a great 'gift' to society. As with the Ik, goodness, in practice, means 'filling one's own stomach'; the difference is that an Ik does not pretend that such 'goodness' is good for anyone else. An American Dream that does not spell out the moral consequences of unmitigated self-interest threatens to turn the next generation of Americans into wilding machines." (Derber, The Wilding of America, p. 101)

Badaracco mentions a simple sleep test as a possible method for evaluating moral dilemmas. Literally, a man who conducts himself ethically can sleep soundly, but those who conduct themselves immorally have insomnia. According to this theory we should rely on our intuition in order to conduct ourselves ethically. But he refutes those simplistic theories. "Everyone knows people who sleep quite soundly even though they have the ethics of bottom-dwelling slugs. They may be masters of rationalization or denial, they may be sociopaths and lack of conscience, but they can look themselves in the mirror and live in peace with whatever perfidy they have committed. During the Holocaust, a good number of doctors spent their days committing atrocities in the concentration camps, and then sat down to quiet family dinners. In contrast, responsible people sometimes lie awake at night precisely because they have done the right thing. They understand that their decisions have real consequences, that success is not guaranteed, and that they will be held accountable for their decisions. They also understand that acting honorably and decently can, in some circumstances, complicate or damage a person's career. In short, if people like Hitler sometimes sleep well and if people like Mother Teresa sometimes sleep badly, we can place little faith in simple sleep-test ethics." (Badaracco, Defining Moments, p.44-5) The limited experience of the author of this book concurs perfectly with Badaracco's point of view, as almost always the immoral businessmen think that they are ethical, invulnerable, and above the law, while the ethical executives spend many white nights attempting to solve intricate ethical dilemmas which are unavoidable in the business world.

The ethical men respond to forces that are deeply rooted in the soul, whether cultural, psychological, emotional, or practical. But the most important force is the force of personal experience, as expressed by the French saying: 'l'homme est un apprenti la douleur est son maitre et nul ne se connait tant qu'il n'a pas souffert', or 'man is an apprentice pain is his master and nobody knows himself until he has suffered'. We become ethical sometimes after having suffered a traumatism caused by an immoral act done to us. We can be moderately ethical as long as we have not suffered, but after suffering personally we become fanatic about ethics. When we feel on our own flesh the pain of a flagrant ethical transgression, which causes a substantial loss of money, trust or friends, we cease to treat mockingly ethical crimes, as when we see somebody fall we often laugh, but if we fall ourselves, then it becomes serious.

Luckily, as the immoral cases perpetuate more and more, we will soon reach a status where everybody will be affected by ethical crimes, and we will discard the maxim that 'suckers do not die but are just replaced'. If all of us will be suckers in one way or another, it will be time to act, as unfortunately we do not act until we reach an extreme condition. For example, the inflation rate in Israel had to reach the astronomic amount of 500 percent annually in 1985 in order to convince us to adopt a drastic turnaround plan, which could have been adopted five years before with much less damages.

Everybody has to decide at a certain moment which way he chooses to follow, the ethical route or the other. It is true that nobody is 100 percent or zero percent ethical, but all of us are fundamentally ethical or unethical. In defining moments the ethical character is formed; it can be influenced by others, by the environment, education, etc., but ultimately every person has to decide for himself. By being promoted as an executive with large responsibilities, or by encountering complex situations, we reach the crossroad of ethical decisions, as business ethics is not an academic theory but a constant fight that has to be fought every day. The more complex the cases, the sooner we arrive at ethical conclusions. We can always leave a company that is unethical; there is always a trade-off between conscience and remuneration, but then the conscience of an ethical man can never be bought. We can be flexible on some minor points, but when the chips are down we have to decide how to proceed, as there is never ambiguity on the basics of ethics.

The moments that define our ethical character according to Badaracco, are vivid, acute, crystallized, intensifying, or as Montaigne says: 'one movement when it is watched closely, can reveal the whole character of a person'. The moments, or the movements, reveal also the past, as the seeds of ethics are in the past. Schindler had such a moment, Petain had it, De Gaulle had it, Sadat had it, Begin had it. Begin, the former leader of the Etsel, who was always perceived as an extremist, gave Sinai to Sadat in order to achieve peace. De Gaulle, who was perceived as an ultranationalist, gave Algeria to the Arab Algerians, sacrificing the French colonists. Businessmen do not need to reach ethical decisions on life and death, their decisions are not disclosed most of the time in the press, and their ethical dilemmas are rarely described in the professional literature. Their internal struggle has no glory and their victory does not give them any medals. Therefore, this struggle is much more valorous as it is conducted in the shade, in many cases to the detriment of their well-being, their wealth, their career, or their family.

Pascal writes in his Pensees that – the heart has its reasons that reason does not know. We do not know for sure why we become ethical; in many cases it is at the opposite of appearances or image. An exemplary family man such as Eichmann can become a monster, while a libertine like Schindler can save thousands of Jews while risking his own life. The moral way can be influenced by the origins of a person, but in any case we cannot say that the zodiac signs decide the morality or ethics of a person, as even two twins can live with totally different ethical concepts. According to the Jewish religion, every person can choose his own conduct, as God gives the liberty of choice to everyone. This is in contradiction to the oriental fatality, which prescribes that everything is '*mektoub*', written in heaven. This also contradicts the excuses of many businessmen, who claim that they could not act differently as it was already predestined.

An ethical reasoning presupposes a person who is mature and considerate. Can a young man be ethical? Of course, although the temptations of a young man are stronger, and his character is less formed, as he has less experience. But we meet in the modern business world many ethical young men and women, as well as extremely unethical men more than 70 years old. Nevertheless, it is recommended by to Aristotle and other ethics philosophers, to increase ethical education in order to assist the young in surmounting the unethical temptations they encounter throughout their career. What matters after all is the moral and ethical character, which can be formed in family circles, at school, in the army, at university, or through volunteer organizations. We tend to think that the young have an idealistic image, the mature have a cynical approach, women are more moral than men, etc., but ultimately what matters are the individual cases, as we should not have prejudices in this domain, as well as in all other domains. "This approach builds on Aristotle's empiricism, rather than Plato's abstractions, for resolving difficult ethical decisions. It shifts the focus of ethical deliberation from abstract principles to issues of personal character, from logic toward psychology, from the universal to the individual, from the intellectual toward the emotional, from objective truths to personal choice and commitment, and from the marble temple on the hill to the hurly-burly of everyday life. In all these ways, the perspective of this framework is much closer to literature than to the grand principles." (Badaracco, Defining Moments, p.53)

This is why the author of this book is convinced that reading ethical oriented literature can contribute considerably to forming ethical character, as philosophy is too abstract, especially for practical businessmen. It is hard to believe that a businessman who has enjoyed reading and was influenced by Pagnol, Zola, Racine, Ibsen, Moliere, Hugo, Brecht, Shakespeare, Cervantes, Agnon, or other authors quoted in this book and in other ethical works could behave unethically in business. Or as Kenneth R. Andrews says in his article "Ethics in Practice" (Ethics at Work, Harvard Business Review, Andrews, Ethics in Practice, p. 40): "Great literature can be a self-evident source of ethical instruction, for it informs the mind and heart together about the complexities of moral choice. Emotionally engaged with fictional or historic characters who must choose between death and dishonor, integrity and personal advancement, power and responsibility, self and others, we expand our own moral imaginations as well."

It is true that Zola was perceived in his epoch as very immoral, and the reading of his novels was prohibited in many circles, therefore, we should not define too narrowly the borders of ethical literature. Sartre, Giraudoux, Mauriac, Dostoyevsky, Proust, and Pirandello are ethical as well in the sense that their work and the problems treated by them can encourage intellectuals and businessmen to think about the basic values of life. From the moment we think seriously we can find ethics, by the road to Damascus or by existentialism, as ethics is universal. It is not uniquely Catholic, Jewish, Protestant, Buddhist, Communist, Socialist, Capitalist, or Nihilist; it is the aggregation of all the theories and practices of ethics. Man is fundamentally the same in Paris, New York, Brisbane or Tel Aviv, and the struggle between ethical and unethical men is a struggle that has been going on for thousands of years, from the days of Moses, Aristotle, Jesus, Mohammed, Kant, Etzioni and many others. It's a struggle with different nuances, with an acerbic polemic, but with a definite goal, with a known issue, which we believe is near.

A striking aspect of ethics in business is the courage that is necessary to behave ethically and the solitude of the ethical decisions. "A travers ces temoignages, nous voyons qu'il existe une grande solitude devant la décision... La lutte contre la corruption ou la violence a un coût élevé. La résistance qui semblait impossible devient un choix vital pour certains... Nous avons été frappes par l'extrême courage de beaucoup. Ils opposent une résistance éthique dans des situations difficiles, parfois au réel péril de leur liberté physique ou même, cela s'est vu, de leur vie: refus du mensonge, de la compromission. De tels témoignages d'hommes et de femmes debout donnent un profond relief a l'engagement humain. La lumière est particulièrement éclatante lorsqu'elle brille dans les ténèbres." (Dherse, L'Ethique ou le Chaos, p.47) "Throughout this testimony, we see that there exists a great solitude in facing the decision... The struggle against corruption or violence has a high cost. Resistance, which seemed impossible, becomes a vital choice for some... We were struck by the extreme courage of many. They oppose an ethical resistance in difficult situations, sometimes at the real peril of their physical liberty or even, we have seen it, of their lives: denial of lying, of compromise. Such testimony of brave men and women give a profound depth to human engagement. The light is particularly bright when it shines in the dark."

"Dans le cœur de l'homme, dans la fragilité et dans la force, se joue et se réalise l'éthique de l'action. Le cœur est le lieu par excellence de la relation. Ce cœur est vulnérable. Il peut devant la dureté du monde soit se blinder, soit s'ouvrir, soit témoigner. Le plus souvent, il doit trouver un chemin entre une juste protection devant la violence, l'œuvre de dégradation ou de mort, et l'ouverture ou il devient source de vie pour autrui. Le cœur blesse peut devenir cœur ouvert." (Dherse, L'Ethique ou le Chaos, p.133) "In the heart of men, in its fragility and in its strength, is the ethics of action devised and realized. The heart is the best place for this relation. This heart is vulnerable. It can in front of human hardness either be hardened, or be opened, or give testimony. Most often, it can find a way between justified protection against violence, the work of degradation or death, and the opening where it becomes the source of the life of other people. The wounded heart can become an open heart."

This is therefore one of the most profound sources of individual ethics, as the wounds of life open the hearts of some and harden the hearts of others. Those wounds can bring about mistrust, resulting from past treason. A wounded man can become a wounding man; this is what Dherse and Minguet call 'la grande chaine des blesses qui blessent a leur tour', 'the long chain of the wounded that wound themselves', or as Hillel the sage has said – whatever you have done to others will be done to you.

What is the goal of human economic activity? This cardinal question has to be analyzed psychologically. Is the economic man a completely rational man who seeks only to augment his well-being, or has he other goals in his agenda, such as gratitude, megalomania, malice, goodness and social empathy? "In the End of History and the Last Man, I argued that the human historical process could be understood as the interplay between two large forces. The first was that of rational desire, in which human beings sought to satisfy their material needs through the accumulation of wealth. The second, equally important motor of the historical process was what Hegel called the 'struggle for recognition', that is, the desire of all human beings to have their essence as free, moral beings recognized by other human beings... All human beings believe they have a certain inherent worth or dignity. When that worth is not recognized adequately by others, they feel anger; when they do not live up to others' evaluation, they feel shame; and when they are evaluated appropriately, they feel pride...

Natural wants and needs are few in number and rather easily satisfied, particularly in the context of a modern industrial economy. Our motivation in working and earning money is much more closely related to the recognition that such activity affords us, where money becomes a symbol not for material goods but for social status or recognition... The entrepreneurs who create business empires do not do so because they want to spend the hundreds of millions of dollars they will earn; rather, they want to be recognized as the creators of a new technology or service. If we understand, then, that economic life is pursued not simply for the sake of accumulating the greatest number of material goods possible but also for the sake of recognition, then the critical interdependence of capitalism and liberal democracy becomes clearer... Liberal democracy works because the struggle for recognition that formerly had been carried out on a military, religious, or nationalist plane is now pursued on an economic one. Where formerly princes sought to vanquish each other by risking their lives in bloody battles, they now risk their capital through the building of industrial empires. The underlying psychological need is the same, only the desire for recognition is satisfied through the production of wealth rather than the destruction of material values." (Fukuyama, Trust, p. 358-360)

The challenge of the economic ethical movement is to tie the recognition that businessmen and tycoons want to achieve to an ethical base, and that recognition, which is not at the same time ethical, should be perceived in a negative way. Only success that was achieved in an ethical way would bring the recognition that businessmen seek so eagerly. The Hebrew proverb - טוב שם טוב משמן טוב , 'tov shem tov mishemen tov', 'it is better to have a good reputation than a large fortune' - has to be applied literally, provided that the good reputation can be achieved only ethically. Unfortunately, too many cases prove that it is possible to eat the cake and leave it intact, and businessmen who behaved in an extremely unethical way have nevertheless an excellent reputation, and are perceived as 'la creme de la creme' of the economy of their country, while the Don Quixotes who try to oppose them are treated as squealers, crazy, or enemies of the people.

After having analyzed ethics from many different angles, we should try to analyze the influence of psychoanalysis on the conduct of businessmen, and we could start with Freud, who is often treated as the modern enemy of morality. "In the writings of most ethicists, Freud, if he is mentioned at all, is treated as the chief modern enemy of morality, whose work is best ignored or flatly condemned in the process of getting on with the task of doing traditional moral philosophy, unimpeded by the sorts of depth-psychological considerations that have transformed everyday morality outside the academy." (Wallwork, Psychoanalysis and Ethics, p. 2) If human nature is selfish and a man tries only to satisfy his interests and pleasures, there is no possible moral unless moral is the facade of selfishness and we are moral only to satisfy our ego. In other words, we can sacrifice ourselves, give up our material interests and our pleasure if we satisfy the intellectual interests that enlarge our ego, but we act always in order to satisfy our interests. We can delay the satisfaction of our pleasures, suffer pains and even martyrdom, if we hope to obtain other pleasures in a near or remote future or even in paradise.

"Freud points out that no departure from the rule of the pleasure principle is entailed. 'Even religion is obliged to support its demand that earthly pleasure shall be set aside by promising that it will provide instead an incomparably greater amount of superior pleasure in another world' (SE 14 [1915] :311). With this example, Freud seems to recognize that in its pleasure seeking, the ego looks at what will give it satisfaction in life as a whole, taking a broad range of considerations into account. This would seem to allow the individual, whether religious or not, to embrace a non-egoistic act if it is part of a life plan adopted as the self's way to ultimate happiness. For example, someone might discipline his baser tendencies and sacrifice his more immediate interests in order to obey the rules of moral and professional conduct laid down by his chosen profession, all because he thinks that life as a doctor, lawyer, teacher, accountant, or scientist will make him happy, even taking into account the burdens of arduous training and the occasional need for 'selflessness' and 'dedication' required to care adequately for patient or client or to achieve sought-after results. (same, p. 121)

The intellectual dilemma of whether a man is moral by altruism or by selfishness is completely superfluous if all we want to achieve is that everybody will act ethically. In the extreme case, we could try to transform ethical conduct into a reflex, exactly like hunger or thirst. Or we could reconcile the theories of the greatest philosopher of ethics, Aristotle, with the allegedly worst enemy of morality, Freud, by substituting the term 'happiness' for 'pleasure'. "Significantly, Freud signals his shift to qualitative hedonism linguistically by substituting 'happiness' (das Gluck) for 'pleasure' (die Lust). The term das Gluck in its colloquial German sense resonates with eudaimonia in Greek and felicitas and beatitudo in Latin. Like them, it carries rich connotations of the goal of life being fulfillment, excellence, well-being, and self-realization. Choice of the term implicitly conveys the message that it takes more for a person to be pleased with life as a whole or with the self (conscious and unconscious, past, present, and anticipated) than a string of separate agreeable sensations of the same monotonous sort, differing from one another only in their intensity and duration." (same, p. 130) Freud maintains that only a person who achieves maturity and builds a strong character by way of qualitative transformation of his personality is capable of defeating the predominance of the quantitative factors. "To pursue happiness as an inclusive goal through such activities as artistic creativity, intellectual work, sensuality, love, and aesthetic appreciation is to enjoy each of these activities as contributing something qualitatively unique to a life plan." (same, p. 133)

In a word, Freud imagines the possibility of obtaining individual happiness through the sublimation of subconscious desires, by obtaining intellectual pleasures, even by the satisfaction of others' desires, or by moral conscience. The final form of the narcissism of Freud is in the positive attitude toward oneself, the respect of oneself, self-esteem, Selbstgefuhl. It is this attitude that motivated Joan of Arc to mount the scaffold and motivated John Proctor in 'The Crucible' to die in order not to give up his self-esteem.

"PROCTOR, with a cry of his whole soul: Because it is my name! Because I cannot have another in my life! Because I lie and sign myself to lies! Because

I am not worth the dust on the feet of them that hang! How may I live without my name? I have given you my soul; leave me my name!

DANFORTH, pointing at the confession in Proctor's hand: Is that document a lie? If it is a lie I will not accept it! What say you? I will not deal in lies, Mister! Proctor is motionless. You will give me your honest confession in my hand, or I cannot keep you from the rope. Proctor does not reply. Which way do you go, Mister?

His breast heaving, his eyes staring, Proctor tears the paper and crumples it, and he is weeping in fury, but erect.

DANFORTH: Marshall!

PARRIS, hysterically, as though the tearing paper were his life: Proctor, Proctor!

HALE: Man, you will hang! You cannot!

PROCTOR, his eyes full of tears: I can. And there's your first marvel, that I can. You have made your magic now, for now I do think I see some shred of goodness in John Proctor. Not enough to weave a banner with, but white enough to keep it from such dogs. Elizabeth, in a burst of terror, rushes to him and weeps against his hand. Give them no tear! Tears pleasure them! Show honor now, show a stony heart and sink them with it! He has lifted her, and kisses her now with great passion.

REBECCA: Let you fear nothing! Another judgment waits us all!"

(Miller, The Crucible, p. 251)

One has to have the character of John Proctor in order not to be intimidated by inquiring committees of McCarthy, the NKVD, or the Inquisition. Those examples are very pertinent in the business world of today, where ethical managers suffer sometimes martyrdom from their companies and colleagues in cases where they have to act according to their conscience and against the immediate interests of the company. They are almost always motivated by a sense of self-esteem, which is much stronger than the pursuit of pleasures and happiness, at the risk even of their lives. If the happiness (eudaimonia) or the pleasure (Lust) that they obtain comes to the detriment of their well-being it is because the value that they attach to their principles is predominant. It is the executives of this caliber who should manage the companies of the 21st century, and not the unscrupulous or the spineless executives who often manage the business world of today.

Freud maintains that only sociopaths, psychopaths, or extreme narcissists have no feelings toward others, which is necessary for morality. According to Freud the ego is irreducibly social. Nevertheless, Freud attacks the maxim 'love thy neighbor as yourself' and would like to substitute for it 'love thy neighbor as he loves you'. In this manner, we could base a much more realistic form of ethics than that of Judeo-Christian religions, which are often not implemented as the standards are too high and unpractical. "The principle of nonmaleficence, not supererogation, guides Freud's moral views and suggests to him that we would all be better off trying to put into practice the moral minimum – enunciated by the maxim primum non nocere, 'above all, or first, do not harm' – rather than trying unsuccessfully to realize the high moral aspirations frequently associated with the law of love. But though Freud is firmly opposed to acts of supererogation without regard to self-concern and our obligations in special relations, it is not inconsistent with his position to have as a general principle mutual aid – that is, the notion that one should go out of one's way to assist someone, even a stranger, when the cost to oneself is not unreasonably great." (Wallwork, Psychoanalysis and Ethics, p. 206) Freud is not as idealistic as Kant, and according to him we are not born as moral beings and morality does not come naturally. "Freud, who on the most abstract level balances the principle of Eros with that of Thanatos, the life instincts with the death instincts, never forgets that along with benevolence, human beings also have a natural tendency to be brutal, violent, cruel, and egoistic and that, unless carefully monitored and guided, sublimated and repressed, these aspects of human nature can be as powerful as, and often more powerful than, other-regarding moral motives. Accordingly, Freud holds no truck with the sort of easy optimism of the self-realization psychologists." (same, p. 342)

9
INTERNATIONAL ASPECTS

"We should rid our ranks of all impotent thinking. All views that overestimate the strength of the enemy and underestimate the strength of the people are wrong."
(Mao Tse-Tung, Quotations, The Present Situation and Our Tasks, December 25, 1947)

Many theories have been proposed in order to prove that there could be a difference in the ethical norms in different countries. What is customary in Italy is not so in Switzerland, the norms in the United States are different from those in Colombia, in Japan from those in Thailand, in Israel from those in Iraq, in South Africa from those in Nigeria, and so on. It is evident that there are various nuances in the practice of business ethics in all the countries of the world, but there are very few differences in the ethical concepts in the world. In the same manner that it was possible to establish the universal human rights of the UN, that the democratic principles are universal, and that the ecological norms are known throughout the world, even if they are not applied universally, it is possible to define universal norms of ethics in business and particularly of ethics in the relations between companies and stakeholders.

One of the criteria for the survival of a society is that it needs to have a common morality for all members of the society. "What follows from this is that there are certain basic rules that must be followed in each society; e.g., don't lie, don't commit murder. There is a moral minimum in the sense that if these specific moral rules aren't generally followed, then there won't be a society at all. These moral rules are universal, but they are not practiced universally. That is, members of society A agree that they should not lie to each other, but they think that it is permissible to lie to the members of other societies. Such moral rules are not relative; they simply are not practiced universally. However, multinational corporations are obligated to follow these moral rules. Since the multinational is practicing business in the society, and since these moral norms are necessary for the existence of the society, the multinational has an obligation to support those norms." (Madsen, Essentials of Business Ethics, Bowie, Business Ethics and Cultural Relativism, p. 376)

One of the aspects of ethics in international business is ethics toward employees, which varies from country to country. "Employees should be regarded as full partners, rather than as hired labour. Their voice should be

86

taken into account, directly or indirectly, through employee representatives on the Board of Directors, when deciding on company policy. Evidently, such participation in the decision-making process should be accompanied by participation in the ownership of the firm ... The socio-economic approach to participation was institutionalized mostly on the European continent, especially after the Second World War. The clearest example is provided by the German system of 'Mitbestimmung', but also French, Dutch, and Belgian economic law contain some specific models." (Harvey, Business Ethics, A European Approach, Gerwen van, Employers' and employees' rights and duties, p.76)

One of the most important criteria for the conduct of companies in international business is the differentiation between the laws and ethics in the different countries. "Moral problems are often raised in multi-national or transnational companies: which law should they obey, when the legislation of the headquarters' country is not the same as that of the subsidiary's? This question can be solved by the distinction between legality and morality. If the legislation of the country a firm is operating in is different, but is just, it must be followed because, by so doing, one contributes to that country's common good. If there is no law, or if it is not in accordance with moral criteria, one must always follow the moral criteria." (Harvey, Business Ethics, A European Approach, Argandona, Business, law and regulation: ethical issues, p.129)

De George claims that in case of divergent ethical opinions, the companies that want to act with integrity have to act according to their own ethical norms, even if the norms in the foreign countries are less strict. In particular, we should not justify a mode of conduct as 'everybody does it'. If the act is wrong, transgresses the law, or is not ethical, we should abstain from committing this act and we should act according to our conscience. "In sum, a central difference between conducting business on a national level and conducting it on an international level is the absence in the latter setting of restrictive background institutions. In this situation a company without integrity – without a developed sense of what is ethically prohibited – seeks to promote its own interest in whatever way it can. Companies that feel constrained only by law and not by ethics in the United States feel few constraints in the international area. They feel no obligation beyond obeying the local laws in each country in which they operate, and then only to the extent that the laws are effectively enforced. Only their own perceived interests guide them when they stand outside the jurisdiction of national laws. That some companies do operate in this way is a fact; that all do is not; and that any should be allowed to so act is a defect calling for a remedy." (De George, Competing with Integrity in International Business, p. 27)

Ethics in international business is influenced by different cultures, moral customs, political regimes, development level, financial situation, and economical structure. De George develops ten ethical norms for the activity of multinational companies:

1. Multinationals should do no intentional direct harm. They are responsible for making due compensation for any harm they do, directly or indirectly, intentionally or unintentionally.
2. Multinationals should produce more good than harm for the host country.
3. Multinationals should contribute by their activity to the host country's development.
4. Multinationals should respect the human rights of their employees.
5. To the extent that local culture does not violate ethical norms, multinationals should respect the local culture and work with and not against it.
6. Multinationals should pay their fair share of taxes.
7. Multinationals should cooperate with the local government in developing and enforcing just background institutions.
8. Majority control of a firm carries with it ethical responsibility for the actions and failures of the firm.
9. If a multinational builds a hazardous plant, it has the obligation to make sure that it is safe and that it is run safely.
10. In transferring hazardous technology to LDCs, multinationals are responsible for appropriately redesigning such technology so that it can be safely administered in the host country.

We remember the embittered reactions of the French defense companies that were forced to abstain from giving bribes in order to facilitate the selling of French armaments, according to the law of 1999. This decision was taken as a result of intensive pressure from the U.S., which adopted the Foreign Corrupt Practices Act in 1977 after the incident where Carl Kotchian, the CEO of Lockheed was accused of having paid $12.5M to Japanese agents and government officials of the Japanese government in order to obtain a contract of Nippon Air for the Tristar airplanes of Lockheed. The U.S. exercised very heavy pressure on the other exporters of armaments to prevent them from benefiting from the unjust advantages resulting from their fraudulent conduct. Finally, those countries have adopted similar laws to the U.S. law to enforce ethical conduct toward government officials of the importer governments. This case of the export of ethics to other countries is a very encouraging one, as otherwise it could have discouraged the U.S. government from receiving other ethical laws, which would not have been followed by their foreign partners. Twenty two years have elapsed between the adoption of the U.S. law against bribery in other countries and the adoption of the French law, which shows that it is never too late to do good.

The English treat the same subject in a humorous manner in the TV series Yes Minister, which describes the trials of the British minister James Hacker and his chief of cabinet, Sir Humphrey Appleby. The minister discovers that the British government has received a contract from an Arab country by paying bribes. He is scandalized by his discovery and tries to clarify the facts with Sir Humphrey.

"Humphrey. Are you telling me that BES got the contract through bribery?'

He looked pained. 'I wish you wouldn't use words like 'bribery', Minister.'

I asked if he'd prefer that I use words like slush fund, sweeteners, or brown envelopes.

He patronisingly informed me that these are, in his view, extremely crude and unworthy expressions for what is no more than creative negotiation.

'It is the general practice', he asserted.

I asked him if he realised just what he was saying. After all, I ratified this contract myself, in good faith.

'And in that communique I announced to the press a British success in a fair fight.'

'Yes,' he mused, 'I did wonder about that bit.'

'And now,' I fumed, 'you are telling me we got it by bribery?'

'No, Minister,' he replied firmly.

There seemed to be a light at the end of the tunnel. My spirits lifted.

'Ah,' I said, 'we didn't get it by bribery.'

'That's not what I said,' he said carefully.

'Well what did you say?'

'I said I am not telling you we got it by bribery."

(Lynn and Jay, Yes Minister, p. 412)

Will the Europeans implement the new norms or will they find ways to get around them? The eternal dialogue between Don Quixote/Hacker the idealist, and Sancho Panza/Humphrey the practical man, will probably continue endlessly, with much humor and sarcasm...

De George develops ten strategies to face the ethical dilemmas in an environment of international corruption:

1. In responding to unethical activity do not violate the very norms and values that you seek to preserve and by which you judge your adversary's actions to be unethical.

2. Since there are no specific rules for responding to an unethical opponent, in responding ethically use your moral imagination.

3. When your response to immorality involves justifiable retaliation or force, apply the principle of restraint and rely on those to whom the use of force is legitimately allocated.

4. In measuring your response to an unethical opponent apply the principle of proportionality.

5. In responding to unethical forces apply the technique of ethical displacement.
6. In responding to an unethical adversary, system, or practice use publicity to underscore the immoral actions.
7. In responding to an immoral opponent seek joint action with others and work for the creation of new social, legal, or popular institutions and structures.
8. In responding to unethical activity be ready to act with moral courage.
9. In responding ethically to an unethical opponent be prepared to pay a price – sometimes a high price.
10. In responding to unethical activity, apply the principle of accountability.

We can differentiate between profitable and unprofitable companies not by the necessity to follow the minimal ethical norms, as all companies have to conduct themselves ethically even in extreme cases, but in the adherence to ethical norms that are beyond the minimal norms developed by De George. The international companies have to comply to three conditions in order to behave ethically: "Among those in the firm who act with integrity, the top managers are the crucial players. Unless they exemplify integrity, demand it of their employees, and support it throughout the firm, the company cannot – and so will not – act with integrity. However, the personal integrity is not enough. The second theme to emerge is that of ethical displacement. Ethical issues and dilemmas cannot always be resolved at the level at which they appear. For this reason corporate structures and policies are vitally important. Ethical individuals are constrained by the organization, structures, and policies of the companies for which they work. These may either reinforce ethical behavior or thwart it.... The third theme is the urgent need for adequate background institutions to counteract the tendencies toward unfairness of the market, of the free enterprise system, and of perceived self-interest on all levels. Such social, political and economic institutions promote fair conditions of competition wherever they exist and will offset the otherwise unbridled power of multinational corporations and banks worldwide." (De George, Competing with Integrity in International Business, p. 194-5)

In trying to define an international ethics, one should reject the theories of cultural relativism, which maintain that everything is relative and that there is no universal ethics, and those of Hobbes who believed that nations existed in the state of nature and were attempting to fulfill only their own interest without any moral obligation. The international law could be the basis of a universal ethics: "International law also consists in, and depends upon, certain fundamental principles of association, principles discovered in custom where they play the role of moral arbiters and reference points in international affairs. Included among such principles are those of 'legal equality (among states), the right to national self-defense, the duties to observe treaties and to respect human rights, the concepts of state sovereignty and non-intervention, and the duty to cooperate in the peaceful settlement of disputes.' With background concepts such as these, then, international law may be seen to presume aspects of international morality." (Donaldson, The Ethics of International Business, p. 22) Another cardinal source of universal ethics is the Universal Declaration of Human Rights, which ensures rights to employment, social security, education, etc. The fundamental international laws according to Donaldson are:

1. The right to freedom of physical movement.
2. The right to ownership of property.
3. The right to freedom from torture.
4. The right to a fair trial.
5. The right to nondiscriminatory treatment (freedom from discrimination on the basis of such characteristics as race or sex.)
6. The right to physical security.
7. The right to freedom of speech and association.
8. The right to minimal education.
9. The right to political participation.
10. The right to subsistence.

Those rights have to be honored according to Donaldson by all countries, companies and persons. One should not exaggerate in the implementation of the principles of equality in the countries and economies, as they are not equal in all respects. If an international company pays Chinese employees a much lower salary than that of France or the U.S., it is because it adheres to the norms of salaries prevailing in China, otherwise it would not have established a company in this country but in France. The ethical question is whether the company pays salaries that are similar to other salaries in China or if it exploits its Chinese workers in comparison to other workers in the same country. "A multinational must forgo the temptation to remake all societies in the image of its home society, while at the same time it must reject a relativism that conveniently forgets ethics when the payoff is sufficient. Thus, the task is to tolerate cultural diversity while drawing the line at moral recklessness." (Donaldson, The Ethics of International Business, p. 103)

Evidently, the basic ethical norms are common in all countries of the world, and the relativism is in the practice or the degree of implementation of the norms. One should not try to remake the societies in which the multinationals operate, but in no case should they conduct themselves in a manner that is unethical, even if the custom is contrary to the norms. The international ethical norms are therefore absolute and exist beyond the national and international laws.

10
THE PERSONIFICATION OF STAKEHOLDERS

"- Signor Hakham, el asno se cayo al poso!
- No se puede hazer nada, car c'est Hilul Shabat, il est défendu de travailler le jour du Sabbath.
- Ma es su asno, signor Hakham!
- Ah Dio santo! Se deve salvarlo! Mon Dieu, dans ce cas la, Pikuah nefesh dokhe Shabat, pour sauver une âme on peut faire outre du Sabbath."
(Kuento, Judeo-Spanish folk story, told in Ladino, French and Hebrew, by Pauline and Albert Cory)
"- Mister Rabbi, the donkey has fallen into the well!
- We cannot do anything, as it would be the sacrilege of Sabbath if we work on the holy day.
- But it is your donkey, Mister Rabbi!
- Good Lord! We have to save him! It is permitted in the Law to work on Sabbath in order to save a soul."

Jean de Florette (L'Eau des Collines of Marcel Pagnol) has come to settle at Bastides Blanches in Provence, in the property of his deceased mother, which was coveted by Cesar Soubeyran, the Papet - the Father or rather the Godfather, and his nephew, Ugolin. Cesar was the richest landowner in the region and the Bastidians feared them or had their interests to remain in good terms with them. The property had a spring, which was known by the Bastidians, and was blocked by the Soubeyran in order to discourage Jean de Florette from cultivating his land. Nobody told Jean about the existence of the spring, even those who learned that it was blocked by the Soubeyran, as Jean was an 'outsider', to whom nobody has to disclose anything as 'you don't mess with others' business'. The 'insider information' is therefore not disclosed to those who are not insiders, part of the majority, mighty, although Jean had the right to know because the spring was in his property. Cesar sends his nephew to befriend Jean in order to get information on his whereabouts, but he himself does not want to know him, as criminals prefer not to personify their victims, because 'nothing is personal'.

Since the victim is anonymous, Cesar can keep his objectivity, and he tells off Ugolin who knows Jean and has scruples over him. Cesar even manages to prevent Jean from befriending the Bastidians, who lose the last scruples they could have toward Jean, whom they do not know. Pamphile, one of the only Bastidians who wants to tell Jean about the spring, is prevented from doing so by his wife Amelie, who gives him the 'classical' arguments to dissuade him: "La premiere fois qu'il est venu au village, il a essaye de tuer Cabridan a coups de boules... ne t'occupe pas des affaires des autres. Tu as besoin d'avoir des clients... C'est pas un bossu de Crespin qui te donnera du travail. Justement, dit-elle le Papet est venu. Il veut que tu lui refasses la mangeoire de son mulet." (Pagnol, Oeuvres Completes III, Jean de Florette, p.822) "The first time that he came to the village, he tried to kill Cabridan with bowls... do not mess up with others' business. You need to have clients... It is not a hunchback form Crespin who will give you work. By the way, she said, the Papet has come. He wants you to mend the manger of his mule."

Anything goes: calumny, as it is Jean himself who received the bowls on his hump; Omerta – don't speak and don't mess with other people's business; intimidation, your livelihood can be endangered; xenophobia – as Jean is from Crespin, he is not one of ours...; and finally corruption, as the Papet buys his silence by giving work to Pamphile.

The story is well known, Jean dies while trying to dig another well, Cesar and Ugolin buy at a bargain price the property from the widow. After having 'rediscovered' the spring on the property, they cultivate carnations, which need a lot of water, and get even richer. When the widow's and Jean's daughter Manon learns later on that the Soubeyran and all the village knew that the spring existed and it was blocked, she decides to avenge herself by obstructing the spring that gives water to the whole village. In so doing, many villagers are ruined, and the property of the Soubeyran is also devastated. In a splendid confrontation with the Papet and the villagers, they learn from Manon that the Papet has concealed from them that Jean was the son of Florette, who was born in the village of the Bastides.

"(Manon) 'Oui, c'était Florette Camoins, qui était née dans la ferme ou son fils est mort!'
'Oyayaie!' dit Pamphile, consterne, 'personne ici ne l'a jamais su!'
(Manon) 'Le vieux voleur, la-bas, l'a toujours su, et Ugolin aussi le savait...'
(Le Papet) 'Qu'est-ce que ça change?'
Pour eux 'ça changeait tout'. Avoir abandonne à son triste sort un paysan amateur venu de Crespin, c'était en somme de bonne guerre, mais la victime, c'était le fils de Florette des Bastides; non pas un locataire ou un acheteur etranger, mais le proprietaire d'un bien de famille, acquis par un heritage maternel." (Pagnol, Oeuvres Complètes III, Manon des Sources, p. 1028)

"(Manon) 'Yes, it was Florette Camoins, who was born in the farm where her son has died!'
'Oyayaie!' said Pamphile, with consternation, 'nobody here knew it!'
(Manon) 'The old thief, over there, has known it all the time and Ugolin also knew it...'
(Le Papet) 'How does it change anything?'
For them 'it changed everything'. To have left to his sad fate an amateur farmer who came from Crespin, was ultimately a good fight, but the victim,

was the son of Florette from the Bastides; not a tenant or a foreign buyer, but the owner of a family wealth, acquired by a maternal inheritance."

Toward the end of the second part of the book (Manon des Sources), Cesar learns that Jean was his son whom he had with Florette, who was not able to reveal it to him as he was posted far away in the army and her letter got lost. Cesar dies from the shock of knowing that he caused the death of his own son...

It is very easy to rob or kill victims who you do not know personally, who are strangers and weaklings. Those victims can be minority shareholders, Polish Jews, or strangers from the neighboring village. The criminals will always find excuses to justify their crimes – he is a foreigner, he tried to throw bowls on Cabridan, he is a speculator anyhow, he spoils the water that I drink – anything goes. But ultimately, the crimes return almost always to the criminals as a boomerang, and from the moment that you act immorally, sooner or later you will be the victim of the immoral norms. The Jewish religion can be summarized according to the Mishna in one sentence: Love thy neighbor as yourself - (ואהבת לרעך כמוך). And Pagnol, the great humanist, is convinced that a crime against a stranger (who on top of it is a hunchback and an intellectual) is ultimately a crime against your own son. We have therefore to try to prove that the individual stakeholders or minority shareholders are like us and personify them as much as we can to the executives and controlling shareholders. We have to do our utmost to divulge the maximum information to the public, as only light can uncover criminals who prefer to act in the dark.

One of the reasons for the 'neat' conscience of the companies' executives when they wrong the individual stakeholders or minority shareholders is the lack of personification of those people who are in most of the cases too small to endanger the position of the executives. It is much easier to harm somebody who you do not know and do not respect, especially when you are convinced that you act rightfully. The executives of the companies have a direct interest in their companies; they conceive their missions beyond the immediate profits, and give allegiance to the majority shareholders who have often founded the company, control it and can remunerate the executives.

Jackall describes an act of conscience of an executive of a chemical company who had to decide if they had to spend $25 million to eliminate the halogenated hydrocarbon from the water or cause the death of 20 people in a million who would drink the contaminated water. "I don't know how to answer that question as long as I'm not one of those twenty people. As long as those people can't be identified, as long as they are not specific people, it's OK. Isn't that strange? So you put a filter on your own house and try to protect yourself. Impersonality provides the psychological distance necessary to make what managers call 'hard choices'." (Jackall, Moral Mazes, p.127) It is very difficult to imagine the Holocaust and the fact that six million Jews were exterminated by the Nazis and their European collaborators. Therefore, every year, on the commemorative date of the Holocaust, ceremonies are held throughout Israel to commemorate and say the names of those who were killed. Different organizations have started to gather all the names of the dead in order to immortalize them, and to publish them on the Internet. Steven Spielberg has dedicated all the profits of his film 'Schindler's List' and a part of his personal fortune to document thousands of stories about the Holocaust as told by survivors. If the Nazis have succeeded in their Satanic mission it is by depersonifying their Jewish victims, and by hiding their fate.

Personification and exposure are very efficient safeguards against crimes, but also against immoral acts. Pagnol and Spielberg fortify the hypotheses of this book, as illustrated by Jackall. From the moment that minority shareholders would have direct access to the Boards of Supervision of the companies, to the Institute of Ethics, to the Internet, to the press, it will be impossible to transgress their rights, as they will have names; they will be known; their photos will be seen; their fate will be made public when their rights will be violated. In the same way it will be necessary to personify and publish all the unethical acts of the businessmen and companies toward their shareholders and stakeholders. We will publish their names and their wrongdoing. We will point our fingers at them in their community. Their family will be ashamed of their acts. They will not be able to hide behind their present anonymity, and the personification might make them honest persons.

One of the cases that can best illustrate the personification and absurdity of the utilitarian theories is the famous case of the Ford company, which decided that it would be less costly to risk the lives of 180 persons who would buy the defective Pinto model rather than add the cost of $11 to each car. "To see more clearly how utilitarianism ignore considerations of justice and rights, consider how Ford's managers dealt with the Pinto's design. Had they decided to change the Pinto's design and to add $11 to the cost of each Pinto, they would in effect, have forced all the buyers of the Pinto to share in paying the $137 million that the design change would cost. Each buyer would pay an equal share of the total costs necessitated by this aspect of the Pinto design. On the other hand, by not changing the Pinto's design, the Ford managers were in effect forcing the 180 people who would die to absorb all of the costs of this aspect of the Pinto design. So we would ask: Is it more just to have 180 buyers bear all the costs of the Pinto design by themselves, or is it more just to distribute the costs equally among all buyers? Which is the fairer way of distributing these costs?" (Velasquez, Business Ethics, p. 81)

This dilemma has no economic solution. The answer is very simple; it resides in the degree of personification that the engineers, managers, or shareholders of Ford see in those 180 persons who would die as a result of their economic decision. If they envision their sons and daughters among the dead, they would not make this decision in any case, even if it were rational and economic, as they would be convinced that 'all are their sons' and 'love thy neighbor as yourself'. But if they perceive the dead as anonymous people without names and faces, who have nothing to do with their loved ones, they will make the same decisions as the Papet in 'Jean de Florette' or Joe Keller in 'All My Sons'.

We can kill for $11, for 30 denarius or for $10,000. According to that logic, the hired killer has the highest respect for human life, as he asks for the higher price. Even Sparafucile in Rigoletto is ready to spare the life of the Duke, as Madalena his sister thinks that he is handsome. The hired killer is impressed by the personification of the Duke and is ready to kill in his place an unknown man. Sparafucile, like some of the companies' executives, is willing to commit a crime if it is toward an unpersonified victim. The personification of the shareholders and stakeholders becomes therefore a major cause to safeguard their interests, as it is much more difficult to wrong them if we know them and appreciate or like them. But, in many cases in modern business the victim is ultimately the abused party who tries to fight the mighty ones. This reminds us of Rigoletto, who has ordered Sparafucile to murder the Duke in order to avenge the abuse of his daughter. The one who dies ultimately is his daughter Gilda, who sacrifices herself in order to save the Duke whom she loved. She presents herself as an unknown person to Sparafucile, who kills her instantly.

"Rigoletto: Dio tremendo! Ella stessa fu colta
dallo stral di mia giusta vendetta!
(A Gilda) Angiol caro, mi guarda, m'ascolta,
parla, parlami, figlia diletta!
Gilda: Ah, ch'io taccia!
A me, a lui perdonate!
Bendedite alla figlia, o mio padre!
Lassu in cielo, vicina alla madre,
in eterno per voi preghero.
Rigoletto: Non morir, mio tesoro, pietade.
Mia colomba, lasciami non dei,
no, lasciami non dei."
(Piave, Rigoletto, end of the opera)

"Rigoletto (to himself): Oh, horror, she herself
has been struck by my vengeance.
(to Gilda) Dear angel, look, listen to me, speak to me beloved.
Gilda: Ah, that I must be silent forever!
Forgive me, forgive him!

Bless your daughter, O father.
In heaven, beside my mother,
I soon shall be,
And there we'll pray for you.
Rigoletto: Do not die, my treasure.
My dove,
Don't leave me."

Would the remorse of Rigoletto, Joe Keller and the Papet be similar to the remorse of the executives who will despoil the rights of the stakeholders? Maybe in the near future, not because they will be more ethical, or because they will read this book, but merely because after mass despoiling of the rights of the stakeholders, they will arrive by statistical probability to the stage that they will despoil the rights of their own family or that they will be despoiled themselves by their colleagues. Only the personification (and the probability) will convince the businessmen who are not ethical that it is more profitable ultimately to be ethical, as when there will be hundreds of thousands of 'Pintos' that can kill or injure people, the probability will reach the threshold of the businessmen.

When we mention the word personification, we incorporate all its meanings, even in the negative sense of minority shareholders, who sometimes while being simple and honest men act more rapaciously than the worse of the majority shareholders. The Internet in many cases reveals this rapacity, this vulgarity, this egoism, which puts a question mark on the essential dilemma of this book. Is it worthwhile to safeguard the rights of minority shareholders or stakeholders if on the average they are just as unethical as the executives and majority shareholders? Emile Zola describes in his book 'Le Ventre de Paris' - 'The Belly of Paris' the conduct of Lisa Quenu-Macquart who finds herself in an ethical dilemma that would make a good case study on ethics. Florent, her husband's brother, has fled from the Devil's Island where he was imprisoned because of subversive conduct toward the regime of Napoleon III. He has the right of his part of the inheritance and she decides to give it to him, by fundamental honesty. She wants to give him the money, but Florent insists that she keep it in her butcher shop. "Vous avez tort, dit-elle, comme pour conclure. J'ai fait ce que je devais faire. Maintenant, ce sera comme vous voudrez... Moi, voyez-vous, je n'aurais pas vecu en paix. Les mauvaises pensees me derangent trop." (Zola, Le Ventre de Paris, p. 106) "You are wrong, she said, as to conclude. I have done what I had to do. Now, it will be as you wish... You see, I would have never lived in peace. Malicious thoughts disturb me too much."

Lisa is the epitome of honesty; her conscience does not reproach her of anything; she does not owe a penny, is not part of any skullduggery; she buys and sells good meat, she does not charge more than her competition... The dishonest people are people like Saccard her cousin the financier, the hero of L'Argent, the speculators, those who despoil the poor people. She is a proud 'minority shareholder' who despises the 'majority shareholders', the mighty. "C'est bon pour nos cousins, les Saccard, ce que tu dis-la. Ils font semblant de ne pas meme savoir que je suis à Paris; mais je suis plus fiere qu'eux, je me moque pas mal de leurs millions. On dit que Saccard trafique dans les demolitions, qu'il vole tout le monde. Ca ne m'etonne pas, il partait pour ça. Il aime l'argent a se rouler dessus, pour le jeter ensuite par les fenêtres, comme un imbécile… Qu'on mette en cause les hommes de sa trempe, qui réalisent des fortunes trop grosses, je le comprends. Moi, si tu veux le savoir, je n'estime pas Saccard… Mais nous, nous qui vivons tranquilles, qui mettront quinze ans a amasser une aisance, nous qui ne nous occupons pas de politique, dont tout le souci est d'élever notre fille et de mener à bien notre barque! allons donc, tu veux rire, nous sommes d'honnêtes gens!" (same, p. 238-9) "It is good for our cousins, the Saccard, what you say here. They pretend to ignore that I am in Paris; but I am prouder than them, I don't care about their millions. They say that Saccard speculates in real estate, that he steals from everybody. It doesn't surprise me; he started like that. He likes money to roll with it on the ground, in order to throw it afterwards from the windows, like a fool… I understand that people of his kind who earn exorbitant fortunes have questionable conduct. For myself, if you want to know it, I don't estimate Saccard… But we who live quietly, who will need fifteen years to achieve an easy life, we who are not preoccupied by politics, whose only concern is to raise our daughter and row our boat properly! Come on, you are kidding, we are honest people!"

And it is this honest woman, who ultimately finds the political discussions of Florent despicable, who cannot stand the smell of fish that Florent brings to the table as it prevents her from eating, she – who probably has the smell of pork from her butcher shop. She thinks that Florent eats too much but he doesn't enjoy it. He cannot even get fatter, the miserable, as he is eaten up by his malice. The honest lamb Florent has become a wolf in the imagination of Lisa, when she sees that she can profit from the inheritance. "Elle s'était approchée de la fenêtre. Elle vit Florent qui traversait la rue Rambuteau, pour se rendre à la poissonnerie. L'arrivage de la marée débordait, ce matin-la; les mannes avaient de grandes moires d'argent, les criees grondaient. Lisa suivit les épaules pointues de son beau-frère entrant dans les odeurs fortes des Halles, l'échine pliée, avec cette nausée de l'estomac qui lui montait aux tempes; et le regard dont elle l'accompagnait etait celui d'une combattante, d'une femme resolue au triomphe." (same, p. 242-3) "She approached the window. She saw Florent cross Rambuteau Street and reach the fish shop. The tide overflowed this morning; the mannas glistened like silver, the fishmongers' auctions were at their peak. Lisa followed the pointed shoulders of her brother-in-law entering the Halles, his back curved, with a nausea of the stomach that reached his temples; and the look with which she accompanied him was a look of a warrior, a woman resolute to win."

Florent was condemned because of his smell of fish, of his 'malice', but really because these excuses gave her the legitimacy to steal his part of the inheritance that she coveted without admitting it, as she was honest. Exactly like those who condemned Captain Dreyfus to exile to the same Devil's Island where Florent was imprisoned, because of his Jewish smell, his treason, his innocence. And Zola, who 20 years later condemns the honorable and honest men who have judged Dreyfus in 'J'accuse'; blames Lisa of her treachery and honest people of their covetousness, after the policemen take Florent to prison. "Les bandes de lard entrevues, les moities de cochon pendues contre les marbres, mettaient la des rondeurs de ventre, tout un triomphe du ventre, tandis que Lisa, immobile, avec sa carrure digne, donnait aux Halles le bonjour matinal, de ses grands yeux de forte mangeuse. Puis toutes deux se penchèrent. La belle Mme Lebigre et la belle Mme Quenu échangèrent un salut d'amitié. Et Claude, qui avait certainement oublie de diner la veille, pris de colère a les voir si bien portantes, si comme il faut, avec leurs grosses gorges, serra sa ceinture, en grondant d'une voix fâchée: 'Quels gredins que les honnêtes gens!' " (same, p. 424) "The packs of bacon, the half porks hanged over the marble, put over there roundness of bellies, a whole triumph of bellies, while Lisa, motionless, with her imposing dignity, gave to the Halles the good morning, with her large eyes. Then both of them stooped over. The beautiful Mme. Lebigre and the beautiful Mme. Quenu said a friendly hello to each other. And Claude, who certainly has forgotten to dine yesterday, furious to see them so healthy, decent, with their large bosoms, gripped his belt, while growling in an angry voice: 'What scoundrels are the honest people!' "

But the simplistic segmentation of Lisa between simple and honest people and rich and corrupted people has no value, as we should not personify the minority shareholders as weak and honest. The majority shareholders can be more honest than the minority shareholders and this book does not intend to idealize the honesty of the weak. Those weak masses can become wolves when they have the opportunity, exactly like Lisa has become a wolf to Florent. Human nature is the same, among the mighty and the weak. The only reason to safeguard the interests of the stakeholders and minority shareholders is for justice and ethics to prevail and allocate the same rights to the strong as to the weak, exactly like in the democracies. The same rights, even if they abuse them, even if they do not deserve them. For it is impossible to pronounce an ethical judgment on the personal value of every one of us. We can always find excuses why we have to abolish the rights of others, legitimate or not, as we are wolves or lambs subsequently or simultaneously, depending on who describes the case.

11
THE PREDOMINANCE OF VALUES AND ETHICS FOR CEOs

"Conscience is but a word that cowards use,
Devis'd at first to keep the strong in awe:
Our strong arms be our conscience, swords our law.
March on, join bravely, let us to't pell-mell;
If not to heaven, then hand in hand to hell."
(Shakespeare, Richard III, Act V, Scene III, 310-314)

In order to promote a change of attitude toward ethics, one has to start probably at the top of the companies, the CEOs, as it is they who ultimately decide the ethical climate of their companies. Unfortunately, companies are the last vestiges of dictatorial regimes. Most of the world, especially after the collapse of the Soviet Union, is ruled by democracies; even the political parties elect their candidates in 'primaries'. All western countries have laws on equal rights of genders, races and religions. Only one domain of human activity remains dictatorial – the companies, where the CEOs have absolute power together with the majority shareholders who rule the companies.

The business world has a great admiration for youth and one often sees CEOs or analysts under the age of 30, or at most 40, in many high-tech companies and Wall Street investment banks. But at this age, very often, men and women have not yet formed an ethical character that has proven its integrity in the most adverse business conditions. The temptation is very acute to transgress moral codes, especially when young people have not received a humanistic upbringing and if they are motivated uniquely by their career. On the other hand, more mature managers with impeccable integrity cannot reach the highest positions, often because of their age and more often because of their integrity.

The most important feature of a businessman has to be his moral integrity, especially in fiduciary positions such as CEOs, vice presidents, or investment bankers and analysts, who are responsible for financing tens or hundreds of millions of dollars. It is imperative to broaden humanist education in the universities, including ethics courses. The astronomical sums of remuneration to top-level businessmen are at the base of corruption. Unfortunately, there are not enough businessmen who cannot be corrupted in any case. For most of the others, it is only a relative question, as corruption and ethical deviation vary from case to case and do not have to be flagrant in each case. As all humans cannot be moral 100 percent all the time, most of businessmen rationalize that even if they are ethical by 60 percent in half of the cases, it is better than the average. If they are obliged to behave unethically, they prefer it to be toward weaker groups that cannot retaliate, and the stakeholders and minority shareholders are amongst the weakest groups.

As there are no businessmen who have all the good qualities, although many of them think so, we have to ask ourselves what are the most important qualities. Should we place the highest value on businessmen who are the most brilliant, efficient or charismatic or those who obtain the best financial results? Or do we favor the most ethical businessmen? Nowadays, ethics is at the lowest level of preferences for some of the managers, but we should transpose it to the highest level, at the same level of the operational qualities. The best manager, with the most brilliant results, who does not behave ethically, will in the long run cause more harm to the company than the ethical manager who is less brilliant but who has nevertheless adequate operational qualities.

We should establish a coefficient of E x P, whereas E is Ethics of the company and P its Profits or Performance. In this formula, we should optimize E x P. This cannot be achieved when E or P are too low, or even if P is 100 percent but E is 0 percent, as the result would be O. The application of this formula could revolutionize the business philosophy, as nowadays E is not at all part of the coefficient in most of the companies, and certainly not at the same level of P. This result could be achieved only if the stakeholders and minority shareholders would insist on it and would not work with or in companies and purchase their shares if they are not managed ethically.

Even the most rapacious minority shareholders, who are interested only in immediate profits on their investments, will reach in the long run the conclusion that only ethics can safeguard their interests. As, in the jungle of the business world where only the strongest survive, the minority shareholders who are not organized and who do not have any protection will always lose in the long run, exactly like gamblers in casinos who do not have a fair chance against the bank. Those 'speculators' would never dare wander into a dangerous district where police are not present, as even if they are very strong individually, the mob is always stronger than them. And they should not expect to be rescued in business by the 'police' of the shareholders. The law, the SEC, the norms, and the conscience of the majority shareholders and the executives have a limited responsibility, exactly like the companies, whose limit is their interests. The legal system and the SEC have their own agenda and are very limited in their ability to safeguard the interests of minority shareholders.

"As a former vice-president of a large firm says: 'What is right in the corporation is not what is right in a man's home or in his church. What is right in the corporation is what the guy above you wants from you. That's what morality is in the corporation.'... Actual organizational moralities are thus contextual, situational, highly specific, and, most often, unarticulated." (Jackall, Moral Mazes, p.6) This dilemma, brought forward by an executive of a large company, emphasizes the need for the predominance of ethics of the CEOs. For many managers, ethics in business is merely their boss' wishes. The boss is a concrete person, while morality is an abstract concept, and if we want to promote ethics in business, it is mandatory that the executives will behave ethically.

The origin of this full obedience to the boss principle comes from the patrimonial bureaucracy, which was prevalent in the courts of kings, where personal loyalty was the norm and not loyalty to the organization. Nowadays, the executives are at the base of the bureaucratic ethical norms, although they comprise only 10 percent of the salaried. The CEO is surrounded by his 'court' of managers who are completely loyal, as loyalty is the most precious characteristic. They have to be 'one of the gang'. In return for full loyalty to the superior, the chief is supposed to protect the subordinates in the organization, exactly like in the feudal epoch. Jackall finds a stunning analogy between the CEOs and the kings, assisted by their subordinates who are the 'barons'. "The CEO of the corporation is the king. His word is law; even the CEOs' wishes and whims are taken as commands by close subordinates on the corporate staff, who turn them into policies and directives." (Jackall, Moral Mazes, p.21) The most interesting subject of conversation of the managers is the speculation on the plans of the CEO, his intentions, his actions, his style and his public image.

In this environment, which is closer to the court of Louis XIV than to modern democracy, we do not have to wonder if the convictions of the executives become suspect 'Everybody has a right to his convictions, as long as he leaves them at the door of the company'. We have to mingle in the masses, be a 'team player' and not be brilliant, otherwise we'll become a threat to our colleagues. We have to align ourselves to the prevailing ideology, even if it is in contradiction to our personal beliefs. We should not make waves, we have to concur with the ideas of the majority; we do not have to argue with the orders of our boss even if we are convinced that we are right. All those observations, based on extensive research of Jackall and many others, concur completely with the results of the 33-year experience of the author of this book.

And we reach the appalling conclusion of Jackall, who resumes the ethos of successful businessmen: "The ethos that they fashion turns principles into guidelines, ethics into etiquette, values into tastes, personal responsibility into an adroitness at public relations, and notions of truth into credibility. Corporate managers who become imbued with this ethos pragmatically take their world as they find it and try to make that world work according to its own institutional logic. They pursue their own careers and good fortune, as best they can, within the rules of their world. As it happens, given their pivotal institutional role in our epoch, they help create and re-create, as one unintended consequence of their personal striving, a society where morality becomes indistinguishable from the quest for one's own survival and advantage." (Jackall, Moral Mazes, p.204)

One should not be a prophet in order to understand where this state of affairs can lead. The degeneration of the totalitarian regimes is inevitable in history as in business. The complete devotion to an 'absolute monarch' is bound to lead to corruption, to abuse of rights of minority shareholders, employees, environment, and finally to the infringement of the law. Absolutism is at the base of all evils, and there is no reason why it should subsist in its last bastion – the business world. There will be no safeguard of the interests of the minority shareholders, as long as the CEOs will continue to conduct themselves as Byzantine pashas or as a Roi Soleil. The Sun Kings of today are sent to a lunatic asylum, a place not unlike some of today's companies, where the talk of the day in the board rooms is not business strategy but rather why the CEO is in a bad mood.

During the Six-Day War the Egyptians officers reported to their headquarters that they were advancing toward Tel Aviv, while they were fleeing from the Israeli army, because they were educated to conduct themselves as Yesmen, and their chiefs did not appreciate the truth if it was disagreeable. Six years later, on the eve of the Yom Kippur War, the Israeli intelligence officers all believed that the Arabs were not going to attack, in spite of all the contrary information that was gathered, as this was what was expected from them by their chiefs. The two armies have learned their lessons, but the armies of businessmen are still at the court of Abdul Hamid. Will we need a defeat like that of the Ottoman Empire in order to change our norms of conduct? The modern theories, like those of 'In Search for Excellence', advocate diversity of opinion, democratic management, ethics in business, and the respect of the rights of all the stakeholders of companies. Unfortunately, those theories are not practiced in many cases, as can be proven in a large number of cases. It is of course impossible to prove quantitatively the degree of ethical conduct of companies, but it would be interesting to analyze what is the profitability of the investments of minority shareholders in unethical companies and compare it to the profitability of the investments of the majority shareholders and the CEOs in the same companies.

We could argue that there is no need to change the autocratic norms of companies, but rather to change the sovereigns to be ethical. It would be much easier for them to institute the ethical norms because of the loyalty of their subjects. Unfortunately, as Diogenes who is still looking for justice, we are still looking for the humanistic monarch in order to render him absolute power. Until we find him, we have to satisfy ourselves with democracy, in parliament as in companies. We are submerged by books written by or about CEOs of the most successful companies, where we can read of all their qualities, but those who know them well can testify that they are in many cases retrograde, mean and petty tyrants. A Hebrew proverb speaks about the difference between a mountain and a monarch: when you look at a mountain from a distance - it looks small, but when you approach it - it looks big, and with the monarch it is the opposite… This book advocates that it is better to have a CEO primus inter pares, surrounded by VPs who can keep their initiatives, raise original ideas, and make decisions, rather than a small Napoleon, who looks literally small when you are close to him, is surrounded by vassals who prostrate to him, without ever seeing, hearing or speaking.

An example of an ethical CEO is Al Casey, who embraced the motto: 'If something can go right, it should'. This motto is the opposite of Murphy's Law, and Casey proves how throughout his brilliant career as CEO of American Airlines, Times Mirror, the US Postal Service and other organizations, he was able to implement his ethical concepts, although it forced him in some cases to quit the jobs in order not to compromise with his ethics. "An axiom of Casey's Law: if you want something to go right, the foundation of your dealings with others must be total integrity. I emphasize, at the risk of sounding self-righteous, the word total. This is not a matter of blind allegiance to some idealistic code of conduct; it's simply that a lack of integrity – however seemingly innocuous or minor the deviation – will eventually come home to haunt you and your company." (Casey, Casey's Law, p.64)

"My mother used to say, 'Just imagine that what you're about to do or say is going to be the headline in tomorrow's paper. Would I be proud of you, Albert?' It was a tried and true question, but Mother constantly impressed it on us. 'I'm not going to be there to help you all the time,' she would say. 'But you must always do the right thing. And you must never shame your parents or your family.' Everyone in the business world ought to be able to agree that treating customers, employees, and suppliers ethically is good business. But corporations often put tremendous, sometimes impossible, pressure on their employees to improve the bottom line. Now they must learn to put equal pressure on their employees to take the ethical high road in meeting their goals and objectives. 'Only a virtuous people are capable of freedom,' George Washington once said." (Casey, Casey's Law, p.310-311) Aristotle suggested that to be virtuous we have to make an example of a virtuous man. The example of Al Casey and many other executives in the U.S., U.K., France, Israel and other countries could help us to find the ethical and practical path, provided that we succeed in discerning the truly ethical businessmen from those who pretend to be ethical.

Many people maintain as a self-fulfilling prophecy that the business world is an immoral jungle and that businessmen are cynically and uniquely motivated by their interests. If people will keep saying it only this kind of businessmen will enter into the business world, and the prophecy will be fulfilled. On the other hand we should not be deluded that everything is for the best, but we have to see things as they are, and try to find remedies for the diseases of the business world and its leaders. "Not long ago in an undercover investigation in New York, 106 bribes were offered to public officials, and 105 were accepted. I would like to be able to tell you that the one who declined was a man of honor, but no, he turned down the bribe because he thought it was too low. Such amusing stories should not make one cynical." (Williams, Ethics and the Investment Industry, p.32)

The predominance of the ethical role of the CEO is much more pertinent if we notice that the executives are elected very often by a Board of Directors that they control. Executives try to stay in their positions as long as possible, earning salaries 150 times higher than the average salary of their employees. They decide in a group such decisions that as individuals they would have never decided. "Inflated billings, shortcutting workplace safety, tax evasion, secret dumping of toxic waste, even deadly products – apparently all can seem acceptable when the decision is made by a group. This is how good people end up making harmful decisions in corporations. This is how corporate managers, whose personal morality, conscience, or religion would prevent them as individuals from ever willingly placing others' lives in jeopardy for a few dollars of profit, will do exactly that in the corporation. Good people end up taking such harmful actions because, when they enter the corporate environment, they come under great pressure to accept the corporate morality, to allow it to dominate their personal morality. And the corporate morality, as we have seen, is a soulless morality defined by the single commandment: 'Maximize the bottom line!" (Estes, Tyranny of the Bottom Line, p. 102) But society does not sanction nor is it upset by the crimes of companies, as there is a double standard for the robber who steals a few hundred dollars and the company that commits a fraud of millions of dollars. "Little crime gets pursued and prosecuted with vigor. Big crime often gets excused; when it is prosecuted the penalty is barely felt. And as a society, we teach our children the morality that wealth and power excuse corruption, while poverty makes it more sinful." (same, p. 104)

Having good values is the software of the success of a good CEO, while the hardware are the financial and operational results. Values are the intangible, the qualitative component of business - honesty, good service, good products, good relations with employees, stakeholders and the community. "All happy families resemble one another, said the Russian writer Tolstoy. Like happy families, values-driven companies resemble one another in important ways. All have discovered the process of qualitative improvement. All follow a well-defined implementation path. All commit at the top, communicate, educate, set standards, align structure and systems. All recognize performance. Values are a commonplace miracle, fully visible, partially seen. These simple operating qualities, vigorously pursued, release 10,000 elevated acts every day. Their power is available to anyone, yet only a few see its full potential." (Harmon, Playing for Keeps, p. 111)

Values can differ from company to company, but the ethical motivation of the executives who have established them is universal. Since its foundation by Eleuthere du Pont in 1802, Du Pont has committed itself to maintaining the security of its employees. The level of work accidents is 40 times less than the average level of the American industry and 10 times lower than the average level of the chemical industry in the U.S. American Steel and Wire Corporation has an employee motivation policy, which could be resumed in the levels of a pyramid: Job Security, Pay Program, Benefits, Training, Development, Communication, Involvement, Measurement, Recognition. For the company, like for Fukuyama, recognition is the highest level of motivation. The values of Intel are: Risk taking, Quality, Discipline, Customer Orientation, Results Orientation, Great Place to Work; and for Disney the values are: Safety, Courtesy, Show, Efficiency.

Values are of the utmost importance in times of crisis, as in the case of 3Com, where the French CEO Benhamou has succeeded in turning around the company in a spectacular way, while enforcing a detailed values system: "In bold capital letters it talked about people as OUR MAJOR ASSET. It stressed the need to Value the Individual. The conventional wisdom was certainly 'to save those happy thoughts for a happier day after we get through this.' Instead, Benhamou challenged himself and his team to be judged by those values during the worst crisis most of them had faced. Topping the list of seven values was 'Act with Honesty and Integrity.' The definition gave explicit guidance, almost as if written for such a crisis. 'Be honest in all our dealings. Tell the truth. Make clear commitments among ourselves and with our customers and partners. Meet those commitments. Communicate openly." (Harmon, Playing for Keeps, p. 212)

Values from the time of Du Pont until the time of Benhamou are at the base of business ethics and the key for the adherence of the business world to the ethical norms would probably be in the combination of the values of the business leaders with a favorable attitude of their environment toward those norms. The success of those ethical companies is flagrant proof that you can conduct yourself in a different manner in the business world and reach a very high level of profitability, while keeping your ethical standards. What matters is not what the leaders believe or declare but how they act, as there was too much abuse until now of the beliefs and ethical codes that in many cases were not implemented seriously. The proof of ethics is therefore in the facts, in the example, in the perseverance, in devotion. "From CEO to solo contributor, values energize work and enrich life. Although values-driven leaders have a thousand faces, their stories resonate with complementary themes. Values-driven leaders change the way we look at work. They uncover standards we didn't see. They create traditions that shape behavior. They transform routine into adventure, careers into voyages of self-discovery. Above all, they inspire others by revealing the power of a commonplace miracle called values." (Harmon, Playing for Keeps, p. 273)

The primordial question is therefore if the ethics of the executives will become the principal motivation of the businessmen of the new Millennium. There are certain indications that this is already the case in many companies. "A manager's personal values and strength of character have become urgent issues for the corporation. In a recent survey by Korn/Ferry and Columbia University Graduate School of Business, over fifteen hundred executives from twenty countries rated personal ethics as the number one characteristic needed by the ideal CEO in the year 2000. As Delbert 'Bud' Staley, former Chairman of NYNEX, remarked, personal integrity is a business leadership essential: 'We have to depend on every one of our employees for the good reputation of this firm.' So, too, Johnson & Johnson's Jim Burke has asserted that most individuals in his company welcome the emphasis on high ethical standards which their Credo represents. 'After all,' he said, 'everybody wants to believe in something." (Nash, Good Intentions Aside, p. 7) Influential groups of businessmen, such as the Business Roundtable, the American Management Association and the Conference Board, sponsor ethical programs. They have arrived at the conclusion that it is one of the most important goals of the modern business world, following the scandals of the 80s and 90s, the heavy fines that the companies had to pay, the destructive effect on the routine of companies and the moral of employees, the frauds, and the bad reputation of the business world.

On the other hand, there is a large number of businessmen who worship the 'street fighters', as if we were in the West Side of New York at the epoch of the fights between opposing gangs. Commendable characteristics for an executive are to be a 'killer of competitors', a 'shark', or 'quick-and-dirty'. From the moment that we perceive ourselves in a state of war with competition where everything is permitted as in 'cut-throat competition' and 'fight on life and death', we create for ourselves motivations of survival like we do in war, and in 'war like in war' - a la guerre comme a la guerre. "Like individuals in life-threatening situations who will violate even the most basic moral tenets in order to survive, the manager or company with a survival ethic will justify actions whose moral implications run counter to their stated moral commitment based on a sense of 'having had to do it." (Nash, Good Intentions Aside, p. 55) The translation of this state of affairs is catastrophic for ethics of the company, but we can notice an evolution that started five or ten years ago: "Walk on whomever you can to get ahead. Squeeze your suppliers dry, manipulate your customers into accepting second-best, waste shareholder dollars on the maintenance of status in an effort to establish your image – oh yes, and stay within the laws and customs of the land. Today's marketplace is not so naive or meek as to accept such behavior without resistance. Suppliers become overnight competitors, customers move on, and shareholders are much more aggressive in demanding an honest accounting. Consumer and environmental groups, somewhat dormant during the last Reagan administration, have recently increased their activism. Thus others are provoked to impose heavy legal or quasi-legal constraints on managers' exploitative tendencies. Laws on fairness and honesty become the only practical ethical controls. This approach to motivating ethical behavior is both inefficient and ineffective." (same, p. 69)

It is practically impossible to impose ethical conduct by law, inter alia because the large companies will almost always win the litigation, due to their power, and to the fact that it is very difficult to codify ethical conduct in legal terms. Most of the ethical dilemmas of executives cannot even be detected by the legal system. Nash proposes to ask oneself six questions in case of ethical dilemmas in order to augment the moral sensibility: "Is it right? Is it fair? Am I hurting anyone? Could I disclose this to the public or a respected mentor? Would I tell my child to do this? Does it pass the stink test?" (same, p. 130) It is improbable that CEOs, like Joe Keller in All My Sons by Arthur Miller, would have conducted themselves unethically if they would have asked themselves those six questions, especially the question on setting an example to your children. This ethical pressure would have to outweigh the other pressures which are much more tangible on the CEOs, such as 'winning isn't everything. It's the only thing.' You are forced to achieve profitable results in every quarter, while the moral dilemmas are much less urgent. In order to move those two pressures closer, which are certainly not at two different poles, we could once again cite one of the greatest authors of the 20th century: "F. Scott Fitzgerald's statement that the mark of a first-class intelligence is the ability to sustain in one's mind two opposing ideas simultaneously is to the point. Bottom-line thinking can only operate constructively if it is balanced by an intelligent reference to the qualitative, ethical values on which responsible decision making is based." (same, p. 138)

But the best argumentation for the ethical conduct of a CEO is that if he conducts himself in an unethical manner toward his customers, suppliers, employees, or the government, he will conduct himself in the same manner also toward the majority shareholders who have appointed him to his position. It is almost impossible to remain ethical toward certain segments and unethical toward others. The deceitful will tend to pass on his deceit toward everybody, and those who will lose the most will be those who appointed him, but it will be too late for them to remedy the situation. The hypocrites are much more dangerous than the deceitful, as they are judged by their declarations. Hearing them, you could think that they are the most ethical executives in the world, as they rationalize their lack of ethics: "There is not a manager or human being alive who has not offered one of the following excuses for failure to act with integrity: 'Nobody's getting hurt'. 'Everybody does it. That's just the way things are done.' 'Everybody understands what's really going on.' 'I can't afford to do otherwise.' 'Nobody cares about this anyway.' 'That's not really an ethical issue.' Whenever such rationalizations are voiced, it's time to take a second look at your behavior or that of your company. Nine times out of ten you are in a type B situation. Problems in Business Ethics – Type A (The Acute Dilemma): Situations where you do not know what is the right or wrong thing to do. Type B (The Acute Rationalization): Situations where you know what is right, but fail to do it. It must be recognized that although top management tends to deal predominantly with Type A decisions, and mid-to first-level management with Type B, most managers face both kinds of moral challenges." (Nash, Good Intentions Aside, p, 126-7)

"A faithful man will be richly blessed, but one eager to get rich will not go unpunished." (Proverbs, 28:20) It is often deceiving to notice how a simple sentence of the Bible can summarize the entire content of a book or thesis… Nevertheless, in trying to analyze the conduct of the CEOs and the reasons that cause them to commit immoral acts, we can see that those who are eager to get rich and obtain immediate results are almost always inclined to act against ethics. "The impulse and obligation to stimulate efficiency corrupt a manager's moral capacity in three basic ways:

1. Once the assumption is made that expediency in its narrowest sense is a manager's first obligation, there is little incentive or legitimacy for taking a critical look at moral issues. Better to adopt a 'no-time-for-ethics' pragmatism…

2. Short-term mindsets encourage self-delusion. Nothing succeeds like success, but often only in the short term. According to the title of Robert Frost's poem, 'Happiness Makes Up in Height for What It Lacks in Length', no position, however euphorically high, guarantees protection from future mistakes of judgment. Thus the tragic heroes once taught us. You make a good deal. You're riding high. No time for a postmortem on the decision, go on to the next. Overconfident and ready to accelerate the pace, you begin to make mistakes in judgment which cumulatively catch up with you only after they are beyond your control. Only a long-term view of career and performance can provide an antidote to the heady live-for-the-present high that success can encourage.

3. Short-term orientations invite greedy orientations."

(Nash, Good Intentions Aside, p. 167)

As a CEO, you enter into a short-term whirl of promotion, and you have never the time and opportunity to pay for the mistakes that you have made. You are paid a very high salary that suppresses all your scruples. You are given warrants and shares of the company in order to participate in the quarry, exactly like Aristide Saccard, who participates avidly in the quarry in La Curee by Emile Zola. "The legal system tends to reinforce the delusion of infallibility. An individual engaged in corporate wrongdoing is neither as easily detected nor as likely to be punished as are other types of criminals. Fines and other punishments for corporate crimes are far less harsh than for street crimes. A drug addict who stole a bicycle in Central Park received a four-year prison sentence. A drug company whose managers covered up the fact that one of its products had resulted in four deaths and many illnesses paid a $25,000 fine and no individual was indicted for criminal charges. Until recently, the insider-trader who stole millions while his company laundered drug money received a slap on the wrist. In an ego-driven environment a manager's capacity for retaining sensitivity and a respect for others is seriously undermined. Reinforced by a totally inequitable culture and compensation system, along with ego-massaging perks, a manager can mistake corporate hierarchy and financial position for good judgment and ethical conduct. When reality is this muddled, it can seem unremarkable to condone conflict-of-interest activities, cheating, cover-ups, mudslinging, bribery, gouging, price-fixing, exploitation of the little guy, and unsafe production processes, all of which stem from an inability to respect the other person's rights and needs." (same, p. 192-3)

This explains how CEOs behave in many cases in the modern business world. They think that they can never lose, that they are infallible, above the masses, protected by the majority shareholders and their lawyers. The CEOs have almost no fear that their conduct toward stakeholders and minority shareholders will be blamed, or that they will ever be condemned. They participate in the quarry, eating the leftovers of the majority shareholders, and leaving only the bones for the minority shareholders.

12
THE METHODOLOGICAL APPROACH OF THE BOOK

"Theories are like nets: only those who throw them, will fish."
(Novalis)

This book and the previous book by the same author 'Business Ethics - The Ethical Revolution of Minority Shareholders', hereinafter 'the author's books', are based on very extensive theoretical and empirical research on activist business ethics and case studies on wrongdoing to stakeholders and minority shareholders in the U.S., France and Israel. They suggest practical proposals that can be implemented without delay, although it is impossible to prove irrefutably that those proposals would be received favorably by the managers of the companies and by the majority shareholders. The companies that will agree to adopt the proposals will probably not be hit by a potential collapse of the international stock markets in the future and will serve as a model of mutual trust between the stakeholders, shareholders and managers of the companies.

We should first examine the methodological basis of the author's books. Feyerabend in his revolutionary book 'Against Method' described his thesis in the following terms: "My thesis is that anarchy contributes to progress, whatever is the sense that we give it... we can use hypotheses which contradict well confirmed theories and/or well established experimental results. We can move forward science by proceeding with counter-induction... A scientist who desires to enlarge to maximum the empirical content of his concepts, and who wants to understand them as clearly as possible, should consequently introduce other concepts: i.e. he should adopt a pluralistic methodology." (Feyerabend, Contre la Methode, Against Method, in French, p. 25-27)

The author's books question entrenched practices in the business world, innate ideologies, interests of groups who control the modern economy. They try to promote democratic principles in the business world, the last bastion of the world totalitarian regimes, where the will of the CEO is the Bible, where the interests of the majority shareholders who control the company are unshaken. 'The more things change the more they stay the same', 'We cannot argue with success', 'My boss's will is my ethics', 'We have to maximize our profits, whatever the ethical costs may be', are the preferred maxims of some businessmen. We do recall in the past other maxims in other fields which sounded also unshakable, like - 'Earth is flat as this is what we see', 'We cannot argue with the legitimacy of the Bourbons as they rule already for a few hundreds years', 'We should not revolt against the British as they are our own blood', 'The 1948 borders of Israel do not exist as they were not recognized by the UN'. This method of argument to sanctify the prevailing situation without allowing any new or unorthodox ideas is common to business as it was common to politics, religion, and sociology throughout history. The author of this book condemns this method and proposes new ideas, as he believes that nothing is sacrosanct, and especially not the unethical conduct of many companies in the business world.

The theoretical concepts and laws of the author's books, the cases which are based on intensive empirical research of thousands of documents, the new organizations proposed for the safeguard of the interests of the stakeholders and minority shareholders - the Board of Supervision and the Institute of Ethics - were developed and verified in an empirical way. The reasoning of these theories was examined under all its angles, after having analyzed the conduct, the psychology, the beliefs, and the sociological aspects of businessmen in the context of the organizations in which they perform. The theories were established from the basis of the individual conduct and interactions between the businessmen. The book 'Business Ethics - The Ethical Revolution of Minority Shareholders' proved that there are laws that are very defined and that manage the conduct toward minority shareholders in Israeli, American or French companies. Those are not exceptional cases but the norm in many companies, which is illustrated by qualitative cases, without being able of course to quantify them.

As the author's books do not propose a change of law toward all companies, but the establishment of voluntary organizations, which could benefit the stakeholders and minority shareholders, it is not necessary to quantify the cases of abuse, and the companies that always conduct themselves ethically will not have to suffer from the new proposals. On the contrary, they will be made as examples and will take part in the ethical funds and increase their good ethical reputation. The argumentation of the books is therefore founded on the theoretical and empirical aspects and weaves like a backbone throughout the chapters. The ethical cases are necessary, as otherwise the theories would have been unfounded, and on the other hand the theoretical concepts are necessary, as otherwise the cases would not conclude anything and would be only descriptive literature. The author's books propose therefore a sophisticated solution to the problem of the safeguarding of the stakeholders and minority shareholders, which could revolutionize the present state of affairs, characterized by frequent abuse of their rights.

Modern theories on ethics, the safeguarding of the interests of the stakeholders of the companies, and the struggle against the abuse of the rights of minority shareholders, are very unpopular in certain circles, as every benefit for the underdogs is after all a loss for the tycoons, who control without adequate opposition the modern business world, in a world where mergers, acquisitions, and multinationals are at the base of 'progress'. The analysis of a brilliant philosopher like Feyerabend, who questions everything, can be very refreshing and timely in order to reinforce the new theories of the author of this book. "The proliferation of theories is beneficial for science, while uniformity impoverishes the critical power. Uniformity puts also in jeopardy the free development of the individual." (Feyerabend, Contre la Methode, p.32) "The examples of Copernicus, of the atomic theory, of the Voodoo, or of the Chinese medicine, prove that even the most advanced theory, and apparently the surest, is not protected from a transformation or from a total reject by the concepts that the vanity of ignorance has already thrown to the garbage of history. This is how the knowledge of today can become the fairy tale of tomorrow, and the most ridicule myth can eventually become a very solid element of science." (Feyerabend, Contre la Methode, p.53)

It would be possible to criticize the new theories of the author's books that do not concur to all the facts to which they apply, but this is the case also of many scientific theories. The analyzed cases in these books cannot be indicative of all the possible cases. If they describe the abuse of the rights of minority shareholders, we should not be requested to describe other cases where the rights of minority shareholders were respected, in the name of scientific objectivity. The only aim of the cases is to illustrate the theories presented in these books, and indicate that if they would have been applied, we could have prevented eventually the abuse of the rights of the minority shareholders in those cases or in similar cases. "Never is a theory in accordance with all the facts to which it applies, but however it is not always the theory which is in default. The facts are themselves built up by much older ideologies, and a break between the facts and the theories can be the sign of progress. It is also a first step in our attempt to discover the principles which guide implicitly the familiar observations." (Feyerabend, Contre la Methode, p.55)

If we would have to wait to formulate new theories that they should be irrefutable, we could never change anything. Because the senses perceive the earth as flat and not moving, we should not conclude that this is the truth, and we should not wait for the invention of ultra-modern telescopes in order to prove that the earth is round and revolves around the sun. If there are some people who argue that the more things change the more they stay the same, we should not conclude that this should be the state of affairs. We cannot always have irrefutable arguments in order to change the state of affairs. "It is clear that the commitment to new ideas should be provoked by other means than arguments. By irrational means, such as propaganda, emotion, ad hoc hypotheses, and an appeal to prejudices of all kinds. We need those 'irrational means' to sustain what is only a blind belief – until we shall find the auxiliary sciences, the facts, the arguments which transform this belief in solid 'knowledge'." (Feyerabend, Contre la Methode, p.165-6) And Feyerabend concludes that: "progress can be accomplished only if the distinction between what should be and what is, is considered as a temporary point of view, rather than as a fundamental frontier." (Feyerabend, Contre la Methode, p.183)

The subject of these books is interesting and pertinent and their author tries his best to develop it, inspired by Popper who said: "I do not care much of the methods which a philosopher can use (or anybody else) as long as there is an interesting problem and that he sincerely tries to resolve it." (Popper, La Logique de la Decouverte Scientifique, The Logic of Scientific Discovery, in French, p.13) The theories, which are developed in the author's books, may be valid only for a certain period, until they will be falsified, as the verification can be based only on the bibliography of these books, the experience of the author and the analyzed cases. But it is preferable to present the theories on business ethics and the safeguarding of the rights of stakeholders and minority shareholders, that may be falsified in the future, rather than to sanctify the prevailing situation and declare that what exists is what should exist. Or as Popper says, "I am inclined to think that scientific discovery is impossible if we do not have a belief in ideas purely speculative and sometimes completely vague, a belief that nothing guarantees from a scientific point of view and which is, in this measure, 'metaphysical'." (Popper, La Logique de la Decouverte Scientifique, p.35)

And he concludes: "The old ideal of episteme, the ideal of an absolutely certain and demonstrable knowledge was revealed as an idol. The demand for scientific objectiveness makes it inevitable that every scientific exposition would remain necessarily and forever as a try-out. It is only in our subjective experiences of conviction, in our personal confidence, that we can be 'absolutely certain'. With the idol of certainty (which includes the imperfect certainty and probability) falls one of the defenses of obscurantism, which puts an obstacle on the way of scientific progress. As the tribute rendered to this idol does not only repress the audacity of our questions, but also jeopardizes the strictness and honesty of our tests. The erroneous conception of science is revealed in the thirst for accuracy. As what the scientist does, is not the possession of knowledge, irrefutable truths, but the obstinate and audaciously critical search for truth." (Popper, La Logique de la Decouverte Scientifique, p.286-7)

The author's books are based on qualitative and inductive research. They are not based on statistics to analyze their concepts, and the ideas of the author have been translated to hypotheses, which were analyzed in order to test their validity at least in partial conditions. In inductive theories, "Hypotheses are both provisional and conditional." (Strauss, Qualitative Analysis, p.12) The verification of the author's books is based on professional and personal experience. Strauss recommends confronting the principal problems in the elements of the cases, by trying to sort out the principal problem that consists of the largest number of elements. We should know how to integrate all those elements in a principal theory. It is necessary that the integration of the first project should be coherent before continuing to the second project.

Is it legitimate to base the author's books on case studies? All the professional education of the author, starting with his studies at INSEAD, seminars at IMD, and throughout his career is a continuation of thousand of cases, read, studied and lived, assembled patiently to give a fascinating outlook on business administration. "The case study has long been stereotyped as a weak sibling among social sciences methods. Investigators who do case studies are regarded as having deviated from their academic disciples, their investigations as having insufficient precision (that is, quantification), objectivity, and rigor. Despite this stereotype, case studies continue to be used extensively in social sciences research... The method also is a frequent mode of thesis and dissertation research in all of these disciplines and fields." (Yin, Case Study Research, p.XIII) "In general, case studies are the preferred strategy when 'how' or 'why' questions are being posed, when the investigator has little control over events, and when the focus is on a contemporary phenomenon within some real-life context." (Yin, Case Study Research, p.1) The purpose of the author's books is to analyze why and how companies do not act ethically toward their stakeholders and minority shareholders. Not how many companies (all, the majority, a negligible percentage...), not which companies (large, small, public, private, high-tech, low-tech, banks or others), not to what degree (they transgress all the rights, part of them, which part), not where (in France, the United States, Italy, Israel, Sweden or Nigeria, although, due to the experience of the author of these books, the cases described are from France, the United States and Israel, but are not indicative or exclusive).

The thesis presented by the author of these books is satisfied with the explanation of how in certain cases, which do not represent all or the majority of the companies in such and such country, the companies abuse the rights of the minority shareholders and why they do it. The case studies should be objective, without introducing sentiments, and cannot generalize scientifically from one or two concrete cases. "The case study, like the experiment, does not represent a 'sample', and the investigator's goal is to expand and generalize theories (analytic generalization) and not to enumerate frequencies (statistical generalization)." (Yin, Case Study Research, p.10) "One rationale for a single case is when it represents the critical case in testing a well-formulated theory (again, note the analogy to the critical experiment). The theory has specified a clear set of propositions as well as the circumstances within which the propositions are believed to be true. To confirm, challenge, or extend the theory, there may exist a single case, meeting all of the conditions for testing the theory." (Yin, Case Study Research, p. 38) The evidence drawn from many cases could be stronger, but it is needed to find the equilibrium between the detailed analyses of one or a few cases from the more superficial analysis of a large number of cases.

Yin concludes that the best cases have to comprise the following features: "Engagement, enticement, and seduction – these are unusual characteristics of case studies. To produce such a case study requires an investigator to be enthusiastic about the investigation and to want to communicate the results vividly. In fact, the good investigator might even think that the case study contains earth-shaking conclusions. This sort of enthusiasm should pervade the entire investigation and will indeed lead to an exemplary case study." (Yin, Case Study Research, p.152)

The methodology adopted in the author's books tries to build a bridge between theories and practice, as "methodology is not only a scholarly word for 'research methods' but a study of the relation between the theoretical concepts and the conclusions which apply to the real world... the methodology does not furnish any mechanical algorithm permitting to construct or validate theories, and, as such, is closer to art than to science. We converge equally on the fact that the economical theories should at any time confront reality which is the ultimate referee of truth, but that the empirical verification is so difficult and ambiguous that we cannot hope to find many examples of decisively invalidated theories by repeated refutations." (Blaug, La Methodologie Economique, The Economic Methodology, in French, p.VI) Blaug employs the term induction "in its strictest logical acceptance: a reasoning which uses premisses containing information on certain elements of a category with the goal of proceeding toward the generalization of the whole category, including, consequently elements of the category which have not been studied." (Blaug, La Methodologie Economique, p.16)

We cannot conclude from a prevailing state of affairs that this state of affairs should prevail, as for example - that we cannot argue with success. "It is David Hume in his book 'Treatise of Human Nature', who a long time ago pronounced the proposition that we cannot deduct what should be from what is, that expositions which are descriptive and factual could bring or imply only other expositions which are descriptive and factual and never norms, ethical judgments, or recommendation to do something. This proposition was justly called the 'guillotine of Hume' (Black, 1970, p.24), in the way that it establishes a rigorous logical distinction between the domain of facts and the domain of values." (Blaug, La Methodologie Economique, p.113-4) Blaug does not maintain that ethics in business has an absolute value and is subjective, being promoted by interesting parties. "The economy of the well-being is, after all, this branch of economy interested by the ethical criteria which permits us to decide if an economic status of the world is more desired than another, and to speak of a positive economy of the well-being is to use literally a paradoxical language." (Blaug, La Methodologie Economique, p.128)

The relations between companies and stakeholders and minority shareholders have a crucial importance for all of us, as even if we do not invest our money in the stock exchange, our pension funds do, and the collapse of the shares' price in the stock exchanges, which could result from the continuous abuse of minority shareholders, would have fatal repercussions over the world economy and we could end up in a world recession much stronger than the recession of the 30s, which will affect all of us. The modest contribution of the author's books, the propagation of their statements, laws and theories, and the partial adoption of their recommendations could contribute to reducing the risks of the fatal repercussions mentioned earlier, which will occur inevitably if nothing is done to amend the insufferable situation.

13
THE INEFFICIENT EXISTING SAFEGUARDS OF THE STAKEHOLDERS' INTERESTS

"Que el mundo fue y sera una porqueria, ya lo se…
(En el quiniento seis y en el dos mil tambien.)
Que siempre ha habido chorros, maquiavelos y estafaos,
Contentos y amargaos, valores y duble…
Pero que el siglo veinte es un despliegue
De maldad insolente, ya no hay quien lo niegue.
Vivimos revolcaos en un merengue
Y en un mismos lodo todos manoseaos…

Hoy resulta que es lo mismo ser derecho que traidor…!
Ignorante, sabio o chorro, generoso o estafador!…
Todo es igual. Nada es mejor.
Lo mismo un burro que un gran profesor.
No hay aplazaos ni escalafon,
Los inmorales nos han igualao.
Si uno vive en la impostura y otro roba en su ambicion,
Da lo mismo que si es cura,
Colchonero, rey de bastos, caradura o polizon…"

(Enrique Santos Discepolo, Tango, Cambalache/The Junk Shop)

"The world was and will be a filthy place, I know it…
(It was in 506 as it will be in the year 2000.)
As there have always been diabolical villains and crooks,
The contented and the disgruntled, honorable men and swindlers…
Because the twentieth century is a display
Of insolent wickedness, nobody can deny it.
We live wallowed in debauchery
All floundering in the same mud…

Nowadays there is no difference in being honest or a traitor…!
Ignorant, wise, tramp, generous or crook.
All is the same. No-one is better.
No difference, dolts as great professors.
No putting it off, no getting on with it either;
We are on the same footing with the corrupt.
Some men may be living out a lie, others are ripping off everyone;
We are all in the same boat; the priest,
The mattress-maker, the card-shark, the cheeky, the good-for-nothing…"

This chapter is a summary of the three chapters dealing with this topic in the book 'Business Ethics - The Ethical Revolution of Minority Shareholders', namely: The Inefficient Safeguards of the Minority Shareholders, The Attitude of Society, The Excessive Privileges of the Majority Shareholders. The author of the two books found it appropriate to include this summary in the book 'Activist Business Ethics' because of the relevance of these chapters and the prevailing situation to the need of adopting activist business ethics.

Discepolo has summarized in his shivering poetry what many of us believe is the present hopeless situation where the mighty rulers of the modern economy abuse the rights of the small stakeholders and shareholders. While presuming that the judges are incorruptible, we have to admit that individual, weak, minority shareholders, who do not have the time, means, and the assistance of the best lawyers, do not have much opportunity to win a case against the tycoons of finance. In paraphrasing the title of the film 'The Untouchables', which tells the story of how Al Capone was sent to jail by untouchable government agents, who could not be corrupted, we notice how the norms have evolved nowadays and how the large companies are now untouchables, as the minority shareholders cannot touch them or undermine their power if they have to confront them in court.

The purpose of this book is to render the unethical businessmen 'untouchables' in the religious sense of the word, like the caste in India, so that nobody would approach them, associate with them, or pay any attention to them. This attitude would be in contradiction to the present veneration that they enjoy from many of their colleagues. The unethical businessmen will be ostracized and apprehended by their Achilles' heel, which is the importance that they give to their image in society. Universities will refuse their donations. They will receive no more honorary doctorates or Legion of Honor. Impossible to imprison them due to their power, they should be treated socially as Mafia outcasts.

All that is legal is not necessarily ethical, and all that is unethical is not necessarily illegal. It could be legal to pour toxic materials into a river, but this is certainly unethical and harmful. Laws can change, but ethics is much more immutable. "Even more, laws themselves must be governed by moral criteria, which gives rise to the classic distinction between just and unjust laws. Thus, a law that violates a person's dignity (sanctioning slavery, for example) is not just and therefore cannot be accepted and observed... a just law... must be observed, not for merely practical reasons (to avoid punishment, for example) but also for moral reasons: there is an ethical obligation to observe it." (Harvey, Business Ethics, A European Approach, Argandona, Business, law and regulation: ethical issues, p. 128-129) We should educate people to behave ethically exactly as we educate them to obey the laws. Aristotle has said that in order to know how to conduct we have to observe a just person. This maxim is somehow difficult to observe in the modern business world, but we can nevertheless compare ourselves to businessmen, who are relatively ethical.

"Ethics is above law and is also the source of the power of the law to oblige morally. Laws are not something sacred, as Latin culture sometimes pretends: they are no more (and no less) than an instrument at the service of the common good of society. They are not an obstacle that must be knocked down, jumped over or bypassed. They should be respected as a condition for the proper functioning of society, and even as a condition for personal freedom. (This notwithstanding, it must be recognized that in practice many laws may be defective or even immoral, and therefore not compelling.)" (Harvey, Business Ethics, A European Approach, Argandona, Business, law and regulation: ethical issues, p.130) This is the reason why in the polemic between legality and ethics in business, the ethical considerations should be predominant, because ethics is above the law, it is almost universal and immutable, while laws are conjunctural, national and often unjust.

One of the most acute dilemmas of managers is the dilemma between cases, which a priori seem equally ethical, but from different angles. Not the dilemmas between just and unjust situations, as in this case the choice is obvious, although it is not so simple for many businessmen. But the dilemma between two just positions is much more intricate, as it is incrusted in our basic values. "Four such dilemmas are so common to our experience that they stand as models, patterns, or paradigms. They are: Truth versus loyalty, Individual versus community. Short-term versus long-term. Justice versus mercy." (Kidder, How Good People Make Tough Choices, p.18) Kidder and many other authors on ethics prefer ultimately truth to loyalty, as it is better to divulge cases that are not ethical than to remain loyal toward a management that is not ethical.

The author gives examples of loyalty toward Hitler, Mao, Stalin, Sadam Hussein, or even Richard Nixon, which caused great damages to humanity, but we should also mention the fate of those who preferred truth over loyalty and who ended up in suffering atrociously. Between the individual and community he prefers community, although he mentions that if he were a Soviet citizen he would perhaps prefer the individual. Between short-term and long-term he prefers long-term, as we see how the financial scandals of the '80s, which were based on immediate gains in the short-term, were detrimental to society. And if he would have to choose between justice and mercy, Kidder would have opted for mercy, which signifies for him compassion and love. As he can imagine a world so full of love that there would be no need for justice, but he cannot imagine a world so full of justice that we would not need any more love.

The issue of double standards is emphasized in this book in the most acerbic manner, because in order to conduct ourselves ethically we should apply our ethics first of all toward the weak, the poor, the strangers, the stakeholders and minority shareholders, who do not have in most cases the possibility to confront the mighty majority shareholders in court. Clemency toward the mighty at the expense of the weak is the height of hypocrisy, and unfortunately this is what is practiced in many cases where the mighty and rich are brought to justice. If a poor thief steals a few hundred dollars he is sentenced to jail for many years, but if an Israeli financial tycoon is found guilty of manipulating the price of the shares of his bank, causing the Israeli minority shareholders and the state of Israel billions of dollars in losses, he is not even sent to jail.

The ancient maxim, which says 'if it ain't illegal, it must be ethical', is completely erroneous, as the difference between ethics and law is as the difference between the enforceable and the unenforceable. "Law is a kind of condensation of ethics into codification: It reflects areas of moral agreement so broad that the society comes together and says, 'This ethical behavior shall be mandated.' But Moulton's distinctions also make something else clear: When ethics collapse, the law rushes in to fill the void. Why? Because regulation is essential to sustain any kind of human experience involving two or more people. The choice is not, 'Will society be regulated or unregulated?' The choice is only between unenforceable self-regulation and enforceable legal regulation... Surely a powerful indicator of ethical decay is the glut of new laws – and new lawyers – spilling onto the market each year." (Kidder, How Good People Make Tough Choices, p.68-69)

History is full of examples of how kingdoms, which were lacking ethics, have collapsed, and how regimes that were governed by so-called very humane laws and an exemplary constitution which were not implemented, as in the case of the Soviet Union, have also collapsed. The economic anarchy which prevailed in Italy in the `80s is another example of how the lack of obedience to the law, or even more to ethics, could be harmful to the economic progress.

Should we obey immoral laws? The Nuremberg tribunal has categorically decided – no! But where is the limit between disobedience and anarchy? The English, who judged at those trials, were confronting at the same time the disobedience to the laws of the British Empire from the same Jews who were the victims of the Nazis and wanted to immigrate to Israel. The British arrested thousands of illegal immigrants who returned to their homeland after having survived the Holocaust, and sent them back to Europe or imprisoned them in concentration camps in Cyprus until 1948. The Americans had racist laws enforced until the '70s and only the Civil Rights Movement, headed by Martin Luther King, succeeded in shaking the American conscience and changing the laws and the implementation of the laws.

The companies are ready to invest considerable amounts in trials, which are much larger than the damages they would have to pay to the minority shareholders or the government institutions. GE preferred to pay $30 million in direct and indirect costs during a trial in which the government sued them for the amount of $10 million in damages for price fixing. Ultimately, the company was acquitted, and those who most benefited from the trial were the lawyers, while the shareholders, the government and other stakeholders lost. And this is the case of a trial against the American government. How can we ask from a poor individual shareholder to finance such astronomical sums, while the company will opt almost always to prefer the trial where it feels strong in comparison to the shareholders?

According to Monks, the decision of companies to obey or disobey the law is simply a profit and loss decision. The company checks if the cost of infringement of the law actualized by the probability to be discovered, brought to justice, and punished (there is almost no risk to be imprisoned), is equal to the cost of obedience to the law. If the cost is inferior, the company will prefer to infringe the law. This is why it is imperative that at the head of each company should stand an ethical CEO, with impeccable integrity and ethics, who will not just calculate impersonal feasibility studies on the benefits of obeying the law. We could try to make audits on the adherence to laws, augment the damages paid by companies, and so on, but the companies, with their infinite funds, their masses of lawyers and experts, and their immeasurable patience will win almost inevitably in court against the government, the stakeholders and the minority shareholders. They feel themselves stronger than all those organizations and individuals, and the only way to beat them is to change their attitude de profundis.

The Jewish religion teaches us that a just person builds a fence around the law, as the ethical man has to observe the ethical norms, which are much wider than the law. On the other hand, the modern lawyers seek loopholes in the law and try to reduce the implementation of the law to a minimum, which is in complete contradiction to Jewish law. It is therefore, practically impossible to rely only on the law, which many influential companies and lawyers try to reduce to a minimum, and we have to adhere to the ethical rules which are much wider than the law.

An extremely important aspect, which prevents the minority shareholders in most of the cases to resort to the law, is the time elapsing between the wrongdoing and the decision of the court. Besides the resources that the shareholder lacks, the risk that he incurs, and the loss of health, this excessively long time makes a trial almost prohibitive. In 1990 Kuwait was invaded by Iraq. The country was looted, thousands of citizens were murdered or mistreated, many others fled the country. A country that was once one of the richest in the world was completely ruined. The United States, which decided to intervene, did so only six months after the invasion, while it was practically too late. We say that time is of the essence, and time is an essential factor in international relations as it is also with the rights of minority shareholders. Even if the law can assist ultimately the minority shareholders, if it occurs many years after they lost their money, it is too late to remedy effectively the wrongdoing.

Of all the maxims that differentiate law from ethics, the most salient is probably caveat emptor, which means that the buyer should always beware. Everything is therefore permitted to the seller if it is legal, and it is the buyer of the product or of the stock who should beware not to be wronged. The author of this book maintains that if it is impossible to rely upon the ethics of the seller, it is preferable to abstain from buying the product or the stock, even if it is a bargain, as it is preferable to pay a higher price to an ethical seller than a lower price to an unethical one. The reason is that if you have to beware of the quality, the delivery, the service and so on, the effective price of the unethical seller is much higher than the effective price of the ethical seller.

Nevertheless, there is some evolution in this respect, and the tendency today in many cases is to make the seller beware and advise the buyer of potential defects of the products. This occurs mainly if there is a law requiring it like in the pharmaceutical industry or in the case of McPherson v. Buick in 1916. But do we need to disclose everything to the public? "We need to ask, 'Why in the case of physicians and therapists, as well as for other professionals such as attorneys, clergy, and journalists, is confidentiality so well protected in the law?'…. The duty to warn is limited in these relationships precisely because it is important to protect privacy and fairness, on the one hand, and encourage people to utilize professional help, on the other hand. Thus society forgoes certain benefits that might be derived from disclosure in order to protect other interests." (May, Business Ethics and the Law, p. 19-20)

Ethical thinking and character bring about the ethical conduct, which is different from legal conduct, as the law defines what is permitted and prohibited, while ethics defines what should be done. If the law in the 21st century will be driven by ethics as maintained by certain specialists, it is needed to make a thorough reform in the legal system.

Monks describes in his outstanding book 'The Emperor's Nightingale' the seven panaceas that are supposed to safeguard the corporate accountability. Those panaceas are really not effective cures, although they give a false sense of comfort that is more dangerous than the total lack of cure. The first panacea is the CEO philosopher-king, who is supposed to distribute evenly the goods of the company amongst the stakeholders. Unfortunately, the CEOs today exercise near-monarchic power, and they are free to advance their own personal interests in compensation, even to the point of harming the interests of shareholders. "Institutional Shareholder Services (ISS) found that, in 1992, the top 15 individuals in each company received 97 percent of the stock options issued to all employees. Business Week wrote for all to read that 'the 200 largest corporations set aside nearly 10 percent of their stock for top executives', adding that 'in almost all cases, moreover, it's the superstar CEO who takes the lion's share of these stock rewards." (Monks, The Emperor's Nightingale, p.62) The second panacea says that if a state and/or federal charter sets proper limits, then the corporation can serve the common good. This chart is effectively very weak and is practically non-existing in multinationals.

The third panacea is the independent directors. Those directors are nominated by independent committees and are elected by the shareholders, but in most cases they are effectively appointed by the CEOs of the companies. "Yet true independence – as well as true nominations and elections – remains elusive. How can an individual selected for a well-paying and prestigious job, notwithstanding his or her compliance with the most exhaustive legal criteria of 'independence', be expected to stand in judgment of those who accorded him this favor in the interest of an amorphous group of owners? Only men and women of the highest character can do this, but the best solutions cannot depend on character alone... Directors are not 'nominated', they are selected by the incumbent directors (however independent) and the chief executive officer. Shareholders do not 'vote', whether or not they mark a slate card; only those named on the company proxy will be elected. Ultimately, independence is a matter of personal character... the search of such a director requires that we be modern-day Diogenes, lamp in hand. This is not acceptable. We cannot have a system that depends on the luck of stumbling across an occasional honest man." (Monks, The Emperor's Nightingale, p.53-4)

The fourth panacea is the Board of Directors, well-structured boards, that rank high as a favored solution to governance problems. Monk believes that even corporations with perfectly independent directors and perfectly structured boards can remain insensitive to the needs of the public. The fifth panacea is independent experts. "The experience with 'experts', however is disheartening. The tendency to generate opinions satisfactory to present and prospective customers is strong. 'Fairness' opinions – whether of the prospective value of Time Warner stock, or in the leveraged buyouts that were the source of the Kluge, Heyman, and many other fortunes – have turned out to be wrong, not by percentages but by orders of magnitude." (Monks, The Emperor's Nightingale, p.55)

The sixth panacea is the free press. The most acute problem of this panacea is the large percentage of the press' revenues that derive from advertising, which may impair the impartiality of the press in regard to companies that finance huge advertising budgets. Furthermore, Westinghouse has recently acquired CBS, Disney owns ABC, GE owns NBC, Time Warner owns Fortune and McGraw-Hill owns Business Week. The situation is similar in France and Israel. It is true that there is no protocol of the sages of the media, but it is difficult to expect critics on an unethical company from a newspaper which is owned by a public company and which can be subjected to retaliation in the future with juicy stories on the owners of the newspaper, written by another newspaper which is owned by a competitor company.

The seventh panacea is multiple external constraints, such as the economic constraints of competition and law, the impact of the tax and regulatory schemes, and the constraining influence of social values on corporate decision making. Adam Smith has recommended to rely on the invisible hand that will arrange everything. It is the same blessed hand that brought the worst recession ever in 1929, all the economic crises, stock exchange scandals, inefficiencies in the legal and governmental system, the reliance on the SEC that will solve everything and so on. All those 'cures' are only panaceas, which cannot cure the wrongdoing to minority shareholders. Only new organisms can cure the illnesses of the existing system, as all the other cures have proved to be in most cases worthless panaceas for safeguarding the interests of stakeholders and minority shareholders.

Minority shareholders themselves have today a distribution that varies significantly from the past. The institutional shareholders have, according to Monks, 47.4 percent of the capital of the American corporations, $4.35 trillion in 1996, 57 percent of the capital of the 1,000 largest companies, and half of this capital or 30 percent of the whole capital is held by public funds or pension funds. "In mutual funds (more formally known as investment companies), the 'independent directors' are chosen under the provisions of the federal Investment Company Act of 1940. They are paid extremely well for services that basically consist of deciding whether to ratify the investment management contract (with a firm whose principals invited them to serve as directors), and they almost invariably vote to do so. In other words, mutual fund trustees are paid so much too much for doing so little that they are unlikely to disturb their sponsors." (Monks, The Emperor's Nightingale, p.148) The fiduciaries of the funds must not be nominated and paid by the companies that they are supposed to control.

A basic factor in the need of the preponderance of ethics over the law is the ignorance of many shareholders of basic terms in the prospectus of companies, which are for them like Chinese. The law and the SEC regulations maintain that if all the important issues are disclosed in the prospectus - the companies have performed legally, even if the most important issues are disclosed in such a way that it is almost impossible to notice or understand them. Furthermore, even according to GAAP's rules, a company can attribute 'extraordinary' costs, due to a restructuring or purchase of a company, whose main assets are intangible, as costs which are treated separately in the financial statements, and which analysts do not take usually into consideration in the valuation of the company. This gives the possibility to companies and to those who control them to do whatever they like in the financial statements and in the prospectuses, while strictly obeying the regulations of the SEC and of GAAP.

Minority shareholders, and especially small investors, who do not understand anything in these intricacies, buy the shares at inflated prices at the stock exchange or at a shares' offering, and often the shares subsequently collapse, while the company has not committed any illegal act. The SEC has decided to change its rules and asks now from the companies to publish a prospectus in a comprehensible language to the average stockholder, and in parallel the rules of the financial reports on the extraordinary costs are being revised. Those changes are done due to the fact that according to Compustat for the US industrial companies, the value of the tangible assets amounted to 62 percent of the market value in 1982, while in 1992 it amounted only to 38 percent!

As far as the author of this book could analyze, most of the public companies traded in the stock exchanges of the US, France and Israel, are controlled by groups of shareholders who own less than 50 percent of the shares of the companies. If the minority shareholders who are effectively the majority would be conscious of their power, and if the boards would be elected only in proportion to the ownership while the remainder of the members would be elected by activist associations, this could revolutionize the modern business world, safeguard the rights of minority shareholders, and prevent the abuse of the shareholders by oligarchies backed by the executives of the companies.

The 'proletariat' of the shareholders, who are not organized, are too often abused, and the time is appropriate for them to get organized directly or through the activist associations, in order to exert their legitimate power and preserve their rights. There is no reason whatsoever that the last vestige of oligarchies, the business world, would remain immune to the democratic evolutions and revolutions that prevail nowadays throughout most of the countries of the world.

The evolution toward participation in the control of companies by minority shareholders is in progress, although very slow, but nevertheless we could notice a tendency, which is reinforced every day. "The California Public Employees Retirement System, the New York State Common Retirement Fund, and the Connecticut State Treasurer's Office have jointly pressured several dozen firms to put a majority of outside directors on their boards' nominating committees... In the future, major shareholders will include employees as well as institutional investors... we may even witness a general restructuring in corporate ownership, one that induces managers to shift their allegiance from the wealthy to the less advantaged: Pension funds and other institutional investors already account for approximately 40 percent of the shares traded, with 10 percent of the nation's households commanding most of the rest... the demand for a global managerial ethics will become increasingly urgent. American managers will have to compete not only on the basis of technique but of democratic values as well." (Kaufman, Managers vs. Owners, p.196-8)

The class actions are very limited in their scope, rewards and efficiency. They are time consuming, and some people even alleged that they benefit mostly the lawyers that handle the cases. Still, until more efficient vehicles are devised, many shareholders resort to class actions.

The origin of the abuse of minority shareholders comes mainly from the greed of some of the majority shareholders, who in some cases has no limit. Those majority shareholders believe that they can do anything, risk more and more, since they find themselves unpunished, while remaining within the very large margins of the law. The minority shareholders who are wronged do not learn the lesson and continue to invest in companies that are conducted in an unethical manner. This is why it is needed to examine in depth the legal protection of those minority shareholders and its efficiency, in order to verify if the law suffices for their protection, or if the minority shareholders need an ethical protection, which has a much wider scope.

Members of society have a tendency to overlook events that do not concern them directly, and it is against this indifference that one has to fight, as an immoral ambiance has a tendency to penetrate to all domains thus affecting all members of society. One is always a client, or a minority shareholder, or a supplier, or at least a member of society, who is affected by ecological crimes or others. An immoral ambiance will make all of us victims, exactly like a totalitarian regime turns ultimately against the majority of its citizens.

Peters and Waterman reinforce the importance of the moral element in our life by affirming: "We desperately need meaning in our lives and will sacrifice a great deal to institutions that will provide meaning for us." (Peters and Waterman, In Search of Excellence, p. 56) And they continue: "an effective leader must be the master of two ends of the spectrum: ideas at the highest level of abstraction and actions at the most mundane level of details." (same, p. 287) And thus, like Don Quixote, the leader has to possess a vision: "Attention to ideas – pathfinding and soaring visions – would seem to suggest rare, imposing men writing on stone tablets." (same, p.287)

If the majority of businessmen maintain that you cannot argue with success and that everything is permitted to obtain this success, there could still exist a minority that maintains that the absolute value is ethics and it is despicable to succeed by despoiling the rights of minority shareholders, stakeholders and, ultimately, everybody. The author of this book believes that this minority is probably right. They will ridicule us as they have done to Don Quixote, they will fight us as they have done to The Enemy of the People, but finally, the truth of the minority will be perceived as self-evident, as democracy, as Human Rights, as equality of mankind, black, yellow or white, men and women, Christians, Moslems or Jews, Americans, French, British, Dutch or Israelis.

Guido Corbetta, in one of the rare articles on the ethical questions in the relations between companies and shareholders divides the most common forms of ownership of medium-sized and large companies in four categories:
"1. Family-based capitalism: ownership is concentrated in the hands of one or a few families, which are frequently related to one another. Sometimes one or more members of the family is directly involved in running the company... This form of ownership is particularly common in Italy, but there are large family businesses practically everywhere.
2. Financial capitalism: ownership is concentrated in the hands of one or just a few private and public financial institutions which, through a system of cross-holdings, control companies and intervene in their management... Ownership also implies powers to appoint management and steer corporate strategy... This form of ownership (with some slight differences) prevails in Germany, Japan and some other countries like Holland and Switzerland; it is rapidly becoming more common in France too.
3. Managerial capitalism: ownership is shared among numerous stockholders, none of whom exercises any significant control over the activity of the managers who run the companies. The management of these companies therefore becomes a kind of self-regenerating structure... It is particularly important in the Anglo-American business world.
4. State capitalism: through central and peripheral agencies or corporations set up ad hoc (as in the case of, for instance, IRI and ENI in Italy), the state has direct control over the companies. The existence of this form of capitalism clearly stems from a certain view of state intervention in the economy. In Italy, France and Spain there are major groups belonging to this category...

In cases of family-based capitalism and financial capitalism, for example, boards of directors are appointed by the majority shareholder or by a coalition of shareholders who are often themselves members of the boards, which appear to be the real organs of corporate governance. In cases of managerial capitalism, board members are instead 'co-opted' by the management itself. Save a few noteworthy exceptions, the choice falls on people whose most important characteristic appears to be their willingness to endorse without question whatever proposals the top managers who are also board members may submit. The Board of Directors thus eventually loses its role as collective organ of corporate governance and often becomes a false front used to give greater authority to decisions made by others."
(Harvey, Business Ethics, A European Approach, Corbetta, Shareholders, p.89-90)

We have dealt at length throughout this book on the differences between the different types of shareholders, especially the majority or controlling shareholders who are called in Corbetta's article the 'governor' shareholders and the minority or small shareholders who are called in Corbetta's article the 'investor' shareholders. The characteristics of both categories are summarized as follows:
"We define our shareholder as a 'governor' when:
- the percentage share of capital stock owned is high;
- development of the firm is substantially dependent on the economic resources made available by the shareholder and, likewise, the economic fortunes of the shareholder depend significantly on the firm's profitability;
- the shareholder exercises his or her power to intervene in decision-making processes by appointing the firm's management, steering corporate strategy and monitoring and appraising the management's performance;
- any decision to sell the shareholding is limited by sentimental reasons, in the case of family businesses, or by complex strategic assessments which may occasionally even have implications for national equilibrium (as was recently the case with operations conducted in Germany and France).

We define the shareholder as an 'investor' when:
- the (percentage) share of capital stock owned is small, often a fraction of a percentage point;
- the link between the development and profitability of the firm and the fortunes of the shareholder is not very close: the company gathers its resources from a very large number of shareholders, each of whom makes only a limited contribution to the firm's needs; likewise, the income of each individual shareholder does not come from the dividends distributed by the firm;
- there is little likelihood that shareholders' opinions about management appointments and corporate strategy will influence decisions. On a practical

level a 'shareholders' democracy' – i.e. effective control over management by numerous small shareholders – is not feasible;
- the decision to sell the shareholding is taken only on the basis of assessments of returns. 'Abandoning' is often preferable to 'expressing dissent' and, even more so, to 'remaining bound'."
(Harvey, Business Ethics, A European Approach, Corbetta, Shareholders, p.92)

The management of management-controlled companies is reluctant to hand over many of their autonomy to the shareholders. This increases the possibility of anti-company behavior on the part of the managers, who are concerned only with getting the maximum personal gain even when this puts the very survival of the company in jeopardy. Corbetta concludes that the governor-shareholder is not morally justified in using the company for his own ends, not even considering that his own compensation is secondary to that of other stakeholders. This article summarizes in a very efficient way all the analysis of the struggle for power and the different sets of interests between the majority and minority shareholders, and emphasizes the risks that the small shareholders incur from not controlling in fact the companies, thus enabling the majority shareholders to misuse their power and to wrong the other shareholders.

The author of this book is convinced that the present state of affairs regarding minority shareholders in France, Israel and the United States is to their detriment, in all the possible contexts. In family-owned companies, they cannot influence the decisions which are taken by the 'Grandes Familles', the richest families, and which favor uniquely those families and rarely the other shareholders. The members of the family are elected to the key managerial positions in the companies, even if they are incompetent, the families do all that is necessary to keep their effective control over the companies, even if it is to the detriment of those companies. As the families have many ramifications to their investments, they can cause the collapse of the price of the shares in one company and enable another company to buy it for an extremely low price.

The 'governors' are convinced that if they are strongly involved with the companies, they control it and they supply it with funds, they have the right to do whatever they want with 'their' companies, and the minority shareholders are treated like speculators, who are not interested in the well-being of the companies but rather in a quick return on their investment. Even if this is true in certain cases, this does not decrease the rights of the minority shareholders, who are in many cases interested in the fate of the company no less than its governors. The cases of the managerial companies are even more dangerous for minority shareholders as the directors jeopardize the company itself in order to increase their personal benefits.

The democracy of the shareholders is completely utopic, the shareholders can shout, protest, be indignant, criticize or threaten on the Internet or in the shareholders' meetings, yet their influence is in most cases nil in all categories of the companies. This is the reason why they have to obtain new rights, even if they do not request it yet. In many cases the minority shareholders collaborate unknowingly with the majority shareholders in order to despoil their own rights. They have the opportunity to participate in shareholders' meetings, which are in many instances a ridiculous circus, manipulated very skillfully by the majority shareholders, who are assisted by the management of the companies.

And even if they participate in the meetings, which is very rare, they have no chance to win against the oiled machine of the owners who control the companies. Many cases illustrate those statements and show how it is possible to eliminate from the protocol touchy questions and answers to minority shareholders, how is it possible to treat as a ridiculous Cassandra troublemakers who disclose the schemes of the owners, thus even augmenting the adhesion of the other shareholders, and how ultimately the minority shareholders cooperate unknowingly or against their wishes in the schemes of the majority shareholders.

The collaboration of the victim with the aggressor is a well-known psychological fact, but the purpose of this book is to eradicate this mentality, which is too widespread, by eliminating the excessive rights of princes, dukes or majority shareholders to the detriment of the minority shareholders. The modern democratic evolution should not stop at the door of the business world. The kings do not amuse themselves anymore, as in Le Roi S'amuse of Victor Hugo, adapted to the opera Rigoletto by Piave, the tyrants have disappeared in most countries, it is high time that the 'droits du seigneur' of 'first night privileges' will disappear from the Medieval courts of the companies as they have disappeared from the court of the duke of Mantova.

Milken, the indisputable hero of the financial world of the '80s, perceived himself as above the legal and moral constraints and thought that they were good only for the 'footsoldiers' – in our case the minority shareholders, the less influential, the less creative, less aggressive, less visionary. There are therefore double standards for the footsoldiers and for the Knights, just as in the Middle Ages. This is the core of this book, how to evolve from the dark and unhealthy epoch of the Middle Ages, where a large part of the business world is still wallowing, to the Renaissance period of the years 2000, and to have the same standards for minority shareholders, as were achieved for minorities all over the civilized world, by Human Rights, the welfare society and democracy. Time is of the essence, as the situation is getting worse instead of improving.

The world economy becomes more and more concentrated in the hands of a small number of huge organizations, which control the economy, without being adequately controlled by the governments and the citizens, and least of all by the shareholders. In 1994, 1,300 companies have participated in mergers amounting to $339 billions. And today the mergers are even larger. The modern empires of companies are much more influential than the monopolies of the Carnegies and the Mellons. The profits of Wall Street in the last years of the century were stunning. The volume of the financial transactions of the `90s is 40 times higher than the productive economy of the US, while the volume of transactions of CS First Boston is higher than the GNP of the US. The SEC has not the necessary funds to control effectively those giants and the only safeguard against them is ethics.

Majority shareholders, executives and members of the Boards of Directors benefit from insider information, which is not accessible to minority shareholders. If the insiders utilize this information to buy or refrain from buying shares of the companies, they commit a despoliation of the rights of the minority shareholders. They risk nothing in buying the shares, as they know in advance that their prices will increase as a result of good financial results, a merger or a scientific discovery. On the contrary, if they sell their shares before the publication of negative financial results, they do not incur losses from the collapse of the shares' price.

"The game, then, like the manipulated market that is the outcome, is unfair – unfair to some of the players and those they represent – unfair not only because some of the players are not privy to the most important rules, but also because these 'special' rules are illegal so that they are adopted only by a few of even the privileged players." (Rae, Beyond Integrity, Werhane, The Ethics of Insider Trading, p. 518) Even worse, the insiders register their companies in Delaware, which enables them to benefit from a complete freedom of action in the governance of their companies. "Delaware, for example, has few constraints in its rules on corporate charters and hence provides much contractual freedom for shareholders. William L. Cary, former chairman of the Securities and Exchange Commission, has criticized Delaware and argued that the state is leading a 'movement towards the least common denominator' and 'winning a race for the bottom'." (Rae, Beyond Integrity, Jensen, Takeovers: Folklore and Science, p. 530)

If this is the case, does the SEC advise the shareholders of the risks that they incur when they buy shares of companies registered in Delaware? Does it try to change the corporate laws of this state?

The present state of affairs is unfortunately like in the Fables of Aesop and La Fontaine, as human nature has not changed since those ancient times. The mighty always find reasons to abuse the rights of the weak - weird, legitimate or even moral. This is why there is a constant abuse of the rights of the weak by the powerful, and the weak have to suffer the consequences of their 'crimes', as they trouble the water of the wolves, they speak ill of them, and they have too many brothers. In order to punish their crime to want to drink in the same waters as the wolves, they almost always lose, as they are allowed to invest their money but they are prohibited from sharing the profits with the mighty.

14
INTERNET, TRANSPARENCY, ACTIVIST ASSOCIATIONS AND ETHICAL FUNDS

"Denn die einen sind im Dunkeln
Und die andern sind im Licht.
Und man siehet die im Lichte
Die im Dunkeln sieht man nicht."
(Bertolt Brecht, Die Dreigroschenoper, The Threepenny Opera,
Die Schluss-Strophen der Moritat, The Final Verses of the Moritat,
Act III, last scene)
"For the ones they are in darkness
And the others are in light.
And you see the ones in brightness
Those in darkness drop from sight."

This chapter is a summary of the three chapters dealing with this topics in the book 'Business Ethics - The Ethical Revolution of Minority Shareholders', namely: Internet and Transparency as Ethical Vehicles, Ethical Funds, Activist Associations, 'Transparency International', 'Adam'. The author of the two books found it appropriate to include this summary in the book 'Activist Business Ethics' because of the relevance of those new vehicles to the need of adopting activist business ethics.

The activists shareholders, who are more and more influential, can communicate via the Internet, which enables free, instantaneous, interactive communication between shareholders, between shareholders and companies, and between shareholders and the organizations that are supposed to safeguard their interests as the members of the Board of Directors, independent directors, fiduciaries, the SEC, etc. In the future, they would be able to ratify decisions that will be submitted to them via the Internet, receive all the required information and financial reports for their decisions from the Internet, and obtain answers to their queries very promptly.

In the business world, as in the political and social world, the tendency is for everybody to mind their own business, and even if the rights of others are wronged they seldom interfere, as they do not want to make enemies, they do not have time for such occupations, or "they didn't help me when I was in need so why should I help them now?" etc. But if it is possible to denounce the crimes without being discovered, there is a tendency to do so, in order to have a clean conscience. The Internet is the best vehicle to do so as it enables you to retain your anonymity while disclosing to the whole world the facts that prior to then were hidden. Light is the worst enemy of criminals who prefer to work in the dark. In some business circles the law of Omerta (Silence, like in the Mafia) prevails, and rarely does someone dare to transgress this law. But the Internet changes this setup, as the whistle-blowers remain concealed and the truth is revealed.

Unfortunately, it is possible to utilize this vehicle also to defame businessmen and companies, manipulate shares, spread rumors and misinform the shareholders by interested parties – the companies, the majority or minority shareholders, competition, or others. As everyone keeps his anonymity, they remain unpunished, although there are some attempts to raise the curtain over those people in extreme cases. Misinformation or not, the minority shareholder has at least the opportunity to be informed about unethical acts performed by the companies or to denounce them in advance. He has only to discern the true and false information, which is better than before when he had no access to the true information.

The ideal would be that companies would be transparent to the stakeholders and shareholders and that everyone would receive simultaneously the same information, whether they are minority or majority shareholders. No more insider information, no more abuse at the detriment of shareholders who live far from the headquarters of the company and who have no access to the information divulged by the insiders to the boards of directors. We could also imagine a black list, established by activist associations and published on the Internet, of companies and persons who do not behave ethically, who went bankrupt, who were condemned by the courts. Accessible to everyone around the world, this list could induce the companies and their executives to conduct themselves ethically and legally, make their utmost effort not to go bankrupt and to repay their debts even if they do not have a legal obligation to do so. It would be recommended to achieve an ethical responsibility of companies, and of their executives and owners, that would not be limited. Responsible executives and companies are the safeguards of the interests of the stakeholders, minority shareholders and the community. The leitmotiv should change from 'I am doing my best to diminish to a minimum my responsibilities' to 'I should behave responsibly toward my employees, all my shareholders, my country, my customers, ecology, and first of all toward my conscience.'

In the present state of affairs, there are too few whistle-blowers who have the courage to denounce overtly the crimes of companies against ecology or the stakeholders, to suffer the consequences, the ostracism of society, and the impossibility to find other jobs. An employee could agree to denounce his company in an extreme case, if there is a danger to the public or to the lives of people. But who would denounce overtly and without getting any remuneration a company that abuses the rights of minority shareholders? Let them solve their own problems; why should I risk my situation, my future, the bread-and-butter of my family, for some 'speculators' whom I do not know and who are attracted only by a quick profit on their investment in shares of my company? They would not have helped me in the same situation, so why should I help them? But if I would have something to gain from the publication of the information and if I do not risk anything, I could do it and also alleviate my conscience. The employees who would do it are only those who have a stronger allegiance to the community and to their conscience than to the company.

We could cite as precedents for the efficacy of denunciations, those that are made to the fiscal authorities and who come almost always from the close environment of the companies. If the IRS finds that it is ethical to encourage the denunciations, why should it not be encouraged also by the activist associations? But does the end justify the means, and can we remain ethical while encouraging denunciations, even of unethical acts? What is the alternative, let the majority shareholders or their companies wrong the minority shareholders? Is it not less ethical, is it a crime to denounce the criminals, or in the words of the Bible cited in this chapter 'The accomplice of a thief is his own enemy; He is put under oath and dare not testify.' There is a moral obligation to testify against a thief, unless you become his accomplice by not revealing his crime, even if you do not dare do so because you are afraid. Ultimately, if we do not find more efficient ways of safeguarding the rights of minority shareholders, we should envisage methods for denouncing unethical acts of companies and render them legitimate without any stigma, as it is probably the only way to resolve problems that could not be resolved otherwise, since crimes are performed usually in the dark.

The companies utilize extreme means to conduct their battles against their adversaries, even if they are dissident shareholders who dare oppose the executives and majority shareholders of their companies. They use the press, public relations agencies, investor relations firms, and even the Internet. But the press could also be used by minority shareholders in cases that could be of public interest. Unfortunately, the newspapers get tired of dealing with complicated cases, and in the long run they drop those cases for lack of public interest, or even as a result of heavy pressure of the companies that threaten to abolish their advertising budgets. An editor prefers a scandalous case of a rape to a tedious case of fraud of minority shareholders, who are often perceived as 'speculators'. But those minority shareholders can also employ public relations firms, which specialize in this domain, or organizations such as ADAM in France, which specialize in the protection of minority shareholders.

Another efficient method that could prevent the abuse of the rights of minority shareholders could be the distribution of rewards to the persons who divulge this wrongdoing of the companies, whether it is unethical or illegal. We enter here into a very problematic domain of the fidelity toward a company where we are employed, as the majority of the whistle-blowers would probably be employees of the companies concerned. Would the denunciations be anonymous like on the Internet? How could we distribute the rewards? And who will distribute them – the activist associations or another organization? Is it ethical to encourage the whistle-blowers? Would it be possible to employ this vehicle to get revenge from companies or executives who have not committed any fraud? How could we verify if the information is correct and make sure that the denunciations do not resemble precedent cases from totalitarian regimes?

The conviction that to denounce is an atrocious crime is inculcated in all peoples and religions. The Jews ostracized in the Diaspora the 'mousser', or the squealer, the person who denounced his brethren to the authorities, even if that brother was a thief or murderer. Everybody knows the awful fate of the squealers who denounce Mafia chiefs to the police. But the American and Italian police would have never succeeded in arresting Mafia leaders without the aid of the squealers of the Cosa Nostra.

Is it moral to denounce a crime committed by the Mafia to the police, in spite of the law of Omerta, which advocates a complete silence? Is it ethical to denounce an immoral act committed toward a customer or shareholder of a company by one of the company's employees? If he does not denounce his chiefs, the employee knows that truth will never be disclosed, and the company will continue to sell airplanes with damaged components, endangering the lives of the pilots, as was the case in many recent cases. Is the employee a squealer? If he believes in God and the Inferno, will he find himself in hell after his death in the vicinity of Judas and Brutus? If he is an agnostic, can he risk his career, the well-being of his family, the respect of his colleagues, in order to save the life of a pilot he does not know or to avoid the losses of a minority shareholder?

The employee will never denounce his superiors if society continues to treat him as a whistle-blower (pejorative connotation in the business world), a tattletale or sneak (pejorative connotation at school), an informer (pejorative connotation from the German Occupation), a stool pigeon (pejorative connotation in the Soviet Union), or a squealer (pejorative connotation from the criminal world). Maybe he would have the courage to denounce immoral acts, if he would be treated as a 'discloser', a neutral term meaning somebody discloses a fact, without a pejorative connotation. In this book the term whistle-blower is used, because otherwise the meaning would not be understood, but the meaning that the author of this book embraces is that of a discloser, and if it does not exist in the dictionary it is high time that it should be invented.

This discloser will not be ostracized but will be appreciated by the society in which he lives, as he will assist it to be cleaner and just. Many of the readers of this book will think of McCarthy who meant exactly the same thing when he urged intellectuals to denounce the 'communists' in order to have a cleaner society with no fear of the rising communism that endangered the existence of the free world. In most cases, nobody forced the people to denounce their friends, but those who did not cooperate did not get jobs and were ostracized.

What is therefore the difference between the proposals of this book and McCarthyism? McCarthy represented the authorities, he acted against the weak. Here is a completely opposite situation where the weak become organized against the powerful. It could be that in the future minority shareholders could become the strongest party, and activist associations would become too powerful. We have seen such inversions in the past in the Soviet Union, where the wronged proletariat became much worse and committed more atrocious crimes than the Tsarist regime that oppressed them. The author of this book believes in democracy and checks and balances, and hopes that the majority and minority shareholders will have a similar power without any one of them subjugating the other, exactly like the minorities are not subjugated nowadays in the United States like they were in the past, yet they do not subjugate the majority as well.

But we are aware that this argument will be raised, similarly to what the Jews in Russia called the 'wronged Kozak', meaning the Kozaks who organized pogroms against the Jews and pretended to be wronged by the persecuted Jews. Those who condemn Brutus, the rebel, the traitor, the squealer, to the pit of hell would have condemned as well the French Revolution which was against the legitimate power of the Bourbons, the American revolution which was against the legitimate power of the British, or the terrorists attacks of the Haganah, Etsel or Lehi in Palestine which were against the legitimate power of the British mandate. Those who condemn the whistle-blowers are in favor of the multitude of the immoral acts that are performed in companies against their stakeholders. The companies should be transparent ethically, without fearing anything from squealers, because when you have a clear conscience you do not need to be afraid to be discovered. Crime likes darkness, and the companies that do not conduct themselves ethically are looking for anonymity.

In order to denounce immoral crimes in companies, as for discovering the crimes of Mack the Knife, we have to be assisted by disclosers, as nobody sees the knives of immoral companies, which keep an impeccable facade and are assisted by the best lawyers and public relations. We need transparency otherwise nothing would ever be disclosed, and the law will never be able to safeguard the interests of the stakeholders, whether they are rich like Schmul Meier or poor like Smith. Therefore, only light can raise the curtain on the unethical acts of companies.

Religious persons should conduct themselves morally as they believe that God examines their acts at every moment and nothing escapes him. For businessmen who are slightly less religious the fear of the disclosure of their acts to the public should replace the fear of God, because if they do not have anything to hide they will not have to fear anything. On the other hand if the employees utilize the liberty of disclosure to reveal the secrets of the companies to the competition or for reasons that have nothing to do with ethics, they would be subject to reprisals, exactly like the newspapers, which benefit from the liberty of the press and cannot disclose state secrets. The employees have to divulge only systematic and permanent cases of abuse that are inherent to the operations of the companies, which wrong the stakeholders, and which are backed by irrefutable documentation. They have to resort to outside bodies only after having exhausted all the internal bodies, which are meant to deal with those cases, such as the ethics officer, the superiors, the executives, the CEO, or even the Board of Directors.

There will always be cases where it will be argued that it is impossible to divulge a case, as it is a state secret or a professional secret whose disclosure could endanger the company or the state. The most renowned case of a disclosure of a crime by act of conscience is probably the case of Colonel Picquart. One needs to have extreme courage in order to denounce his superiors, and bring against him the French army, the government and the majority of Frenchmen. But Picquart, imperturbable, testifies at the trial of Zola, after the latter wrote his famous 'J'accuse', where he accused the French authorities of concealing the truth about the innocence of Captain Dreyfus: "Pendant plus d'une heure, il expose, d'une voix tranquille, comment il a decouvert la trahison d'Esterhazy, les manoeuvres dont il a ete la victime et sa tristesse d'etre ecarte de l'armee. Les révisionnistes lui font une ovation. Après quoi il est confronte avec ses anciens subordonnes, qui, tous partisans de Henry, l'accablent." (Troyat, Zola, p.274) "For more than an hour, he exposes, in a quiet voice, how he has discovered the treason of Esterhazy, the maneuvers that he was victim of and his sadness to be dismissed from the army. The revisionists make him an ovation. After that he is confronted with his old subordinates, whom, all colleagues of Henry, scorn him."

The modern history of business knows many similar glorious pages, where employees have denounced their companies at the risk of their career, their well-being and even their lives.

The transparency of companies will force every employee to ask himself at every moment the question: 'what is my ethical attitude toward this ethical problem?', because the following day his acts will be disclosed in the press or on the Internet, and his family, friends and congregation will learn about his acts. We will not have to ask ourselves anymore if our acts are legal or not, if they concur with the mission of the company and its ethical standards, but how they concur with our ethical standards, as we will not be able to hide anymore in anonymity. It will be like in the senate committees for the appointment of high officials, or with presidential candidates who are obliged to disclose their life transparently. Of course, we would have to beware not to resort to McCarthyism, to the open eye of the 'big brother', or to the denunciations of the sons and colleagues, as in the dictatorial regimes. The companies should be made transparent with measure and moderation and excesses will have to be condemned. Full disclosure should be made only on important cases, where the evidence is irrefutable, where there are no ulterior motives, and after having exhausted all other instance within the company.

The material advantages of the disclosers are often very high and outbalance the risks. In 1986, the US law, 'The False Claim Act' of 1863 was amended, and it encourages the disclosure of companies' fraudulent acts against the government. The discloser can receive up to 25 percent of the money that could be recuperated. The most renowned case is that of Chester Walsh and General Electric. In 1986, a manager of GE had conspired with an Israeli General to steal funds from the US military aid to Israel. The thieves succeeded in stealing at least $11 million, which was deposited in a Swiss bank account controlled by the Israeli General and the GE employee. Some employees of GE asked themselves how millions of dollars were transferred to a company that did not exist in the past. The control system of GE, the US army and the Israeli Army did not succeed in discovering the fraud. In 1992, GE admitted committing fraud and paid a sum of $69 million in fines. Twenty-two GE employees were fired or punished. The discloser of the fraud was Chester Walsh, a GE marketing director in Israel, who succeeded during five years to gather documents, tape conversations and accumulate evidence of the fraud. Walsh and a non-profit organization sued the US government under the False Claims Act and received the sum of $11.5 million, which they shared.

Throughout the centuries, history repeats itself. Disclosers are called squealers and whistle-blowers by the legitimate forces that try to conceal their crimes. Progress is always linked with discoveries and disclosures, which the 'majority' tries to hide. Brutus makes a coup d'etat against a tyrant, although the majority worships Caesar. Galilei says 'e pur si muove' although the Church in 'majority' tries to silence him. The Dreyfusards try to acquit the poor Dreyfus although the 'majority' cannot admit that a Christian officer has betrayed his country. The financial tycoons of modern economy try to hide their actions, which transgress ethics and even the law. The only way to fight the prerogatives of the majority shareholders, to overcome the law of Omerta and to destroy the last bastion of totalitarian organizations, is to fling upon the windows of the companies and to render them transparent to all ethical critics. As the press safeguards the democratic regime; the Internet, the free access to information on companies, the possibility to reveal the cases that transgress ethics by the employees, should safeguard the interests of the stakeholders. The employees have to be the fiduciaries of the stakeholders and minority shareholders, like the quality managers are the fiduciaries of the customers. The Internet restitutes the Athenian democracy, as it is the modern Agora where nothing can be hidden. And when all companies will act openly, will be transparent, will not be able to hide dubious cases, the stakeholders of the companies, and especially the minority shareholders will have the possibility to be treated equitably.

The bibliography of business ethics is clearly divided between the optimists and the pessimists. We have those who are disgusted from the lack of ethics in the business world, the swindles, scams and schemes, and who hardly see a way to get out of this mud that prevailed in the past and will prevail forever. But on the other hand there are those who maintain their hope when they enter into the business world, who notice a favorable evolution, and who are convinced that they can change the negative trends and make an impact in their lifetime. Among those, we can find the businessmen and investors who have started the ethical funds movement, which has gathered tremendous momentum in the last years of the twentieth century.

Will there be any material change between the twentieth and the twenty first century? There is hope that the new ethical vehicles, such as the Internet, the activist associations and the ethical funds will make a substantial change in the negative environment that prevailed in the turn of the century.

The ethical funds were established in the United States, Canada and Great Britain, especially in the last ten years of the twentieth century. In 1999 in the U.S. they had investments of more than two trillion dollars – 2,160 billion US$, 13 percent of all investments under professional management in the United States, invested in 175 funds. Those ethical funds succeed in maintaining better results than the average results in the stock exchange. The performances of the Domini 400 Social Index, comprising 400 ethical shares, beats regularly the S&P 500 and the Russell 1000, representing the average American securities. Europe is not so advanced in this domain as the US. Great Britain has already 34 ethical funds in 1999 with investments of 48 billion sterling pounds, the Netherlands have social responsible investments of more than one billion Euros, slightly more than Sweden, in Switzerland those investments amount to 0.8 billion Euros. The socially responsible funds in France have a much smaller scope – 0.4 billion Euros, in Germany about one quarter of a billion Euros, and in Israel they do not exist.

This book proposes to add as an investment criterion of the ethical funds the ethical relations between companies and minority shareholders. In this manner, investors in ethical funds, who are normally minority shareholders in the companies in which they invest, will be assured that their investment will be treated fairly. Ultimately, if most of the minority shareholders or the small investors will invest uniquely in ethical funds or in companies that behave ethically, we might be able to achieve the Lisistrata effect, when the strike of minority shareholders will force the companies to behave ethically, as without minority shareholders the companies will not be able to raise funds to operate their activities.

ETHICAL INVESTING

Ethical Investing, or socially-screened investing, is the placement of money in mutual funds, stocks, bonds, securities or other investments that are screened to reflect ethical, environmental, social, political or moral values.

Socially conscious investing is a way to build an investment portfolio that keeps pace with your conscience and reflects your beliefs, convictions and desire of change. It may involve avoiding companies with corporate practices you deem unacceptable or supporting acceptable ones.

Socially conscious investing grew from an early desire by many in the religious community to avoid investing in companies that profited from the sale of alcohol, tobacco or gambling products (sin and religious screens). The Pioneer Group, a group of 24 funds, has used a sin screen for almost seven decades, because the founder was a very religious man when he started the fund in 1928.

In the 60s, social investing grew even more popular as investors protested against the war in Vietnam. The Pax World Fund was started by Quakers and Methodists in the 70s to avoid investment in defense contractors in protest over the Vietnam War.

In 1972, the Dreyfus Corporation became the first traditional money-management house to add a socially screened fund, the Dreyfus Third Century Fund, that avoided investments in companies doing business in South Africa, and sought out companies with good records for equal opportunity, safety, health and environmental care.

In the 80s, socially conscious investing entered the mainstream as our emotions were stirred by issues such as apartheid in South Africa, the environment and abortion. In 1982, the Calvert Group offered a fund with extensive social screens - the Calvert's Money Market Portfolio. By 1997, Calvert was offering a family of nine socially screened funds.

The really rapid growth in the number of funds having some type of social and/or environmental screening took place in the `90s. And the pace does not appear to be slowing. In the U.S. alone, there are more than 100 funds with such screening. Ethical Funds are also very popular in Canada, Great Britain, and other countries in Europe.

There are a number of concerns generally shared by social investors. These include local community affairs, ecological and environmental issues, labor relations, minority and gender relations, military production, nuclear weapons and power, product quality and business practices.

Ethical investors, and the advisers who work for them, look at the social record of companies and investments on these issues to determine whether they are acceptable or desirable places to invest.

Researchers maintain that ethical investments can perform as well as conventional investments. In some cases they have performed better. For example, stock prices listed in the Domini 400, an index of 400 socially responsible U.S. stocks, have grown 135 percent since the index was started in 1990 until the end of 1995. By comparison, the S&P 500 increased 120 percent.

The Domini Social Index (SRI) provides a broad market, common stock index for measuring the performance of portfolios with social constraints. The social investment research firm of Kinder, Lydenberg, Domini & Co. (KLD) constructs the DSI by identifying US stocks that pass a multitude of common social screens. The DSI was created on May 1, 1990 by KLD.

Two socially responsible indexes, the Domini 400 Social Index and the Citizens Index outperformed the Standard and Poors 500 Composite Index in 1999. Domini clocked in at 24.5 percent and the Citizens at 29.6 percent while the S&P gained 21 percent in calendar 1999. They have outperformed the S&P on a total return basis since their inception in 1990 and 1994 respectively. Nearly 70 percent of the largest socially responsible funds earned top ratings in 1999.

The most common criteria for investments in ethical funds are:

- Responsibility to the communities in which they operate, including the provision of products and services of long term benefit to the community, e.g. safety equipment. Charitable donations.

- A record of suitability, quality and safety of products and services.

- Adhering to environmental regulations and using technologies and products that are environmental friendly, non-polluting, conserving natural resources and energy, such as woodlands and forests.

- Progressive general approach to customers, suppliers and the public, as well as to industrial and employee relations - employment equity, welfare standards, labor safety practices, child labor laws.

- Operating within countries and regions that support racial equality, adhere to non-discriminatory hiring practices and avoid unreasonable exploitation of people generally.

- Deriving a majority of income from non-tobacco related products.

- Engaging in peace-based, non-military activities.

- Deriving income from activities that are non-nuclear and are not related to the production of nuclear fuel or waste.

Areas of Support of most of the Ethical Funds are: Education and training, Healthcare services and health and safety, Good employee relations, Equal Opportunities Policy, Policy statements audits and openness, Progressive community relationship and strategy, Effective corporate governance, Benefits to the environment, Energy conservation.

Other Areas of Support are: Multimedia and telecommunications, Mass transit systems, Pollution monitoring and control, Process control equipment, Recycling services, Renewable energy, Water management, Animals, Vegetarian foods, New textiles.

Areas of Avoidance of most of the Ethical Funds are: Alcohol, Gambling, Irresponsible marketing, Offensive advertising, Armaments, Oppressive regimes, Anti-Trades Union activity, Third World debt/exploitation, Pornography, Tobacco, Greenhouse gases, Mining, Nuclear power, Ozone layer depleters, Pesticides, Road Builders, Tropical hardwood, Water polluters, Animal testing, Fur, Meat/dairy production.

The basic structure for an ethical fund is as follows: Fund manager who decides what to invest in, Green/Ethical criteria - the stated guidelines and

restrictions which the fund manager needs to be able to act, Share purchase when an investment is made, Ethical committee who monitors share purchases to ensure green/ethical criteria are being adhered to.

The Fund Managers ask companies to report in detail on their environment and social performance. They analyze the ethical information received by companies and conduct additional research from other sources to build up a complete picture in which a 'green' evaluation is made. They avoid companies deriving more than a negligible part of their turnover from oppressive regimes, or the arms, nuclear or tobacco companies.

Community Investing, supporting development initiatives in low-income communities both in the funds' countries and in developing countries, provides affordable housing, create jobs and helps responsible businesses get started. It is achieved mainly through Community Banks, Community Credit Unions, Community Loan Funds and Microenterprise lenders.

Social Venture Capital describes investing that integrates community and environmental concerns into professionally managed venture capital portfolios. The essence of venture capital lies between providing capital and management assistance to companies creating innovative solutions to social and environmental problems, and institutional investors investing on potential one billion dollar technologies.

The Funds aim to strike a balance between good and bad aspects of company activities, emphasize higher standards and positive aspects of corporate behavior, and influence companies to respond beyond the letter of the law to Ethical Criteria, through a system of 'constructive dialogue'.

Ethical Funds tend to avoid most of the largest corporations because they do not pass the ethical criteria. Smaller companies have more room for growth and can adapt more quickly to market changes, although of course they are more sensitive to market conditions.

Companies that perform according to ethical criteria ought to be more efficient, produce less waste, and have a more motivated and productive workforce, with less risk of prosecution, bad publicity, restrictive legislation, etc. The ethical fund managers who are active in their research will know a lot more about the companies they invest in and therefore can make more informed investment decisions.

Most of the Ethical Funds invest in companies that adhere to the Ceres Principles and publicly affirm their belief on their responsibility for the environment in a manner that protects the Earth. The Principles are - Protection of the biosphere, Sustainable use of natural resources, Reduction

and disposal of wastes, Energy conservation, Risk reduction, Safe products and services, Environmental restoration, Informing the public, Management commitment, Audits and reports, Disclaimer.

The Ethical Funds' mission is to be the providers of Socially Responsible Investments (SRI) products and services. In order to achieve this mission, the funds should have a clearly defined business culture and ethical commitment, that consists of the following principles:

- Maintaining the highest ethical standards when dealing with their clients. Placing the clients' interests first, reflecting the social concerns of the clients in their recommendations, and fully disclosing their means of compensation.

- Providing clients with the broadest possible range and highest quality of investment choices, social research, and service options.

- Operating in a fiscally responsible manner. Generating an adequate profit margin, while reinvesting in the continued growth of the funds.

- Encouraging, developing and maintaining a high level of professional standards and education, mainly in Socially Responsible Investing.

- Supporting public education to promote the relationship between financial decisions and the public good. Supporting social activism by providing information on shareholder activism and boycotts.

- Operating in a socially responsible manner. Balancing the interests of all their stakeholders - clients, staff, products suppliers, research companies and local communities.

"Here are some findings from a 1994 survey conducted jointly by Cone and Roper: Seventy-eight percent of adults said that they were more likely to buy a product associated with a cause they care about.
. Sixty-six percent of adults said that they'd be likely to switch brands to support a cause they care about.
. Fifty-four percent of adults said they'd pay more for a product that supports a cause they care about.
. After price and quality, 33 percent of Americans consider a company's responsible business practices the most important factor in deciding whether or not to buy a brand.
The number of people who want to 'vote with their wallets' is growing toward critical mass. There's a paradigm shift occurring. As one indicator, the Council on Economic Priorities' handbook Shopping for a Better World, which rates the products available in supermarkets based on their degree of

social responsibility, has sold over 1 million copies since 1991." (Cohen and Greenfield, Ben & Jerry's Double-Dip, p. 48-9)

The social-performance report of Ben & Jerry's covers: social activism, customers and their needs, environmental awareness, supplier relationships, use of financial resources, financial support for communities, quality of work life. "The social audit is useful to shareholders or prospective shareholders. Theoretically those folks are reading the company's financials. If a shareholder is interested in investing her money based on social criteria as well, she should be able to read the company's social audit and make her investment decision based on being able to compare different investment opportunities. More and more companies are doing social audits in one form or another. The Body Shop and Whole Foods Markets do social-performance reports similar to what Ben & Jerry's does. Other companies publish environmental-impact disclosures and statements of social responsibilities: Patagonia, Reebok, British Airways, Volvo, Philips Electronics, Sony, Compaq, Intel, and IBM, among others." (Cohen and Greenfield, Ben & Jerry's Double-Dip, p. 251)

The firm Kinder, Lydenberg, Domini, established in Boston proposes since 1990 the Domini 400 Social Index, composed of 400 socially responsible American securities. It excludes the fields of tobacco, alcohol, gambling, nuclear, and companies with more than two percent of its turnover in military contracts. In total, half of the securities of the index S&P 500 enter in the composition of the Domini 400. The results are indisputably in favor of the ethical funds: by the end of July 1999, the Domini 400 index increases by 24.08 percent annually against 20.27 percent for the S&P 500. Over five years, the annualized performance amounts to 28.04 percent for the ethical index, which is two points higher than the larger index of Wall Street. Many American companies propose ethical funds to their employees in their pension funds. This has brought up a favorable and durable dynamism for the development of those products.

The rights of minority shareholders are tightly linked to the evolution of the rights of stakeholders. The companies are controlled today in most cases by majority shareholders who own often less than 50 percent of the shares but who manage to control the boards of directors. From the moment that the stakeholders will be represented in the boards of directors, the rights of minority shareholders will also be safeguarded. The majority shareholders justify their absolute control of the company by the fact that they have invested their capital into the company. Nevertheless, Estes and many other authors maintain that the stakeholders invest also in the company, often much more than the majority shareholders.

"But the corporation has other constituents as well: the workers, customers, suppliers, community, and the greater society. These other stakeholders are investors too, and they often risk far more than financial investors. Employees invest in the corporation. They bring their education, skills and experience – often gained at substantial personal expense – to the job. They invest time, energy, and too often their health. They invest their careers, careers that can be effectively wiped out in a casual layoff or relocation decision... Customers invest in the corporation. Their monetary investments are often greater than those of stockholders... Like workers, suppliers are investors too. They may commit production facilities, install special equipment, redesign products, and provide financing to their corporate customers. They have a right to expect fair treatment and a fair return on their investment.

Communities – neighbors, towns, cities, counties, and states – invest in corporations. They provide much of the infrastructure, such as streets and bridges, water and sewer systems, and police and fire protection, without which the corporation could hardly function.... Communities are investors and deserve a fair return on investment as much as stockholders. The nation – society – invests in the corporation. It provides the social capital and structure, without which we would face the brutal anarchy of the cave dweller. Our society supports the democratic system that allows the corporation, and the rest of us, freedom of movement and action. It provides protection for the free enterprise system.

Nations also grant specific benefits to corporations, such as investment incentives, tariff protection, research subsidies, defense contracts, and tax benefits including investment tax credits, accelerated depreciation, and foreign tax credits. Employees, customers, suppliers, communities, and society are all investors, but the corporation is not accountable to them. It reports regularly and comprehensively to stockholders, almost never to other stakeholders." (Estes, Tyranny of the Bottom Line, p. 4-6)

If you analyze which funds effectively finance the company, we shall notice in most of the cases that the funds of the shareholders who control the company contribute only a minimal part of the necessary funds for the functioning of the company. In many cases those who control the company are the executives who have not invested anything in the company even if they own its stocks. In the cases of the founders, they have invested in the initial phases of the company or when the shares' prices were not so high, and those who have invested the largest sums in equity are the minority shareholders who not only are not represented in the boards of directors but also have invested when the shares' prices were very high, mainly at public offerings.

Furthermore, the original investors of the company have often sold their shares on the stock exchange, and the new shareholders have not invested into the company but paid to the other shareholders for their shares. Thus, the company has not profited from the appreciation of the price of the shares, especially if it does not issue new shares. The suppliers, willingly or not, finance the company that utilizes their credit to finance the working capital. The clients finance undoubtedly the company, as it is their revenues that generate the profits of the companies. The creditors finance the company, as their financial leverage finances sometimes two or three times more than the equity. It is superfluous to state that the financing of the community and the state is so high, that in some stages, especially in the first ones it can amount to a third or even more of the total financing.

In the last years, we witness in the U.S., and to some extent also in France, a growing social activism of the shareholders and in many cases they succeed in changing the decisions taken by large companies in the U.S.: "The world-wide phenomenon observed as a growth in shareholder awareness comes under the general term of 'government of companies' or corporate governance. This phenomenon involves an increased interest in two categories of concerns linked to the internationalization of the capital of large industrial and financial conglomerates. The first category of concerns, already well recognized in France, regards questions directly relating to the rights of shareholders: company policy on information, distribution of profits, the organization of the Board of Directors, remuneration and protection of managers, etc.

The second category, not yet well known in our country but more widely discussed on the other side of the Atlantic, covers questions related to the general direction taken by management in response to a movement that could be termed 'social activism of shareholders'... Numerous recent initiatives by shareholders in the United States - 'General Electric sells its aerospace division to Martin Marietta under pressure from the Sisters of Notre Dame de Lorette; - The sisters of the Charity of the Holy World force Kimberley-Clark to sell its tobacco division; - The Lourdes Medical Centre forces the management of Pfizer to change their strategy; - The Sisters of Sainte Catherine de Sienne win a lawsuit against Wal Mart..." (Richardson, World Ethics Report, Leroy, Development of Social Activism amongst Shareholders, p. 161)

In shareholders' meetings in the U.S. there are hundreds of resolutions that are adopted every year as a result of the activism of the shareholders, who are mainly minority shareholders. The most dominant organizations in their activism are religious associations, proactive associations of shareholders, often with women dominance. "The spiritual heart of this movement is a New York non-profit organization, the Interfaith Centre for Corporate

Responsibility… For the last twenty-five years, ICCR has organized a coalition of 275 institutional investors, Protestant, Jewish and Catholic, who together represent a share portfolio with a total of value of 45 billion dollars. This organization co-ordinates the activity and voting of its members at shareholder meetings. Each year, it also publishes the astonishing growth of external proposals put forward by shareholders at general meetings of American publicly-owned companies…

In the United States, ownership of shares is popular and the American financial system is favorably disposed to direct intervention by shareholders in the business affairs of a company. Contributory pension funds are managed by organizations without links to the banking system and they are also subject to managements by vote. In addition, the invested capital allowing a shareholder to propose a motion at a company general meeting is low, being only one thousand dollars. To be included in the agenda of a general meeting, any resolution must also be recorded by the company; and the minutes are controlled by the American Securities and Exchange Commission." (same, p. 162)

The stakeholders and minority shareholders are not conscious of their power, in the same way that the people were not conscious of their strength before Rousseau, Voltaire and the French revolution. A large number of minority shareholders act like Candide and are convinced that everything is for the best in the best of the world, and that they should continue to lose in the long run like the gamblers who lose at the casino. There are very few militant minority shareholders and very few organizations that safeguard their interests like ADAM, managed by Mme. Neuville in France. The power of these individuals and organizations is very limited and if they sue the companies they often lose. But they ignore that they possess the absolute power, the Armageddon weapon, the absolute weapon, and if they use it they could collapse the Philistines' temple. But Samson, who is blind and thinks that he has no power, does not have to die with his persecutors. The minority shareholders can cease to invest in companies that do not behave ethically and in parallel invest uniquely in ethical funds. They could also, if they do not want to incur any risk, invest their money in savings deposits and be satisfied with 5 percent interests per annum.

Majority shareholders and the companies cannot operate without minority shareholders, as the majority shareholders invest effectively in most of the cases only about 30 percent of the equity in order to obtain control of the company and the remainder is invested by the minority shareholders, who own in fact the majority of the shares without having any control of the company. In paraphrasing a well-known 250-year-old maxim, the minority shareholders should say – no investment without representation! Furthermore, the majority shareholders do not lose in most cases from their investment, as they know when to sell and buy the shares with their insider information.

Ultimately, the minority shareholders invest effectively almost all the capital in absolute terms, not in number of shares, as they invest at the highest prices at the offerings, and the majority shareholders manage to recoup all their investments while selling part of their shares at offerings or in the market at high prices, thus risking henceforward only part of their return on investment but not of their capital that they have recouped. In many cases the majority shareholders profit from a collapse of the price of the shares and buy from the panicked minority shareholders shares at 10 percent of their previous prices, thus increasing even more their ownership and their profits.

When the situation stabilizes and the prices of the shares increase again, they sell once more their shares at the higher prices to the new minority shareholders, and, like in a perpetuum mobile, they always increase their ownership and profits to the detriment of the minority shareholders. This circus continues invariably for more than 100 years, as the same norms that prevailed in the times of the Second French Empire and the robber barons still exist in the year 2000. Suckers never die, they are just replaced, and as nobody warns them, least of all the SEC, the rich get richer and the poor get poorer in the stock exchange, and the more it changes the more it remains the same.

It is stunning how democracy has evolved dramatically in the last few years, but how democracy in business has remained retrograde. Heraclites has said that cattle are driven to the water with a stick, and the same law prevails possibly with humankind. There needs to be a catastrophe in order to instigate drastic change, as only after World War II did the world reach the conclusion that the best regime is the democratic regime, and the communist economies needed to collapse in order to change their totalitarian regimes.

The minority shareholders have probably not suffered enough, as the French people before the revolution of 1789, or the American people before the War of Independence in 1766. At the end of the twentieth century the stock exchange has reached new records; many minority shareholders got rich by investing in high-tech companies, and the scandals of the '80s are long forgotten. In searching in the world bibliography for the subject of this book we discover that almost nothing was written previously on this matter, probably because it does not interest the minority shareholders. Do we need a worse catastrophe than in 1929 in order to convince the minority shareholders to take their fate in their hands and exert the power that they can possess?

The author of this book is not so pessimistic and is convinced that even without a catastrophe evolution is inevitable and in five or ten years at most there will be a drastic change in ethics in the relations between companies and minority shareholders. We need to publish theses, books, articles on this subject, we need to introduce new norms, we need to use the Internet and other vehicles to augment the democracy of companies and assist the minority shareholders. We have to remember that there has never been a revolution in the US to abolish racist laws, there has never been a revolution in South Africa to abolish apartheid, and there has never been a revolution in the Soviet Union and its satellites to establish capitalistic democracy.

The dictatorial regimes of Spain, Portugal, Argentina, Chile or Greece have disappeared almost without bloodshed, although they were established in civil wars and bloody revolutions. The reason for this evolution without revolution was that the dictatorial regimes were ostracized and boycotted by the democratic countries, which have also ostracized the regimes of the Soviet Union and South Africa. In the same manner we need to ostracize and boycott the companies that will not conduct themselves ethically in general and toward the minority shareholders in particular.

Minority shareholders are waiting for their leaders, their Martin Luther King, their Nelson Mandela or their Ben Gurion. They are waiting for their 'Altneuland', their 'Contrat Social' or their 'Kapital'. Business ethics is not merely a nouvelle vague, a new wave, an ephemeral fashion, a gimmick, a buzzword. This is the new level of evolution of business, after the taylorism, the marketing, the organization, the quality and the ecology. The time of business ethics has arrived and it will remain forever. But the victory of ethics cannot be achieved without achieving also ethics toward the minority shareholders.

We should however be careful not to succumb to the tendency to pay artificial tribute to ethics as many companies are doing today, by having Codes of Ethics and not practicing them. As it is not politically correct to express oneself with pejorative terms toward women, Afro-Americans or Jews, the majority of businessmen declare their profound allegiance to business ethics but continue to act as in the past in their intimate circles. Eventually, they could hire an ethics officer, ethics consultants, or finance an ethics cathedra, to use them as Adam's leaves to cover the moral nudity of their companies.

We know how the 'robber barons' have alleviated their conscience by donating millions of dollars to build museums, universities or hospitals. According to their ethical norms and the norms of their followers to our days, they can despoil the rights of minority shareholders, cheat their customers and suppliers, destroy the ecology of entire nations, and make amends for it by giving to society a small percentage of what they robbed and usurped. And society, in order to thank them, nominate them as doctors honoris causa, give them the legion of honor, or the award for the best industrialist or exporter.

The only way to act against those ethics criminals is by organizing a campaign led by the activist associations that will ostracize the unethical businessmen instead of envying them, to refuse their donations, to nominate them doctors deshonoris causa and to put them on the black list. For them, appearances are very important and they invest considerable amounts in public relations in order to save face. We should only change their rules of the game, as those who should lead in the business world should be the ethical businessmen. It would be like being members of an exclusive club, where the ethics criminals would not be admitted, even if they try to redeem themselves.

We have already mentioned the activist minority shareholders, but we should emphasize also the worker-owners, as a vehicle to safeguard the rights of minority shareholders. The activist minority shareholders were already responsible for the significant improvement of competitiveness and financial results of many American companies in the last ten years of the century. Companies such as General Motors, IBM, Eastman Kodak, Westinghouse, and Sears Roebuck have improved their performance as a result of an intervention of activist shareholders. The 100 million salaried in the U.S. possess through their pension and other funds the majority of shares of a large number of companies. "There are now over 10,000 American ESOPs, including huge companies such as United Airlines, Avis Rent-a Car, and Weirton Steel, and there is evidence that they are more responsive to their employees and their customers. Studies show that worker-owners are more productive and deliver higher quality, with Avis now number one in ratings of customer satisfaction.

Hundreds of ESOPs and cooperatives, including large worker-owned factories, practice sophisticated forms of workplace democracy. They are proving effective in job creation and retention, and are responsible for saving hundreds of jobs during the epidemic of factory closings in the last decade. According to polls, including one by Peter Hart, economic democracy makes sense to most Americans; approximately 70 percent say that they would welcome the opportunity to work in an employee-owned company. Employee ownership in the United States has grown fifty-fold since 1974, with employees being the largest shareholders in more than 15 percent of all public companies.

The cutting edge is in the Fortune 500, where by 1990 the percentage of employee ownership was 11.7 percent in Ford, 9.3 percent in Exxon, 10 percent in Texaco, 16 percent in Chevron, 24.5 percent in Procter & Gamble, 18.9 percent in Lockheed, and 14.5 percent in Anheuser-Busch. By 1995, employee ownership was higher than 30 percent in huge companies such as Kroger, McDonnell Douglas, Bethlehem Steel, Rockwell International, Hallmark Cards, Trans World Airlines, U.S. Sugar, and Tandy Corporation.

Thirteen percent of the labor force – 11 million workers – are employee owners, more than the number of private sector union members. The total value of stock owned by workers in their own companies now exceeds $100 billion." (Derber, The Wilding of America, p. 158-9)

On the other hand, many companies and university professors maintain that minority shareholders harass the companies in order to extort benefits that are not due to them, claiming that some minority shareholders are 'speculators who are eager to have prompt benefits and have no respect and loyalty toward the companies where they invest'. Therefore, according to them, it is their duty to prevent their schemes by forcing them through the courts to pay damages. If the issue of the minority shareholders is tackled under a strictly defensive angle, we can find many cases in which minority shareholders resort to harassment maneuvers that not only destabilize the management in charge but can also in due term threaten the social interest. As the right to criticize that is recognized for the minority shareholders has only a goal to serve strictly their individual interests, the protest becomes pure harassment reprehensible as other sorts of harassment, such as contractual harassment. Those strategies of harassment have sometimes received some encouragement, notably through the decisions of the Court, especially in cases of class actions.

It is against those alleged harassments that those companies try to protect themselves and the judges justify the companies if they are convinced that the matter is in fact an abuse by the minority shareholders. The minority rights are not evident, even from a legal point of view, and the minority shareholders, who do not want to risk being sued for harassment, have, in the end, only ethics to safeguard their interests. It is very difficult for minority shareholders to prove legally that their rights were wronged. On the other hand it is much easier for companies to prove the opposite case of harassment by minority shareholders, those 'despicable speculators'.

The following is a sample of social investing and consumer activist groups and organizations: 20/20 Vision for protecting the environment, Action against Hunger, The Action Coalition preserving human rights, the American Animal Care Foundation, Center for Biological Monitoring, Center for Defense Information monitoring and criticizing the military, Center for Economic Conversion, Computer Professionals for Social Responsibility, Co-op America provides practical tools for businesses to address social and environmental problems, Council on Economic Priorities, Cruelty Free Investment News, Earth Challenge, Earth Wins, Environmental Defense Fund, The Equality Project, Fair Trade Federation, Friends of the Earth, Grassroots International working for social change, Habitat for Humanity International, Hunger Web, Inner City Press on community reinvestment, Institute for Global Communications, International Co-operative Alliance,

International Federation for Alternative Trade, Macrocosm USA for urgent social and environmental problems, New Uses Council for new consumer uses of renewable agricultural products, New World Village for the politically progressive Internet community, the Nonviolence Web, Nuclear Information and Resource Service, Pax World Service, Physicians for Social Responsibility, The Progress Report, Public Interest research Groups, Rainforest Alliance, Social Justice Connections, Union of Concerned Scientists, Zero Waste America.

Transparency International is a non-governmental organization, operating in about 90 countries and dedicated to increasing government accountability and curbing both international and national corruption. The movement has multiple concerns:
humanitarian, as corruption undermines and distorts development and leads to increasing levels of human rights abuse.
democratic, as corruption undermines democracies and in particular the achievements of many developing countries and countries in transition.
ethical, as corruption undermines a society's integrity.
practical, as corruption distorts the operations of markets and deprives ordinary people of the benefits that should flow from them.

Combatting corruption sustainably is only possible with the involvement of stakeholders, which include the state, civil society and the private sector. Through their National Chapters they bring together people of integrity in civil society, business and government to work as coalitions for systemic reforms. As they outline in their Mission Statement they do not identify names or attack individuals, but focus on building systems that combat corruption. They are playing an important role in raising public awareness and their Corruption Perceptions Index has triggered meaningful reform in many countries.

Transparency International classifies countries according to their level of lack of corruption, giving to Finland in 2000 the grade 10, or first place, for being practically without corruption, and to the other Scandinavian countries the second, fourth, sixth and seventh place. The other countries are: New Zealand (3rd 9.4), Canada (5th 9.2), Singapore (8th 9.1), the Netherlands (9th 8.9) and United Kingdom (10th 8.7), the ten least corrupted countries of the world, with grades of 10 to 8.7. Switzerland is 12th - 8.6, Australia is 13th – 8.3, the United States is 14th - 7.8, Germany is 17th - 7.6 and Spain is 20th - 7.0. France is 21st - 6.7 and Israel is 22nd with 6.6. In five years Israel has deteriorated from 14th place to 22nd place. Japan receives the grade of 6.4 in 23rd place, Belgium 25th – 6.1, South Africa 34th – 5.0, Italy – 4.6 in 39th place, Brazil 49th -3.9 and Turkey 50th - 3.8. Argentina is 52nd - 3.5, Mexico 59th - 3.3, Egypt 64th - 3.1, Romania 68th - 2.9, India 69th - 2.8, Kenya 82nd - 2.1 and Russia – 2.1 in 83rd place. Nigeria is the most corrupted country with 1.2 in 90th place.

Ivan Boesky has declared, before his fall, to the graduates of UCLA that you can be greedy and feel good about it. Perhaps if the temptation would not be so great, he and others would have abstained from their fraudulent conduct and he would have continued to respect the law. We remember what Aristotle has said on moderation and if we could make a wish to the minority shareholders it would be that they would have moderate and not excessive profits, as this is the best safeguard for them and for the majority shareholders to make ethics prevail and keep their integrity, even when they will participate in the control of the companies!

Karl Marx did not believe that the proletariat existed as a class conscious of its rights when he wrote 'Das Kapital'. The minority shareholders, nowadays like the proletariat in the 19th century, are not associated and conscious of their power. Marx has noticed the excessive abuse of power of the capitalists of his time who managed the economy not with the invisible hand of Adam Smith but with an iron fist, which oppressed the masses. It is Dickens, Zola, Hugo and others who have described the sufferance of the masses, but unfortunately modern literature does not pay attention to the wrongdoing to minority shareholders. Marx and Zola have condemned the indifference and injustice of the mighty toward the poor, the weak, those who were not organized.

"Taking the labor theory of value to its logical conclusion, Marx argued that those who did the work produced the value and, consequently, deserved the products of their labors for themselves. In other words, his emphasis on the actual activity of production instead of the commercial value of the end products led him to a conclusion that would have not been tolerable to Adam Smith – that the work itself was everything and the operations of the market were only a systematized form of theft. Marx, in other words, is very much in the line of ancient and religious thinkers who rejected the activity of business as parasitic on the honest labor of the working man... That concept is exploitation, and it is the sense of being exploited that did, in fact, create the class consciousness Marx urged (for example in the American labor union movement) and that continues to appeal so powerfully to so many people in Third World countries, especially former colonies of the great industrial empires." (Solomon, Above the Bottom Line, p. 267)

Nobody advocates to end up with the conclusions of Marxism in order to safeguard the interests of the minority shareholders, although the basic situation is the same – they are the majority of people contributing the most to the economy but sharing only a fraction of their contribution without being represented adequately. The solution should be cooperation between the majority and minority shareholders and the management of the companies. But in order to reach this stage, it is needed that the minority shareholders should sense that they are despoiled in many cases, they should organize in order to safeguard their interests, they should be assisted by the activist associations. We could do it by way of evolution or by revolution. The powerful should reach the conclusion that it is in their best interest not to abuse their excessive rights, exactly like in Great Britain, which has managed to move from absolutism to democracy without revolution.

The revolution for the minority shareholders would be to cease investing in the stock exchange, after having lost their trust in the system. The minority shareholders have the alternative to invest their savings in the banks instead of purchasing shares of companies. They could earn much less, eventually, but they would not incur the risk of being despoiled in fixed games, by fraudulent use of insider information, and by greedy businessmen eager to get even richer at all cost. But if the minority shareholders cease to invest, the stock exchange will suffer from its worse collapse ever, which could end up in a world recession. If we do not want to encounter such catastrophes, we should allow the minority shareholders to exert their rights, share equitably in the companies' wealth, be represented adequately in their organizations, participate in their control, and restitute the notion of fair play in the stock exchange.

15
FUTURE ACTIVIST VEHICLES - THE SUPERVISION BOARD

"Who will guard the guards themselves?"
(Juvenal, Satires)

This 2,000-year-old question, describes the ancient and modern dilemma of the safeguarding of the various interests by guards who have to remain uncorrupted. The book 'Business Ethics - The Ethical Revolution of Minority Shareholders' by the same author proves how in many cases the interests of the minority shareholders are not safeguarded by the Boards of Directors, which are controlled by the majority shareholders, or by committees of independent directors appointed by the same shareholders. Those organisms were supposed, among others, to safeguard the interests of the minority shareholders. The new organism proposed in this chapter, the Supervision Board that will be established in order to support the interests of the minority shareholders, will have to be immune to corruption and to the influence of the majority shareholders. On the other hand the addition of a new organism that will supervise the operations of the company could complicate its operations and make them impossible in cases of deadlocks between the two Boards – the Supervision and the Directors. Which Board does the CEO have to obey? These legitimate issues will be addressed in a very detailed manner in this chapter, which proposes a practical solution to all those dilemmas. But, more importantly, as the present situation is unbearable, and the minority shareholders are despoiled continuously, the establishment of this new board has to be risked in order to respond to the urgent need of the safeguarding of the interests of the minority shareholders. As the new vehicles, the Internet, Transparency, Activist Associations and Ethical Funds are not sufficient to guard their interests; the Supervision Board will be the first guard of the minority shareholders and not the guard of the guards, without lessening the critics of the modern Juvenals who will always criticize such innovations.

The greatest danger for the minority shareholders comes from the holy alliance between the executives of companies and the majority shareholders who appoint and remunerate them. Those executives themselves participate in the quarry, by receiving shares and warrants of the companies in very favorable terms that enable them to get rich without incurring apparent risks. This book will propose to break this link by establishing a new organism – the Supervision Board, in which the shareholders who control the Board of

Directors would be able to appoint at maximum only 50 percent of their members, even when they hold almost all the shares, while the other members will be elected by the other shareholders and by the Institute of Ethics.

The Supervision Board would be able to hire and fire the CEO of the company, and to decide on his remuneration, his bonuses, and the shares and warrants that he will be entitled to. In this manner, the CEO will pledge allegiance to all the shareholders and will have only one target: to succeed in his mission without taking into consideration the breakdown of the ownership of the shares. The members of the Supervision Board will be elected by adjusted voting. If the shareholders, who control the Board of Directors, hold 40 percent of the shares, they will be able to elect only 20 percent of the members of the board of supervision. If the other shareholders present at the shareholders' meeting hold 10 percent of the shares (as the shareholders are scattered throughout the country and do not attend or send their proxies), they will be able to elect only 10 percent of the members of the board of supervision. The other 70 percent will be elected by the National Institute of Ethics. In this manner, the majority of the members of the Supervision Board will always be elected by organisms that are not controlled by the Board of Directors or by the management of the company and will always be able to safeguard the interests of the minority shareholders. The members of the Supervision Board will be elected proportionately to the capital that the minority shareholders have and not by the random proportion of their attendance in the shareholders' assembly. The shareholders who will not vote will therefore be represented by the delegates appointed by the Institute of Ethics.

The functions of the Supervision Board could be inspired by the German Bundesrat, which acts mainly as a Consultative House, but has to give its advice and consent to a large number of laws, as well as to constitutional changes. The Supervision Board will not duplicate the Board of Directors but will control it, as the latter is elected in most of the cases by the majority shareholders, by controlling shareholders with less than 50 percent of the shares, or sometimes even by the executives of the company, if the shareholders are totally scattered and do not control the company. The external or independent directors do not function genuinely in most cases as supervision committees, as they are appointed by the executives, the majority shareholders, or by political bodies in companies controlled by the state.

There could be many ramifications to the structure of the Supervision Board. If the allocation of a maximum of 50 percent of the votes in the Supervision Board to the shareholders who control the Board of Directors seems draconian, it could be possible to amend the adjusting formula in favor of the minority shareholders up to 50 percent of the members of the Supervision Board. In this manner, the shareholders who control the Board of Directors will be entitled to 25 percent of the votes of the Supervision Board if they hold 50 percent of the shares of the company. For shares above 50 percent, the majority and minority shareholders will have the same rights of voting. With 76 percent of the shares, the majority shareholders will have the control of the Supervision Board, with 51 percent of the members (25 percent + 26 percent). The minority shareholders will have to know that if they invest in companies with majority shareholders holding above 75 percent of the shares, they incur a risk of being wronged by them, as they will possess the control of the two boards. But even in those cases, the minority shareholders will be entitled to a double representation in the Supervision Board, and this improves substantially their present situation, when in many cases they are not represented at all in the Board of Directors.

Another alternative could be that the CEO of the company would not be able to get shares and warrants of his company and his remuneration will be uniquely through salaries and bonuses according to the financial and other results of the company. In this manner, the CEO will not be motivated mainly by the valuation of his company but by the satisfaction of the stakeholders of the company, and he will tend to be more ethical and equitable toward the different groups that constitute the company. His allegiance toward the majority shareholders will be lessened as he will not have identical interests with them, and many conflicts between majority and minority shareholders will be avoided. One could nevertheless distribute shares to the CEO and the directors of the company if the Board of Directors and the Supervision Board will jointly agree to it, ensuring in this manner the allegiance of the CEOs to the majority and minority shareholders.

The Supervision Board could have as an additional mission - the safeguarding of the interests of the stakeholders of the company, including the interests of the minority shareholders. We witness recently attempts to appoint stakeholders, such as the community, customers, lenders and others, to the Board of Directors and other organisms of the companies. Those stakeholders could be represented in the future in the Supervision Board, and the Institute of Ethics could appoint the stakeholders' representatives to this board and not only the representatives of the minority shareholders. The stakeholders could be represented in the Supervision Board according to the degree of their participation in the activities of the company. The community that invests particularly in the company by giving it land free of charge, the lenders that lend large amounts to the company as part of a turnaround plan, employees who work in the company for more than ten years, customers and suppliers that constitute a large percentage of the company's activities, and so on, will have the right to be represented in the Supervision Board of the company. Germany and Japan have a representation of certain stakeholders since many years and this could be one of the reasons for their spectacular development.

If one tries to understand the motives that motivate the majority shareholders, we could find that they are interested in power and control, maybe much more than in profits or even abusive profits at the expense of the minority shareholders and other stakeholders. The control of the Board of Directors, that is the main body of management, could suffice them, and they would be willing to share more equitably the profits with the minority shareholders without abusing the rights of the stakeholders. The Supervision Board will verify that the repartition of profits will be done ethically, and its main role will be the ethical control of the company, but in any case not the strategic management, with the only exception that the CEO will have to be nominated by this board, as otherwise his allegiance would be uniquely to the Board of Directors, which is controlled by the majority shareholders.

The Supervision Board will not be a panacea, as its structures will be balanced between the majority and minority shareholders, with a large influence of the Institute of Ethics that will elect part of its members. The minority shareholders themselves have today a distribution that varies significantly from the past. Only the Supervision Boards and the Institutes of Ethics will be able to safeguard, beyond the other organisms, the interests of the minority shareholders.

But even the members of the Supervision Board can be corrupted and behave like men of straw. Berlureau needs a man of straw for a fishy business in Corsica, and he contemplates sending Henri in order to get rid of him. Henri, who had scruples prior to then, plays the game and sells himself to the highest bidder.

"Henri – Mais puisque je vends mon ame au diable, j'ai besoin de deux mille francs pour apaiser mes scrupules.

Berlureau – Ils sont un peu chers vos scrupules.

Henri – C'est qu'ils sont grands, et assez douloureux… Le scrupule, mon cher Ferdinand, est une maladie pénible dont tu n'as probablement jamais souffert. Mais c'est aussi cruel qu'une sciatique. Par bonheur, il existe un très vieux remède, mais dont l'effet est immédiat: c'est le cataplasme d'oseille.

Berlureau (joyeux) – Les remèdes de bonne femme ont toujours été les meilleurs. D'accord.

Bachelet – Il ne faudrait tout de même pas abuser…

Henri – Tu trouves que ce n'est pas MORAL?

Berlureau – Edouard, ne sois pas confus, parce que moi, ça me rassure. Je craignais que l'amnésie ne l'ait rendu inutilisable, et je l'envoyais la-bas pour l'escamoter… Mais puisqu'il a toute sa tête, et qu'il a compris la musique, il peut me rendre de grands services. C'est une affaire très délicate. Les deux mille francs, il les vaut."

(Pagnol, Les Marchands de Gloire, Oeuvres Completes I, p. 153)

"Henri – But if I sell my soul to the devil, I need two thousand francs to appease my scruples.

Berlureau – Your scruples are a little bit expensive.

Henri – It is because they are huge, and quite aching… The scruple, my dear Ferdinand, is a painful sickness from which you have probably never suffered. But it is as painful as sciatica. Luckily, there exists a very old cure, with an immediate effect, the poultice of dough.

Berlureau (happily) – The old women cures were always the best. I agree.

Bachelet – You should nevertheless not exploit the situation…

Henri – You think that it is not MORAL?

Berlureau – Edouard, don't be confused, because I am reassured. I was afraid that the amnesia has made him unusable, and I was sending him there to make him disappear… But as he has got all his senses, and he has understood the tune, he can render me valuable services. It is a very delicate matter. He is worth the two thousand francs."

So, even in the Supervision Board nothing prevents its members from abusing their rights and working as men of straw of the majority shareholders. The independent directors in the Board of Directors are already tempted in many cases to act in favor of the majority shareholders, and this scenario can repeat itself also in the Supervision Board. We should therefore elect to this board members with a reputation of incorruptibility. The organism that will take care of electing most of the members of the Supervision Board and will verify their integrity is therefore the Institute of Ethics.

16
FUTURE ACTIVIST VEHICLES -
THE INSTITUTE OF ETHICS

"A gift from the Danaans, and no ruse?
Is that Ulysses' way, as you have known him?
Achaeans must be hiding in this timber,
Or it was built to butt against our walls,
Peer over them into our houses, pelt
The city from the sky. Some crookedness
Is in this thing. Have no faith in the horse!
Whatever it is, even when Greeks bring gifts
I fear them, gifts and all. 'Timeo Danaos et dona ferentes.' "
(Virgil, The Aeneid, Book II, 62-70)

Is the Institute of Ethics a Trojan Horse? Should the majority shareholders
and the management of companies fear this future vehicle of activist Business
Ethics? Fateful to the pledge of complete transparency, we have to state that
indeed for unethical businessmen this is a Trojan Horse, but for ethical
businessmen and companies the Institute of Ethics would safeguard against
future collapse of the stock exchange.

The Institute of Ethics will not operate as a 'big brother', as a 'revisor', or as a
'Russian Commissar'. This organism will operate voluntarily and have a
mission to avoid the most flagrant cases of obstructing the rights of the
stakeholders and minority shareholders.

By the word 'Institute', we mean either an anemic organization, which does
not have power, comprised of detached men unrelated to the business world,
who do not understand its complexity. It is at least what its opponents will try
to convey. But this book proposes a realistic model, based on a thorough
study of the subject and a profound knowledge of the business world. The
proposed Institute will be very effective, as will be explained in this chapter,
and will have concrete and realistic missions, experienced directors, first class
attendants, and an assured financing. Furthermore, it will keep its
independence and its impartiality like the courts and the judges.

The national Institute of Ethics will be financed by a contribution deducted
from each transaction made at the national stock exchange. The members of
the Institute will possess impeccable reputations and will be elected by the

national courts, but they will not be active businessmen and will not hold any shares in companies.

The safeguarding of the minority shareholders' interests will be parallel to the safeguarding of the underprivileged minorities in the United States, such as Afro-Americans, Hispanics, native Americans, and so on. If we will not take corrective measures to favor minority shareholders and adjust their rights, they will always be despoiled by the majority shareholders, as the Afro-Americans were by the WASPs in the United States.

We witness recently a trend toward voluntary regulation of companies in many aspects of their activities toward stakeholders, employees, customers, the community, environment, and so on. Industries' associations obtain control over its members, which is often more effective than governmental or legal control. "A faster adaptation to changing conditions in industry is possible when not restricted to laws. The quality of the adjustment to specific conditions of an industry is better. Voluntary participation of the member firms of the branch prevents destructive behaviour and secures the efficiency of self-regulation. Some of the disadvantages are: - Informal behaviour of an industry is hard to generalize and codify. - Member firms are rather inclined to agree to non-binding and mild regulations than to obligatory demanding standards. - Not all companies of a certain branch are members of the association. Consequently they are not forced to adhere to the regulations. - Violations of rules are often hard to punish." (Harvey, Business Ethics, A European Approach, Kuhlmann, Customers, p.117) The companies adhere to a 'soft law', established after mutual negotiations that result in an agreement on the rules and ways to punish the transgression of the rules.

In the political and economical world, there are associations more or less formal as the United Nations, the European Parliament, the IMF, GAAT, and so on. But those associations, like the stock exchange, are established and managed by the organisms that they are supposed to control. The Institute of Ethics will be elected by impartial courts and will supervise the companies that will agree to submit voluntarily to its rules. If in the future we will reach a status that only companies supervised by the Institute of Ethics will be able to recruit the best employees, have access to the best customers, receive the best prices from the suppliers, sell their shares to minority shareholders; then most of the companies or at least their first league will abide by the rules of the Institute. The other companies will be treated as outcasts, on the outskirts of society, and will not be able to survive in the long run. The ethical reputation of a company will become one of its most important assets and will be a decisive factor in the valuation of the company.

How is it possible to guard the integrity of the members of the Institute? First of all, by choosing members with impeccable integrity, who could have worked prior to that in companies, but will be prohibited to return to work in business. The Institute will be like an Academy or court, with members elected for life, and when they will want to leave they will be entitled to a pension. They will write ethical codes and supervise their implementation, they will elect a large part of the members of the Supervision Boards, they will give an ethical rating to companies, similar to the creditworthiness rating, ranging from AAA to CCC. The ethical funds will be allowed for example to invest only in companies with an ethical rating of A, and as this rating will be granted by the Institute, it will have financial power of the utmost importance. The National Institutes of Ethics will be associated in an International Institute of Ethics that will establish international ethical codes and exchange information on ethical and unethical companies, ethical funds, unethical executives and directors and so on in the various countries. As the world becomes a global village, a company or an individual who has behaved unethically in one country will not be able to start from zero in another country. Their name will appear on an international black list that will chase them forever, as ethical information will be exchanged by all the National Institutes of Ethics.

The modern structure of business has to be parallel to the political structure, by being democratic and based on the foundation of the separation of power. The legislative power will have to be enlarged in order to include the Institutes of Ethics. The members of the Institutes will have to be independent and have a theoretical and practical background in corporate governance. They will have to be fluent in corporate law, business administration, ethics, accounting (with a special knowledge of the dangers of creative accounting…), etc. But they will need to have active and inquisitive minds, which will not be contented with the unethical conduct of controlled companies.

In the event that a contribution to the Institute of Ethics by a fee on every stock exchange transaction will not be feasible, it could be possible to raise the necessary funds from the ethical funds or the shareholders who will benefit from the privileged information of the Institute, which will be distributed only to the contributors. The operational expenses of the Institute are negligible in comparison to the benefits or prevention of losses to the minority shareholders, as the costs of mistrust and wrongdoing to the minority shareholders amount to billions of dollars and could cause the collapse of the stock exchange securities and lead to a world recession.

The companies will submit an annual report on the ethical and ecological conduct toward its stakeholders and will be responsible for the social results of their conduct. The investors, especially the minority shareholders, employees, suppliers, customers, community and society, will have access to the ethical information that will enable them to decide on their conduct toward the companies based on the ethical reports, in a similar way that they evaluate the operational performance of companies from their financial reports, which give only very partial information on the companies.

The Institute of Ethics could decide to compensate the minority shareholders in case of wrongdoing to their rights by forcing the companies that would want to maintain their ethical rating to reimburse the shareholders of their investment with interests and damages. The most problematic element of investment, the risk, will be neutralized in this way and the minority shareholders will be assured that, unless they resort to the court in order to sue the company, they will have the possibility to recoup the actualized value of their investment if an ethical institution will find their ethical plea justified without the necessity to resort to the expensive procedure of the court and payment of legal fees.

The minority shareholders will be able to attenuate their risks by receiving from companies adhering to the ethical norms quarterly ethical reports, monthly financial reports, audited financial reports, etc. The Institute of Ethics will also conduct statistics and reports on unethical costs and losses incurred by minority shareholders that are estimated as shown by this book at billions of dollars. The minority shareholders will have free access, via the Internet, to the reports of the Institute, that will be assisted by whistle-blowers, anonymous or not, who will expose the unethical conduct of the companies, often done in the shade far away from the public eye. The Institute will publish a black list or a pillory of companies that did not behave ethically, as well as of investment bankers, analysts, auditors, and other consultants, whose reports have harmed the minority shareholders.

The Institute of Ethics can also safeguard the interests of the other stakeholders, such as suppliers, customers, lenders, and the community, but its principal role will always be to safeguard the interests of the minority shareholders. They will intercede in favor of the minority shareholders in every case of an offer to purchase shares and will ensure that unless the companies have received a written consent of 95 percent of their shareholders, they will not be able to enforce them to sell their shares. If they would want to purchase the shares of the minority shareholders at the undervalued current market price, the companies will have to offer them at least the actualized value of their investment. The Institute will have to give its consent to every offer to purchase the shares of the minority shareholders of the companies that will submit to its control, in the same manner that the mergers necessitate the approval of the anti-trust organizations.

The Institute will also nominate the members of the Supervision Board, in cases where the minority shareholders will not vote or give proxies at the shareholders' meetings. In no case will the members of the Supervision Board be elected only by the participants in the vote, which can consist often of only 20 percent of the shareholders. The members of the Supervision Board, representing in this example the other 80 percent of the shareholders who have not participated in the vote, will be nominated by the Institute of Ethics.

The Institute of Ethics will therefore be the main safeguard of the minority shareholders. It will be impartial, very involved, with secured funding and an impeccable reputation. The greatest danger of corruption will be avoided by the fact that its directors would not be allowed to return to the business world, as in the case of managers of government institutions who are tempted to favor certain companies in return for a promise to work for them or the receipt of direct or indirect rewards from them. While keeping the limpidity of its water, the Institute will let many fishes, even small fry like individual shareholders, swim without being disturbed by the sharks that will be kept away by the Institute. Those sharks, who always speak a double talk, will try to prevent the existence of the Institutes in the name of the economic development and of free enterprise, and will try to treat the Institutes as bureaucratic organizations, detached from real business or even anti-business. But the Institutes of Ethics, backed by the minority shareholders and possibly the main stakeholders, who will have access at last to a sympathizing and effective organization, will know how to repel the attacks and to overcome all the doubts.

17
CONCLUSION

"Je fis souffler un vent révolutionnaire.
Je mis un bonnet rouge au vieux dictionnaire.
Plus de mot sénateur! plus de mot roturier!
Je fis une tempête au fond de l'encrier,
Et je mêlai, parmi les ombres débordées,
Au peuple noir des mots l'essaim blanc des idées;
Et je dis: Pas de mot ou l'idee au vol pur
Ne puisse se poser, toute humide d'azur!…
Je bondis hors du cercle et brisai le compas.
Je nommai le cochon par son nom; pourquoi pas?"
(Victor Hugo, Reponse a un acte d'accusation, Reply to a bill of indictment)
"I have swept a revolutionary wind.
I have put a red hat on the old dictionary.
No more noble! no more common people!
I have made a tempest at the bottom of the inkstand,
And I have blended, between the overloaded shadows,
The white swarm of ideas with the black multitude of words;
And I said: No words where the pure flight of ideas
Cannot land on, all humid from the azure sky!…
I have leaped out of the ring and broken the compass.
I have pointed the finger at the pig; why not?"

The author of this book would rather be approximately right than precisely wrong. He prefers to put a red hat on the old dictionary and make a tempest at the bottom of the inkstand, leap out of the ring and break the compass. And most of all - point the finger at the wrongdoers and call them by their name. Having worked for more than 33 years in the business environment, he knows all the tricks of the trade. When those tricks became unethical, he decided to write a thesis and books on business ethics and to be active in this field. However, he soon found out that more activism is needed in order to make an impact in the near future. The dignified, laid-back approach of some business ethicists is not sufficient to change the deteriorating situation, possibly because those ethicists are often academic professors who have not worked in the actual business world and have learned of unethical conduct as a result of research and not of personal experience.

A new revolutionary wind is needed, even if it is not based on 'smoking-gun evidence'. Most of the unethical acts cannot be fully proven, as the wrongdoers prefer to conduct their abuse in the dark, like Mack The Knife. A fresh wind of transparency is essential; new organizations representing the stakeholders and minority shareholders are needed, such as the Supervision Board and the Institute of Ethics; and the democratic use of the Internet has to prevail. Not enough businessmen put ethics at the forefront of their mission. Even less would advocate activist business ethics and not just being satisfied with paying a lip service to the need of codes of ethics. Yet, the New Economy needs even more activist business ethics, as it will become the lingua franca of the international business community, overcoming the gap between nations, cultures and religions.

Businessmen state that they obey the law and it is enough. It is more convenient for them to do so, as the law in many cases is ambiguous, and the best lawyers could be hired in order to impose the will of companies and majority shareholders. The weaker economic groups of society have no chance to use the law in their favor, due to the huge amounts and long periods of time needed in order to win a lawsuit. Activist business ethics is therefore the only safeguard of the stakeholders and minority shareholders, as it transcends the law, frontiers, religions and cultures.

The theories presented in the author's books are based on qualitative research. The unethical businessmen and many academics disregard them as they are not substantiated by quantitative research and at best present, in their viewpoint, a few cases of alleged unethical conduct. The businessmen who have a passive attitude toward business ethics tend to advocate this criticism, as it concurs with good business conduct, which is essentially not revolutionary and conservative. Why should they fight their colleagues, with whom they work, cooperate and share social contacts? As long as stakeholders and minority shareholders will have no power and no backing by influential institutes, the existing situation will prevail.

Those who dare to fight for change will be treated as Enemies of the People, Don Quixotes or Whistle-Blowers. But the lack of ethics undermines the business world and an earthquake is imminent. The stakeholders and minority shareholders are waiting for a strong leadership to organize them, and in the meantime they will inevitably come to the conclusion of 'no investment or collaboration without representation'. Conquered people, oppressed minorities, and underprivileged classes have rebelled in the last century and have brought about a commonwealth of democracies, new social structures, new nations, and modern regimes. The last bastion of dictatorship, the management of unethical companies, will be swept away by activist business ethics, which will become the leit motive of the next decades.

Schopenhauer said: "The truth can wait, for it lives a long life. All truth passes through three stages. First, it is ridiculed. Second, it is violently opposed. Third, it's accepted as being self-evident." Do we have the long life needed to wait for the truth? We are in the first stage of the truth as activist business ethicists are only ridiculed. They are not violently opposed, which shows that they are not feared enough. If we do not write books, theses, articles, novels and plays on these subjects, if we do not lecture in companies, universities, activist associations on those topics, and most of all - if we do not decide to take our fate in our own hands and fight for our privileges, we shall continue to be ridiculed in the years to come. But if the books by this author and similar books, which will be written in the future, will shake the complacency of the unethical businessmen we might reach the next stage and be violently opposed. We are waiting eagerly for this stage to come, as it will announce that the last stage is near and the truth of equality to all business groups will prevail. We are not philosophers and we do not have the time and the long life to wait for this truth to arrive. This is why we do our utmost to shorten the time. Do you, stakeholders and minority shareholders, have the long life to wait for the end of the multitude of cases in which your rights are despoiled, or are you willing to act vehemently at last in your lifetime?

BIBLIOGRAPHY

Aristotle, Ethics, Penguin Classics, 1976

Badaracco, Jr. Joseph L., Defining Moments, When Managers Must Choose between Right and Right, Harvard Business School Press,1997

The Holy Bible, The Old Testament, New International Version, International Bible Society, 2/96

The Holy Bible, The New Testament, New International Version, International Bible Society, 2/96

Blanchard Ken, O'Connor Michael, Managing By Values, Berrett-Koehler Publishers, 1997

Blanchard Kenneth, Peale Norman Vincent, The Power of Ethical Management, William Morrow and Company, Inc., 1988

Blaug Mark, La Methodologie Economique, The Economic Methodology, in French, 2e edition, Ed. Economica 1994

Bollier David, Aiming Higher, 25 Stories of how Companies Prosper by Combining Sound Management and Social Vision, Amacom, 1997

Bonder Nilton Rabbi, The Kabbalah of Money, Insights on Livelihood, Business, and All Forms of Economic Behavior, Shambhala, 1996

Brecht Bertolt, Die Dreigroschenoper, The Threepenny Opera, in German, Universal Edition, 1928, assigned to Brookhouse Music, Inc., 1957

Briner Bob, The Management Methods of Jesus, Ancient Wisdom for Modern Business, Thomas Nelson, Inc., 1996

Burkett Larry, Business by the Book, The Complete Guide of Biblical Principles for Business Men and Women, Expanded Edition, Thomas Nelson Publishers, 1991

Burkett Larry, Sound Business Principles, Includes Ethics and Priorities, Moody Press, 1993

Business Ethics Quarterly, January 1998, Vol. 8 No. 1, The Journal of the Society for Business Ethics

Business Ethics Quarterly, April 1998, Vol. 8 No. 2, The Journal of the Society for Business Ethics

Business Ethics Quarterly, July 1998, Vol. 8 No. 3, The Journal of the Society for Business Ethics

Business Ethics Quarterly, October 1998, Vol. 8 No. 4, The Journal of the Society for Business Ethics

Business Ethics Quarterly, The Ruffin Series Special Issue No. 1, 1998, The Journal of the Society for Business Ethics

Business Ethics Quarterly, January 1999, Vol. 9 No. 1, The Journal of the Society for Business Ethics

Business Ethics Quarterly, April 1999, Vol. 9 No. 2, The Journal of the Society for Business Ethics

Business Ethics Quarterly, July 1999, Vol. 9 No. 3, The Journal of the Society for Business Ethics

Business Ethics Quarterly, October 1999, Vol. 9 No. 4, The Journal of the Society for Business Ethics

Business Ethics Quarterly, The Ruffin Series Special Issue No. 2, 2000, Environmental Challenges to Business, A Publication of the Society for Business Ethics

Business Ethics Quarterly, January 2000, Vol. 10 No. 1, The Journal of the Society for Business Ethics

Casey Al with Seaver Dick, Casey's Law, If Something Can Go Right, It Should, Arcade Publishing, 1997

Cervantes Miguel de, El Ingenioso Hidalgo Don Quijote de la Mancha, Don Quixote, in Spanish, Catedra Letras Hispanicas, 1992

Chatfield Cheryl A., Ph.D., The Trust Factor, The Art of Doing Business in the 21st Century, Sunstone Press, 1997

Cohen Ben and Greenfield Jerry, Ben & Jerry's Double-Dip, Lead with Your Values and Make Money, Too, Simon & Schuster, 1997

Cory Jacques, Business Ethics: The Ethical Revolution of Minority Shareholders, Kluwer Academic Publishers, 2001

Cory Jacques, Beware of Greeks' Presents, in Hebrew, Bimat Kedem Publishers, 2001

Dante, The Divine Comedy, Pan Classics, 1980

De George Richard T., Competing with Integrity in International Business, Oxford University Press, 1993

Derber Charles, The Wilding of America, How Greed and Violence Are Eroding Our Nation's Character, St. Martin's Press, 1996

Devine George, Responses to 101 Questions on Business Ethics, Paulist Press, 1996

Dherse Jean-Loup, Minguet Hughes Dom, l'Ethique ou le Chaos?, Ethics or Chaos?, in French, Presses de la Renaissance, 1998

Donaldson Thomas, The Ethics of International Business, The Ruffin Series in Business Ethics, Oxford University Press, 1992

Driscoll Dawn-Marie, Hoffman W. Michael, Petry Edward S., The Ethical Edge, Tales of Organizations that Have Faced Moral Crises, MasterMedia Limited, 1995

Estes Ralph, Tyranny of the Bottom Line, Why Corporations Make Good People Do Bad Things, Berrett-Koehler Publishers, 1996

Ethics at Work, A Harvard Business Review Paperback, 1991

Etzioni Amitai, The Moral Dimension, Toward a New Economics, The Free Press, 1990

Feyerabend Paul, Contre la Methode, Esquisse d'une Theorie Anarchiste de la Connaissance, Against Method, in French, Editions du Seuil, 1979

Fukuyama Francis, Trust, The Social Virtues and the Creation of Prosperity, A Free Press Paperbacks Book, 1996

Ginsburg Sigmund G., Managing with Passion, Making the Most of Your Job and Your Life, John Wiley & Sons, Inc., 1996

Hall William D., Making the Right Decision, Ethics for Managers, John Wiley & Sons, Inc., 1993

Handy Charles, The Hungry Spirit, Beyond Capitalism: A Quest for Purpose in the Modern World, Broadway Books, 1998

Harmon Frederick G., Playing for Keeps, How the World's Most Aggressive and Admired Companies Use Core Values to Manage, Energize and Organize Their People, and Promote, Advance and Achieve Their Corporate Missions, John Wiley & Sons, Inc., 1996

Harvey Brian, Edited by, Business Ethics, A European Approach, Prentice Hall, 1994

Homer, The Iliad, Penguin Classics, 1987

Homere, Odyssee, Le Livre de Poche, 1960

Hornstein Harvey A., Ph.D., Brutal Bosses and Their Prey, Riverhead Books, 1996

Huckabee Mike, the Honorable Governor of Arkansas, with Perry John, Character is the Issue, How People with Integrity Can Revolutionize America, Broadman & Holman Publishers, 1997

Ibsen Henrik, An Enemy of the People, Modern Library College Editions, 1950

Inoue Shinichi, Putting Buddhism to Work, A New Approach to Management and Business, Kodansha International Ltd., 1997

Jackall Robert, Moral Mazes, The World of Corporate Managers, Oxford University Press, 1989

Jackson Jennifer, An Introduction to Business Ethics, Blackwell Publishers, 1996

Jacobs Joseph J., The Anatomy of an Entrepreneur, Family, Culture, and Ethics, ICS Press, 1991

Jay Antony, Management and Machiavelli, in Hebrew, Ma'ariv Book Guild, 1989

Kafka Franz, The Trial, Schocken Books, 1998

Kafka Franz, The Metamorphosis and Other Stories, Barnes an Noble Books, 1996

Kaufman Allen, Zacharias Lawrence, Karson Marvin, Managers vs. Owners, The Struggle for Corporate Control in American Democracy, The Ruffin Series in Business Ethics, Oxford University Press, 1995

Kelley Michael, On Stone or Sand, The Ethics of Christianity, Capitalism, & Socialism, Pleroma Press, 1993

Kidder Rushworth M., How Good People Make Tough Choices, Resolving the Dilemmas of Ethical Living, A Fireside Book published by Simon & Schuster, 1995

Koran, the Essential, the Heart of Islam, an Introductory Selection of Readings from the Qur'an, Translated and Presented by Thomas Cleary, Castle Books, 1993

La Fontaine, Fables, in French, Folio, Gallimard, 1991

Lawrence William D., with Turpin Jack A., Beyond the Bottom Line, Where Faith and Business Meet, Praxis Books Moody Press, 1994

Leibowitz Yeshayahu, Talks with Michael Shashar, On Just About Everything, in Hebrew, Keter Publishing House, 1988

Lynn Jonathan and Jay Antony, edited by, The Complete Yes Minister, The Diaries of a Cabinet Minister by the Right Hon. James Hacker MP, British Broadcasting Corporation, 1985

Machiavelli Niccolo, The Prince, Bantan Books, 1981

Madsen Peter, Ph.D., and Shafrtiz Jay M., Ph.D., Essentials of Business Ethics, A Collection of Articles by Top Social Thinkers, Including Peter Drucker, Milton Friedman, Robert Jackall, Ralph Nader, Laura Nash, Patricia H. Werhane, A Meridian Book, 1990

Mao Tse-Tung, Quotations from Chairman, Foreign Languages Press, 1966

May William W., Business Ethics and the Law, Beyond Compliance, The Rockwell Lecture Series, Peter Lang, 1991

McLellan David, Karl Marx - His Life and Thought, A Paladin Book Granada, 1973

Miller Arthur, All My Sons, Six Great Modern Plays, Dell Publishing Company, Inc., 1977

Miller Arthur, The Crucible, The Portable Arthur Miller, Penguin Books, 1995

Miller Arthur, Timebends - A Life, Penguin Books, 1995

Monks Robert A.G., The Emperor's Nightingale, Restoring the Integrity of the Corporation in the Age of Shareholder Activism, Addison-Wesley, 1998

Mott Graham M., How to Recognize and Avoid Scams Swindles and Rip-Offs, Personal Stories Powerful Lessons, Golden Shadows Press, 1994

Nash Laura L., Ph.D., Believers in Business, Resolving the Tensions between Christian Faith, Business, Ethics, Competition and our Definitions of Success, Thomas Nelson Publishers, 1994

Nash Laura L., Good Intentions Aside, A Manager's Guide to Resolving Ethical Problems, Harvard Business School Press, 1993

O'Neill Jessie H., The Golden Ghetto, The Psychology of Affluence, Hazelden, 1997

Pagnol Marcel, Judas, in French, Oeuvres Completes I, Theatre, Editions de Fallois, 1995

Pagnol Marcel, Les Marchands de Gloire, The Merchants of Glory, in French, Oeuvres Completes I, Theatre, Editions de Fallois, 1995

Pagnol Marcel, Topaze, in French, Oeuvres Completes I, Theatre, Editions de Fallois, 1995

Pagnol Marcel, L'Eau des Collines, Jean de Florette, in French, Oeuvres Completes III, Souvenirs et Romans, Editions de Fallois, 1995

Pagnol Marcel, L'Eau des Collines, Manon des Sources, in French, Oeuvres Completes III, Souvenirs et Romans, Editions de Fallois, 1995

Parks Robert H., Ph.D., The Witch Doctor of Wall Street, A Noted Financial Expert Guides You through Today's Voodoo Economics, Prometheus Books, 1996

Passeron Jean-Claude, Le Raisonnement Sociologique, L'Espace Non-Popperien du Raisonnement Naturel, Sociological Reasoning, in French, Collection Essais & Recherches, Nathan, 1991

Peters Thomas J. and Waterman, Jr. Robert H., In Search of Excellence, Lessons from America's Best-Run Companies, Warner Books, 1984

Phillips Michael and Rasberry Sally, Honest Business, A Superior Strategy for Starting and Managing Your Own Business, Shambhala, 1996

Piave Francesco Maria, Rigoletto, in Italian, TMK(S), Marca Registrada RCA Corporation, 1974

Popper Karl R., La Logique de la Decouverte Scientifique, The Logic of Scientific Discovery, in French, Bibliotheque Scientifique Payot, Editions Payot, 1995

Pratley Peter, The Essence of Business Ethics, Prentice Hall, 1995

Quintus Smyrnaeus, The Fall of Troy, Loeb Classical Library, 1984

Rae Scott B. & Wong Kenman L., Beyond Integrity, A Judeo-Christian Approach to Business Ethics, Zondervan Publishing House, 1996

Richardson Janice, edited by, World Ethics Report on Finance and Money, Editions Eska, 1997

Scott Fitzgerald Francis, The Great Gatsby, Heinemann/Octopus, 1977

Shakespeare William, Julius Caesar, Oxford University Press, 1959

Shakespeare William, The Merchant of Venice, Oxford University Press, 1959

Solomon Robert C., Above the Bottom Line, An Introduction to Business Ethics, Second Edition, Harcourt Brace College Publishers, 1994

Solomon Robert C., Ethics and Excellence, Cooperation and Integrity in Business, The Ruffin Series in Business Ethics, Oxford University Press, 1993

Strauss Anselm L., Qualitative Analysis for Social Scientists, Cambridge University Press, 1996

Strauss Michael, Volition and Valuation, in Hebrew, Haifa University Press & Zmora-Bitan, Publishers, 1998

Tamari Meir, The Challenge of Wealth, A Jewish Perspective on Earning and Spending Money, Jason Aronson Inc., 1995

Troyat Henri, Zola, Flammarion, in French, Le Livre de Poche, 1992

Velasquez Manuel G., Business Ethics, Concepts and Cases, Fourth Edition, Prentice Hall, 1998

Virgil, The Aeneid, Translated by Robert Fitzgerald, Vintage Classics, Random House, 1990

Voltaire, Candide, Dover Publications, Inc., 1993

Wallwork Ernest, Psychoanalysis and Ethics, Yale University Press, 1991

Ward Gary, Developing & Enforcing a Code of Business Ethics, A Guide to Developing, Implementing, Enforcing and Evaluating an Effective Ethics Program, Pilot Books, 1989

Williams Oliver F., Houck John W., edited by, A Virtuous Life in Business, Stories of Courage and Integrity in the Corporate World, Rowman & Littlefield Publishers, Inc., 1992

Williams Oliver F., Reilly Frank K. & Houck John W., edited by, Ethics and the Investment Industry, Rowman & Littlefield Publishers, Inc., 1989

Wilson Rodney, Economics, Ethics and Religion, Jewish, Christian and Muslim Economic Thought, New York University Press, 1997

Woodstock Theological Center, Seminar in Business Ethics, Ethical Considerations in Corporate Takeovers, Georgetown University Press, 1990

Wright Lesley and Smye Marti, Corporate Abuse, How "Lean and Mean" Robs People and Profits, Macmillan, 1996

Wuthnow Robert, Poor Richard's Principle, Recovering the American Dream through the Moral Dimension of Work, Busines, & Money, Princeton University Press, 1996

Yin Robert K., Case Study Research, Design and Methods, Second Edition, Applied Social Research Methods Series, Volume 5, Sage Publications, 1994

Zola Emile, La Curee, The Quarry, in French, Gallimard, 1997

Zola Emile, L'Argent, Money, in French, Fasquelle, Le Livre de Poche 584, 1992

Zola Emile, Le Ventre de Paris, The Stomach of Paris, in French, Gallimard, 1996

LIST OF ARTICLES

Agle Bradley R. and Van Burren III Harry J., God and Mammon: The Modern Relationship, Business Ethics Quarterly, 1999 (4)

Amiel Barbara, Feminist Harassment, National Review, Rae, Beyond Integrity

Andreas Kurt, Germans and the D-Mark, Richardson, World Ethics Report on Finance and Money

Andrews Kenneth R., Ethics in Practice, Ethics at Work, A Harvard Business Review Paperback, 1991

Argandona Antonio, Business, law and regulation: ethical issues, Harvey, Business Ethics: a European Approach

Arrington Robert L., Advertising and Behavior Control, Journal of Business Ethics, Rae, Beyond Integrity

Auerbach Joseph, The Poletown Dilemma, Ethics at Work, A Harvard Business Review Paperback, 1991

Bandow Doug, Environmentalism: The Triumph of Politics, The Freeman, Rae, Beyond Integrity

Barry Vincent, Advertising and Corporate Ethics, Madsen, Essentials of Business Ethics

Bartolome Fernando, Nobody Trusts the Boss Completely – Now What?, Ethics at Work, A Harvard Business Review Paperback, 1991

Bass Kenneth, Barnett Tim, and Brown Gene, Individual Difference Variables, Ethical Judgments, and Ethical Behavior Intentions, Business Ethics Quarterly, 1999 (2)

Batakovic Dusan T., To Obey Is to Survive, Richardson, World Ethics Report on Finance and Money

Bazerman Max II. and Messick David M., On the Power of a Clear Definition of Rationality, Business Ethics Quarterly, 1998 (3)

Betz Joseph, Business Ethics and Politics, Business Ethics Quarterly, 1998 (4)

Bhide Amar and Stevenson Howard, Why Be Honest If Honesty Doesn't Pay, Ethics at Work, A Harvard Business Review Paperback, 1991

Bicchieri Cristina and Fukui Yoshitaka, The Great Illusion: Ignorance, Informational Cascades, and the Persistence of Unpopular Norms, Business Ethics Quarterly, 1999 (1)

Binmore Ken, Game Theory and Business Ethics, Business Ethics Quarterly, 1999 (1)

Boatright John R., Does Business Ethics Rest on a Mistake? Business Ethics Quarterly, 1999 (4)

Boatright John R., Globalization and the Ethics of Business, Business Ethics Quarterly, 2000 (1)

Bok Sissela, Whistleblowing and Professional Responsibility, New York University Education Quarterly, Rae, Beyond Integrity

Bouckaert Luk, Business and community, Harvey, Business Ethics: a European Approach

Bowie Norman E., Business Ethics and Cultural Relativism, Madsen, Essentials of Business Ethics

Bowie Norman E., Does It Pay to Bluff in Business, Business Ethics, Rae, Beyond Integrity

Brenkert George G., Marketing and the Vulnerable, Business Ethics Quarterly, Special Issue #1, 1998

Brenkert George G., Marketing to Inner-City Blacks: PowerMaster and Moral Responsibility, Business Ethics Quarterly, 1998 (1)

Brenkert George G., Trust, Business and Business Ethics: An Introduction, Business Ethics Quarterly, 1998 (2)

Brenkert George G., Trust, Morality and International Business, Business Ethics Quarterly, 1998 (2)

Brock Gillian, Are Corporations Morally Defensible?, Business Ethics Quarterly, 1998 (4)

Brockway George P., The Future of Business Ethics, Williams, Ethics and the Investment Industry

Buchholz Rogene A., The Evolution of Corporate Social Responsibility, Madsen, Essentials of Business Ethics

Cabot Stephen J., Plant Closing Bill Will Give Many Employees Their Day in Court, Madsen, Essentials of Business Ethics

Cadbury Adrian Sir, Ethical Managers Make Their Own Rules, Ethics at Work, A Harvard Business Review Paperback, 1991

Camdessus Michel, The Financial Crisis in Mexico: Origins, Response from the IMF and lessons to Be Learnt, Richardson, World Ethics Report on Finance and Money

Carr Albert Z., Is Business Bluffing Ethical?, Madsen, Essentials of Business Ethics

Chamberlain Neil W., Corporations and the Physical Environment, Madsen, Essentials of Business Ethics

Child James W. and Marcoux Alexei M., Freeman and Evan: Stakeholder Theory in the Original Position, Business Ethics Quarterly, 1999 (2)

Ciminello Romeo, Banks and Ethical Funds, Richardson, World Ethics Report on Finance and Money

Ciulla Joanne B., Imagination, Fantasy, Wishful Thinking and Truth, Business Ethics Quarterly, Special Issue #1, 1998

Ciulla Joanne B., On Getting to the Future First, Business Ethics Quarterly, 2000 (1)

Collier Jane, Theorising the Ethical Organization, Business Ethics Quarterly, 1998 (4)

COB, International Harmonisation of Accounting Practice, Richardson, World Ethics Report on Finance and Money

Cooke Robert Allan and Young Earl, The Ethical Side of Takeovers and Mergers, Madsen, Essentials of Business Ethics

Corbetta Guido, Shareholders, Harvey, Business Ethics: a European Approach

Cory Jacques, Essay - Business Ethics: The Dream and the Reality, in Hebrew, Beware of Greeks' Presents, Bimat Kedem Publishers, 2001

Danley John, Beyond Managerialism, Business Ethics Quarterly, Special Issue #1, 1998

Davis Philip E., Why Might Institutional Investors Destabilise Financial Markets?, Richardson, World Ethics Report on Finance and Money

De George Richard T., Ethics and the Financial Community: An Overview, Williams, Ethics and the Investment Industry

De George Richard T., Business Ethics and the Challenge of the Information Age, Business Ethics Quarterly, 2000 (1)

Delhommais Pierre-Antoine, Banks – More to Gain than to Lose with the Single Currency, Richardson, World Ethics Report on Finance and Money

Del Ponte Carla, The Fight Against Money Laundering in Switzerland, Richardson, World Ethics Report on Finance and Money

DeMott Benjamin, Reading Fiction to the Bottom Line, Ethics at Work, A Harvard Business Review Paperback, 1991

Des Jardins Joseph R., Privacy in Employment, Moral Rights in the Workplace, Rae, Beyond Integrity

Dodds Susan et alia, Sexual Harassment, Social Theory and Practice, Rae, Beyond Integrity

Donaldson Thomas, Multinational Decision-Making: Reconciling International Norms, Journal of Business Ethics, Rae, Beyond Integrity

Donaldson Thomas, Are Business Managers "Professionals"?, Business Ethics Quarterly, 2000 (1)

Drucker Peter, The Ethics of Responsibility, Madsen, Essentials of Business Ethics

Dunfee Thomas W., The Marketplace of Morality: Small Steps Toward a Theory of Moral Choice, Business Ethics Quarterly, 1998 (1)

Duska Ronald, Business Ethics: Oxymoron or Good Business?, Business Ethics Quarterly, 2000 (1)

Dwyer Paula, Shareholder Revolt, Richardson, World Ethics Report on Finance and Money

Eliet Guillaume, The Three Founding Principles of the Single European Stock Market, Richardson, World Ethics Report on Finance and Money

Endreo Gilles, Protection of Minority Shareholders in France, Richardson, World Ethics Report on Finance and Money

Estola Matti, About the Ethics of Business Competition, Business and Leadership Ethics, June 1998

Etzioni Amitai, A Communitarian Note on Stakeholder Theory, Business Ethics Quarterly, 1998 (4)

Ewing David W., Case of the Disputed Dismissal, Ethics at Work, A Harvard Business Review Paperback, 1991

Fadiman Jeffrey A., A Traveler's Guide to Gifts and Bribes, Ethics at Work, A Harvard Business Review Paperback, 1991

Faugerolas Laurent, Assessment of Stock Options in 1995, Richardson, World Ethics Report on Finance and Money

Ferrell O. C. and Fraedrich John, Understanding Pressures That Cause Unethical Behavior in Business, Business Insights, Rae, Beyond Integrity

Flores Fernando and Solomon Robert C., Creating Trust, Business Ethics Quarterly, 1998 (2)

Foegen J. H., The Double Jeopardy of Sexual Harassment, Business and Society Review, Rae, Beyond Integrity

Frederick William C., One Voice? Or Many? A Response to Ellen Klein, Business Ethics Quarterly, 1998 (3)

Freeman Edward R., Poverty and the Politics of Capitalism, Business Ethics Quarterly, Special Issue #1, 1998

Friedman Milton, The Social Responsibility of Business Is to Increase Its Profits, Madsen, Essentials of Business Ethics

Gaillard Jean-Michel, Retirement Management and Social Responsibility, Richardson, World Ethics Report on Finance and Money

Garaventa Eugene, Drama: A Tool for Teaching Business Ethics, Business Ethics Quarterly, 1998 (3)

Gauthier Frederic, A Summary of the Banking Crises in Central Europe, Latin America and Africa, Richardson, World Ethics Report on Finance and Money

Geisler Norman L., Natural Law and Business Ethics, Biblical Principles in Business: The Foundations, Rae, Beyond Integrity

Gellerman Saul W., Why "Good" Managers Make Bad Ethical Choices, Ethics at Work, A Harvard Business Review Paperback, 1991

Gerwen van Jef, Employers' and employees' rights and duties, Harvey, Business Ethics: a European Approach

Geva Aviva, Moral Problems of Employing Foreign Workers, Business Ethics Quarterly, 1999 (3)

Gibson Kevin, Bottom William, and Murnighan Keith J., Once Bitten: Defection and Reconciliation in a Cooperative Enterprise, Business Ethics Quarterly, 1999 (1)

Gini A. R. and Sullivan T., Work: The Process and the Person, Journal of Business Ethics, Rae, Beyond Integrity

Goodpaster Kenneth E., Business Ethics and Stakeholder Analysis, Business Ethics Quarterly, Rae, Beyond Integrity

Graddy Kathryn and Robertson Diana C., Fairness of Pricing Decision, Business Ethics Quarterly, 1999 (2)

Gross Joseph Prof., From the Desk of the Board of Directors – The New Corporate Law, Directors and Officers, Taxation Issues, in Hebrew, Globes, Israel, July 1999

Gross Joseph Prof., From the Desk of the Board of Directors, in Hebrew, October 1998

Gross Joseph Prof., From the Desk of the Board of Directors, in Hebrew, June 1998

Gross Joseph Prof., From the Desk of the Board of Directors, in Hebrew, March 1998

Gross Joseph Prof., From the Desk of the Board of Directors, in Hebrew, May 1997

Hamilton Stewart, How Safe Is Your Company?, Richardson, World Ethics Report on Finance and Money

Hanke Steve H., Argentina and the Tequila Effect, Richardson, World Ethics Report on Finance and Money

Hanke Steve H., Currency Board for Mexico, Richardson, World Ethics Report on Finance and Money

Hanson Kirk O., A Cautionary Assessment of Wall Street, Williams, Ethics and the Investment Industry

Hartman Edwin M., Altruism, Ingroups and Fairness: Comments on Messick, Business Ethics Quarterly, Special Issue #1, 1998

Hartman Edwin M., The Role of Character in Business Ethics, Business Ethics Quarterly, 1998 (3)

Hasnas John, The Normative Theories of Business Ethics: A Guide for the Perplexed, Business Ethics Quarterly, 1998 (1)

Hendry John, Universalizability and Reciprocity in International Business Ethics, Business Ethics Quarterly, 1999 (3)

Hoffman Michael W., Business and Environmental Ethics, Business Ethics Quarterly, Rae, Beyond Integrity

Hosmer Larue T., Lessons from the Wreck of the Exxon Valdez: The Need for Imagination, Empathy and Courage, Business Ethics Quarterly, Special Issue #1, 1998

Howard Robert, Values Make the Company: An Interview with Robert Haas, Ethics at Work, A Harvard Business Review Paperback, 1991

Husted Bryan W., The Ethical Limits of Trust in Business Relations, Business Ethics Quarterly, 1998 (2)

IMF Bulletin, How to Manage Today's Risks, Richardson, World Ethics Report on Finance and Money

Ishii Hiroshi, A Solution for the Crisis in the Japanese Banking System, Richardson, World Ethics Report on Finance and Money

Jackall Robert, Business as a Social and Moral Terrain, Madsen, Essentials of Business Ethics

Jackall Robert, Moral Mazes: Bureaucracy and Managerial Work, Ethics at Work, A Harvard Business Review Paperback, 1991

James Gene G., Whistle-Blowing: Its Moral Justification, Madsen, Essentials of Business Ethics

Jarrell Gregg A., The Insider Trading Scandal: Understanding the Problem, Williams, Ethics and the Investment Industry

Jensen Michael C., Takeovers: Folklore and Science, Harvard Business Review, Rae, Beyond Integrity

Jones Thomas M. and Verstegen Ryan Lori, The Effect of Organizational Forces on Individual Morality: Judgment, Moral Approbation, and Behavior, Business Ethics Quarterly, 1998 (3)

Kapstein Ethan B., Shockproof: the End of the Financial Crisis, Richardson, World Ethics Report on Finance and Money

Keller G. M., Industry and the Environment, Madsen, Essentials of Business Ethics

Klebe Trevino Linda, Butterfield Kenneth D., and McCabe Donald L., The Ethical Context in Organizations: Influences on Employee Attitudes and Behaviors, Business Ethics Quarterly, 1998 (3)

Klein E. R., The One Necessary Condition for a Successful Business Ethics Course: The Teacher Must Be a Philosopher, Business Ethics Quarterly, 1998 (3)

Klein Sherwin, Don Quixote and the Problem of Idealism and Realism in Business Ethics, Business Ethics Quarterly, 1998 (1)

Koehn Daryl, Virtue Ethics, the Firm, and Moral Psychology, Business Ethics Quarterly, 1998 (3)

Koslowski Peter F., The ethics of capitalism, Harvey, Business Ethics: a European Approach

Kuhlmann Eberhard, Customers, Harvey, Business Ethics: a European Approach

Kujala Johanna, Analysing Moral Issues in Stakeholder Relations – A Questionnaire Development Process, Business and Leadership Ethics, June 1998

Kupfer Andrew, Is Drug Testing Good or Bad?, Madsen, Essentials of Business Ethics

Kwame Safro, Doin' Business in an African Country, Journal of Business Ethics, Rae, Beyond Integrity

Lacour Jean-Philippe, Ces droles de tribunaux de commerce, Those funny courts called tribunaux de commerce, in French, La Tribune, 20 octobre 1999

Lambert Agnes, Les fonds ethiques s'ouvrent aux particuliers, Ehical funds open to the public, in French, La Tribune, 24.9.99

Laurent Philippe, Ethics, Money and Globalisation, Richardson, World Ethics Report on Finance and Money

Lea David, The Infelicities of Business Ethics in the Third World: The Melanesian Context, Business Ethics Quarterly, 1999 (3)

Lei Kai, New Banking Law in China, Richardson, World Ethics Report on Finance and Money

Leiser Burton M., Ethics and Equity in the Securities Industry, Williams, Ethics and the Investment Industry

Leithart Peter J., Snakes in the Garden: Sanctuaries, Sanctuary Pollution, and the Global Environment, Stewardship Journal, Rae, Beyond Integrity

Le Lien Charles, The Labours of Sisyphus – Going Beyond the Project for a Single Currency, Richardson, World Ethics Report on Finance and Money

Leroy Pierre-Henri, Shareholding and Society, Richardson, World Ethics Report on Finance and Money

Levitt Theodore, The Morality (?) of Advertising, Harvard Business Review, Rae, Beyond Integrity

Luijk van Henk, Business ethics: the field and its importance, Harvey, Business Ethics: a European Approach

Mackenzie Craig and Lewis Alan, Morals and Markets: The Case of Ethical Investing, Business Ethics Quarterly, 1999 (3)

Magnet Myron, The Decline and Fall of Business Ethics, Madsen, Essentials of Business Ethics

Mahoney Jack, How to be ethical: ethics resource management, Harvey, Business Ethics: a European Approach

Maitland Ian, Community Lost? Business Ethics Quarterly, 1998 (4)

Maitland Ian, The Limits of Business Self-Regulation, California Management Review, Rae, Beyond Integrity

Marens Richard and Wicks Andrew, Getting Real: Stakeholder Theory, Managerial Practice, and the General Irrelevance of Fiduciary Duties Owed to Shareholders, Business Ethics Quarterly, 1999 (2)

Margolis Joshua D., Psychological Pragmatism and the Imperative of Aims: A New Approach for Business Ethics, Business Ethics Quarterly, 1998 (3)

Marturano Marco, Italian Citizens' Confidence in the Judiciary and State Institutions, Richardson, World Ethics Report on Finance and Money

Marx Gary T., The Case of the Omniscient Organization, Ethics at Work, A Harvard Business Review Paperback, 1991

Mathiesen Kay, Game Theory in Business Ethics: Bad Ideology or Bad Press?, Business Ethics Quarterly, 1999 (1)

McCann Dennis P., "Accursed Internationalism" of Finance: Coping with the Resource of Catholic Social Teaching, Williams, Ethics and the Investment Industry

McClennen Edward F., Moral Rules as Public Goods, Business Ethics Quarterly, 1999 (1)

McCoy Bowen H., The Parable of the Sadhu, Madsen, Essentials of Business Ethics

McMahon Thomas F., Transforming Justice: A Conceptualization, Business Ethics Quarterly, 1999 (4)

Messick David M., Social Categories and Business Ethics, Business Ethics Quarterly, Special Issue #1, 1998

Michelman James H., Some Ethical Consequences of Economic Competition, Journal of Business Ethics, Rae, Beyond Integrity

Milgram Stanley, The Perils of Obedience, Obedience to Authority, Rae, Beyond Integrity

Missir di Lusignano Alessandro, Protecting the Financial Interests of the European Community and Fighting Financial Crime, Richardson, World Ethics Report on Finance and Money

Moberg Dennis J., The Big Five and Organizational Virtue, Business Ethics Quarterly, 1999 (2)

Morley Alfred C., Nurturing Professional Standards in the Investment Industry, Williams, Ethics and the Investment Industry

Morris Christofer W., What is This Thing Called "Reputation"?, Business Ethics Quarterly, 1999 (1)

Movahedi Nahid, Changes in Japanese Capitalism, Richardson, World Ethics Report on Finance and Money

Murphy Patrick E., Creating and Encouraging Ethical Corporate Structures, Sloan Management Review, Rae, Beyond Integrity

Nader Ralph, The Anatomy of Whistle-Blowing, Madsen, Essentials of Business Ethics

Nagel Thomas, A Defense of Affirmative Action, Senate Judiciary Committee, Rae, Beyond Integrity

Nash Laura L., Ethics without the sermon, Madsen, Essentials of Business Ethics

Nesteruk Jeffrey, Reimagining the Law, Business Ethics Quarterly, 1999 (4)

Neuville Colette, Protection judiciaire des actionnaires minoritaires, Legal protection of minority shareholders, in French, Ecole Nationale de la Magistrature, 12 mai 1997

Newton Lisa, The Hostile Takeover: An Opposition View, Ethical Theory and Business, Rae, Beyond Integrity

Nielsen Richard P., Can Ethical Character be Stimulated and Enabled? An Action Learning Approach to Teaching and Learning Organization Ethics, Business Ethics Quarterly, 1998 (3)

Novak Michael, A Theology of the Corporation, The Corporation, Rae, Beyond Integrity

Novak Michael, Virtuous Self-Interest, The Spirit of Democratic Capitalism, Rae, Beyond Integrity

O'Hara Patricia and Blakey Robert G., Legal Aspects of Insider Trading, Williams, Ethics and the Investment Industry

Olasky Marvin, Compassion, Religion and Liberty, Rae, Beyond Integrity

O'Neill June, An Argument Against Comparable Worth, Comparable Worth: An Issue for the 80's, Rae, Beyond Integrity

Orlando John, The Fourth Wave: The Ethics of Corporate Downsizing, Business Ethics Quarterly, 1999 (2)

Pastin Mark and Hooker Michael, Ethics and the Foreign Corrupt Practices Act, Madsen, Essentials of Business Ethics

Pastre Olivier, The Ten Commandments of Corporate Governance, Richardson, World Ethics Report on Finance and Money

Pava Moses L., Developing a Religiously Grounded Business Ethics: A Jewish Perspective, Business Ethics Quarterly, 1998 (1)

Perquel Jean-Jacques, New Markets, Richardson, World Ethics Report on Finance and Money

Pezard Alice, The Vienot Report on Corporate Governance, Richardson, World Ethics Report on Finance and Money

Pezard Alice, Confidence in the Judiciary, Richardson, World Ethics Report on Finance and Money

Phelan John J. Jr., Ethical Leadership and the Investment Industry, Williams, Ethics and the Investment Industry

Philips Robert A. and Margolis Joshua D., Toward an Ethics of Organizations, Business Ethics Quarterly, 1999 (4)

Pierenkemper Toni, The German Fear of Inflation, or Can History Teach Us Lessons?, Richardson, World Ethics Report on Finance and Money

Ploix Helene, Ethics and Financial Markets, Richardson, World Ethics Report on Finance and Money

Purdy Laura M., In Defense of Hiring Apparently Less Qualified Women, Journal of Social Philosophy, Rae, Beyond Integrity

Rak Pavle, Crime and Finance in Russia, Richardson, World Ethics Report on Finance and Money

Reed Darryl, Stakeholder Management Theory: A Critical Theory Perspective, Business Ethics Quarterly, 1999 (3)

Renard Vincent, Corruption and Real Estate in Japan, Richardson, World Ethics Report on Finance and Money

Rivoli Pietra, Ethical Aspects of Investor Behavior, Journal of Business Ethics, Rae, Beyond Integrity

Robin Donald, Giallourakis Michael, David Fred R., and Moritz Thomas, A Different Look at Codes of Ethics, Madsen, Essentials of Business Ethics

Roma Giuseppe, Italy's Moneylenders, Between Illegality and Social Compromise, Richardson, World Ethics Report on Finance and Money

Rorty Richard, Can American Egalitarianism Survive a Globalized Economy?, Business Ethics Quarterly, Special Issue #1, 1998

Russell James W., A Borderline Case: Sweatshops Cross the Rio Grande, Madsen, Essentials of Business Ethics

Sass Steven, Risk at the PBGC, Richardson, World Ethics Report on Finance and Money

Schermerhorn Jr. John R., Terms of Global Business Engagement in Ethically Challenging Environments: Applications to Burma, Business Ethics Quarterly, 1999 (3)

Schneider Jacques-Andre, Pension Fund Management and the Ethics of Responsibility, Richardson, World Ethics Report on Finance and Money

Schokkaert Erik and Eyckmans Johan, Environment, Harvey, Business Ethics: a European Approach

Schumacher E. F., Buddhist Economics, Small Is Beautiful, Rae, Beyond Integrity

Sciarelli Sergio, Corporate Ethics and the Entrepreneurial Theory of "Social Success", Business Ethics Quarterly, 1999 (4)

Senate Finance Commission, Stock Options in France, Richardson, World Ethics Report on Finance and Money

Servet Jean-Michel, Metamorphosis of a Chinese Dollar, Richardson, World Ethics Report on Finance and Money

Sethi Prakash S. and Sama Linda M., Ethical Behavior as a Strategic Choice by Large Corporations: The Interactive Effect of Marketplace Competition, Industry Structure and Firm Resources, Business Ethics Quarterly, 1998 (1)

Seymour Sally, The Case of the Willful Whistle-Blower, Ethics at Work, A Harvard Business Review Paperback, 1991

Seymour Sally, The Case of the Mismanaged Ms., Ethics at Work, A Harvard Business Review Paperback, 1991

Sharp Paine Lynn, Managing for Organizational Integrity, Harvard Business Review, Rae, Beyond Integrity

Shaw Bill, Aristotle and Posner on Corrective Justice: The Tortoise and the Hare, Business Ethics Quarterly, 1999 (4)

Shaw Bill, Community: A Work in Progress, Business Ethics Quarterly, 1998 (4)

Shaw Bill, Should Insider Trading Be Outside the Law?, Business and Society Review, Rae, Beyond Integrity

Shriver Donald W. Jr., Ethical Discipline and Religious Hope in the Investment Industry, Williams, Ethics and the Investment Industry

Singer M. S., Paradigms Linked: A Normative-Empirical Dialogue about Business Ethics, Business Ethics Quarterly, 1998 (3)

Sirico Robert Fr., The Entrepreneurial Vocation, Acton Institute, Rae, Beyond Integrity

Skillen James W., Common Moral Ground and the Natural Law Argument, Rae, Beyond Integrity

Smith H. R. and Carroll Archie B., Organizational Ethics: A Stacked Deck, Journal of Business Ethics, Rae, Beyond Integrity

Smith Virgil, The Place of Character in Corporate Structure, Rae, Beyond Integrity

Smith William, A View from Wall Street, Williams, Ethics and the Investment Industry

Snell Robin S., Obedience to Authority and Ethical Dilemmas in Hong Kong Companies, Business Ethics Quarterly, 1999 (3)

Solomon Robert C., Game Theory as a Model for Business and Business Ethics, Business Ethics Quarterly, 1999 (1)

Solomon Robert C., The Moral Psychology of Business: Care and Compassion in the Corporation, Business Ethics Quarterly, 1998 (3)

Solomon Robert C., Business with Virtue: Maybe Next Year?, Business Ethics Quarterly, 2000 (1)

Soule Edward, Trust and Managerial Responsibility, Business Ethics Quarterly, 1998 (2)

Steele Shelby, Affirmative Action: The Price of Preference, The Content of Our Character, Rae, Beyond Integrity

Takala Tuomo, Postmodern Challenge to Business Ethics, Business and Leadership Ethics, June 1998

Thiery Nicolas, A la decouverte des fonds ethiques, The discovery of ethical funds, in French, La Tribune, 19.10.99

Thiveaud Jean-Marie, Confidence Reigns Supreme, Richardson, World Ethics Report on Finance and Money

Tierney Paul E. Jr., The Ethos of Wall Street, Williams, Ethics and the Investment Industry

Trichet Jean-Claude, Is There an Increase in Risks to the System and How Should We Confront It, Richardson, World Ethics Report on Finance and Money

Tumminen Rauno, Ownership in Environmental Management, Business and Leadership Ethics, June 1998

Uusitalo Eeva and Outi, Marketing Ethics, Business and Leadership Ethics, June 1998

Vanderschraaf Peter, Hume's Game-Theoretic Business Ethics, Business Ethics Quarterly, 1999 (1)

Vanderschraaf Peter, Introduction: Game Theory and Business Ethics, Business Ethics Quarterly, 1999 (1)

Vandivier Kermit, Whu Should My Conscience Bother Me?, In the Name of Profit, Rae, Beyond Integrity

Velasquez Manuel G., Corporate Ethics: Losing It, Having It, Getting It, Madsen, Essentials of Business Ethics

Velasquez Manuel, Globalization and the Failure of Ethics, Business Ethics Quarterly, 2000 (1)

Vidaver-Cohen Deborah, Moral Imagination in Organizational Problem-Solving: An Institutional Perspective, Business Ethics Quarterly, Special Issue #1, 1998

Vidaver-Cohen Deborah, Motivational Appeal in Normative Theories of Enterprise, Business Ethics Quarterly, 1998 (3)

Virard Marie-Paule, Companies: the Hidden Side of the Accounts, Richardson, World Ethics Report on Finance and Money

Waide John, The Making of Self and World in Advertising, Journal of Business Ethics, Rae, Beyond Integrity

Wallis Jim, The Powerful and the Powerless, Agenda for Biblical People, Rae, Beyond Integrity

Walton Clarence C., Investment Bankers from Ethical Perspectives... With Special Emphasis on the Theory of Agency, Williams, Ethics and the Investment Industry

Warner Alison, Banks in a Spin, Richardson, World Ethics Report on Finance and Money

Warsh David, How Selfish Are People - Really?, Ethics at Work, A Harvard Business Review Paperback, 1991

Watson George W., Shefard Jon M., Stephens Carroll U., and Christman John C., Ideology and the Economic Social Contract in a Downsizing Environment, Business Ethics Quarterly, 1999 (4)

Watson Jr. Thomas S., Connecting People: Alternative Futures, Business and Leadership Ethics, June 1998

Weaver Gary R. and Klebe Trevino Linda, Compliance and Values Oriented Ethics Programs: Influences on Employees' Attitudes and Behavior, Business Ethics Quarterly, 1999 (2)

Weithers John G., Ethics within the Securities Industry, Williams, Ethics and the Investment Industry

Wensveen Siker Louke van, Christ and Business, Journal of Business Ethics, Rae, Beyond Integrity

Werhane Patricia H., A Bill of Rights for Employees and Employers, Madsen, Essentials of Business Ethics

Werhane Patricia H., Employee and Employer Rights in an Institutional Context, Ethical Theory in Business, Rae, Beyond Integrity

Werhane Patricia H., Moral Imagination and the Search for Ethical Decision Making in Management, Business Ethics Quarterly, Special Issue #1, 1998

Werhane Patricia H., The Ethics of Insider Trading, Journal of Business Ethics, Rae, Beyond Integrity

Werhane Patricia H., Exporting Mental Models: Global Capitalism in the 21st Century, Business Ethics Quarterly, 2000 (1)

Wicks Andrew, How Kantian a Kantian Theory of Capitalism?, Business Ethics Quarterly, Special Issue #1, 1998

Wicks Andrew C. and Glezen Paul L., In Search of Experts: A Conception of Expertise for Business Ethics Consultation, Business Ethics Quarterly, 1998 (1)

Wilmouth Robert K., Futures Market and Self-Regulation, Williams, Ethics and the Investment Industry

Wokutch Richard E. and Shepard Jon M., The Maturing of the Japanese Economy: Corporate Social Responsibility Implications, Business Ethics Quarterly, 1999 (3)

Wood Donna J., Ingroups and Outgroups: What Psychology Doesn't Say, Business Ethics Quarterly, Special Issue #1, 1998

Wu Xinwen, Business Ethical Perceptions of Business People in East China: An Empirical Study, Business Ethics Quarterly, 1999 (3)

INDEX